FOOD, SEX,
AND POLLUTION

FOOD, SEX, AND POLLU

ANNA S. MEIGS · *Rutgers Univers*

TION · *A New Guinea Religion*

ity Press · *New Brunswick* · *New Jersey*

Library of Congress Cataloging in Publication Data

Meigs, Anna S., 1943–
Food, sex, and pollution.

Bibliography: p.
Includes index.
1. Hua (Papua New Guinea people)—Religion.
2. Food—Religious aspects.   3. Hua (Papua New Guinea
people)—Sexual behavior.   I. Title.
BL2630.H82M44   1983   306'.6'0899912   82–12202
ISBN 0–8135–0968–8
ISBN 0–8135–1306–5(pbk)

British Cataloging-in-Publication
information available

*Photographs on jacket and title page
courtesy of Peter Tarplee*

In memory of my mother
FLORENCE TRUITT WHITE
for her spirit of adventure

CONTENTS

PREFACE

I arrived in Lufa in the Eastern Highlands of New Guinea expecting to do a thesis on divorce. My training had prepared me for a study of social organization, and the literature on Eastern Highlands societies had suggested a need for research on how divorce would affect alliance patterns. As not infrequently happens in real life, I found that my preformulated questions on what I had imagined to be themes of burning importance were regarded by my informants as trivial and beside the point. Instead they wanted to tell me about what they were and were not allowed to eat. Doggedly I persisted in my attempts to unravel the intricacies of divorce and alliance: my attempts were met with good-natured indifference. Finally I gave up and decided to go with the flow.

It became very clear that the symbolic evaluation of food was a major preoccupation of the Hua.[1] Part of the evidence for this was relatively impersonal, furnished by the language itself. For example, two of the Hua words for "ev-

---

1. The possibility that the food rules represent a mechanism of protein distribution in a population known to suffer from an inadequate protein supply (Hornabrook, Crane, and Stanhope 1977) had a great immediate appeal—especially in view of the fact that women of reproductive age and children observe dramatically fewer prohibitions than does any other category. A problem in the nutritional explanation, however, soon became apparent. Consumption of the sweet potato, staple of the Hua diet, is never limited, much less eliminated, except under the rarely invoked condition of a total fast. The foods that were totally restricted to certain people, and actually not eaten by them for extended periods, were ones that formed only a peripheral part of the diet. I concluded that the Hua food rules were not significantly motivated by nutritional factors and abandoned the pursuit of nutritional data. K. V. Bailey (1966), a nutritionist, came to a similar conclusion about the nutritional significance of food taboos among the Chimbu, another Eastern Highlands people.

erything," *do'ado'na* and *rema'atema'*,[2] mean literally "that which can be eaten and that which cannot" and "that which is cooked and that which is not." While any feature "x" in a construction "x and not-x" may mean "everything," it is fair to infer that the choice of the particular "x" reflects something of the speakers' assumptions about what is of central significance in their world. And part of the evidence was truly behavioral. Dozens of informants wanted to talk to me about food restrictions, and in most details they agreed. I found myself recording hundreds of categorical statements about what kinds of food people could eat and under what circumstances they could eat them.

As I continued to record these statements, it became clear to me that questions about food provided a natural approach to more subtle discussions of a variety of social and biological issues. (I may even have entertained the hope that the food rules would provide a point of entrance to the topic of divorce: if I did, I was certainly disappointed.)

I may seem to belabor this point. I do so because I wish to make clear that the focus of this book was dictated not by any theoretical preconceptions of my own, but by the preoccupations of my Hua teachers. The issue of food was presented to me on a platter, and finally I ate what was offered. It was my goal to follow along those paths of inquiry that were opened to me by my consultants themselves.

My fieldwork was undertaken in two villages, Kemerake and Sara, whose combined total population was 377. I lived in each village for nine months. As it turned out, the acknowledged experts on food rules were men, and consequently, my list of consultants contained a preponderance of them. I did some work with most adult males and some females in each of the two villages and can say with confi-

---

2. An apostrophe indicates a glottal stop.

dence that the data recorded here represent a social consen-
sus on a cultural passion. Although it is my impression that
this passion is shared by all the Hua people resident at Lufa,
I do not have sufficient data to substantiate such a claim.
Although Hua women participate in many elements of this
ideology, they are also excluded from large portions.[3]

Hua men were of course not accustomed to teaching
their sexual ideology as represented in food rules to a
woman, and on several occasions I inquired about how
they felt about talking to me. No one seemed to feel this
was any problem provided I did not spread my knowledge
around among the women. Although men cited the fact
that I washed my hands frequently and wore underpants
as some kind of justification of my sexually neutral status, I
think the truth was simpler. First, these rules and this ideology are breaking down and are thus not revered as invio-
lable. Second, although I was obviously a woman, and one
who gestated and lactated before their eyes, I was otherwise so radically different as to disqualify myself sexually.

I am sure the ideological focus on food was traditional,
but was this ideological focus as intense in precontact
times as it is now? Since the 1950s, when the first Australian patrol post was established in the area, Hua males
have been going to the coast for wage labor. With their
departure the male cult, centerpiece of Hua culture, has
suffered a very considerable decline. Initiations are no
longer performed except in abbreviated fashion. Men's
houses are no longer the center of much activity. But the
food rules are to a certain extent still practiced and are ea-
gerly remembered by all males. They represent a neat and
manageable body of data in which are encapsulated much
of the thoughts and ideals of the past. They are something
one can hold onto. Hua males, while lapsing in their obser-

---

3. In an attempt to keep the distinction between female and male
knowledge clear, I try to specify in each case the sex of my informant(s).
Where I leave sex vague as in "Hua believe" or "informants say," both
sexes are intended unless otherwise indicated by the context.

vations of many food rules, use these rules as a tool for talking about traditional culture and as a means of honoring and remembering the past.

This book is about an ideology, a shared complex of beliefs about procreation, nurturance, growth, decay, and the nature of the sexes among the Hua of New Guinea. Careful readers will notice it differs from current ethnographic norms in two ways: the ideology is not explicitly and consistently connected with actually observed behavior, and the ideology seems at many points to abound in contradictions. These disparities raise corresponding questions about the reliability of the "rules" reported here and about their status as mutually contradictory components of the ideology inferred from them.

Surely it is fair to say that an ideology can be inferred *either* from actual behavior or from the texts in which it is enshrined. Not infrequently, and not surprisingly, there is a disparity between behavior and texts, as can be seen in the history of Christian or Marxist theory and practice. The disparity between Hua theory and practice may once have been equally extreme. We cannot know, because many of the Hua rules have very recently fallen into disuse. Again and again my consultants explained that these rules, like many other aspects of traditional culture such as cannibalism and warfare, had declined, casualties of Australian pacification. Some younger men have expressed a speculative and nostalgic interest in reviving these food restrictions, to restore a golden age when all old men were well preserved, a time when wars were fought and life had a meaning it has since lost.

What is the ethnographic value of an ideology uprooted from the praxis from which alone the "true ideology" can be inferred? Are not the results of such an investigation doomed to irrelevance?

A semihistorical account such as mine is justified on two counts. The first is that where only recollections survive, they should not be despised. We do not, for example, reject the writings of Tacitus because they are largely uncorroborated: on the contrary, we value them all the more because they are our only surviving records of events. The second is that there are connections, sporadic and unsystematic as they seem, between what people do today and what they say they used to do. Much eating behavior that seems incoherent and unmotivated in itself—and would no doubt continue to appear so, even if observations were multiplied—acquires a coherent meaning when viewed as an attempt to conform with a set of partially obsolete but not forgotten norms.

I believe my conclusions represent the most cautious possible interpretation of the data. For example, the chain of inference linking the statements of informants to the food rules presented in chapter 1 involved only a stylistic transposition from Hua statements "we do not eat x because of y" to my rule "x is prohibited because of y."

A number of readers may be disturbed at the systematic denial of rules that occurs at what I call "deeper levels." What is the status of rules that are denied, of the levels at which they are denied or validated, and of an explanatory model that can encompass them? A quick answer to this question might be that all cultural rules, being arbitrary, are breakable and hence are broken. It is this which distinguishes them from natural laws. This answer will account for sporadic violations of rules and for the fact that cultural conventions, unlike natural laws, may change over time. It will not account, however, for systematic violations, where one set of cultural norms is superseded by another contemporary set of rules.

My understanding of this conflict, implicit throughout the following discussion, is that "deeper levels" represent *arcane knowledge*, knowledge that is not universally shared. All of us are aware of the contrast between arcane and naive knowledge in Western culture. The difference between the two is usually quantitative. Naive knowledge, the common property of everyone in the culture who speaks its language, is codified in a dictionary. Arcane knowledge is the fruit of more specialized study and is typically codified in technical journals, textbooks, and encyclopedias. The possession of such knowledge, being socially and intellectually restricted, is a common mark of high social status.

A recent treatment of the contrast between dictionaries and encyclopedias claims that in nontechnological preliterate societies this arcane-naive contrast simply does not exist (Haiman 1980b:337). I believe this statement requires qualification. A quantitative difference between naive and arcane knowledge may not be possible without considerable specialization and successful research, but given the social status that arcane knowledge confers, it is inevitable that it should be greatly prized. I suggest that some of what passes for arcane knowledge in secret societies, fraternities, religions, and guilds (and to some extent among Hua males) may not necessarily be a greater collection of facts, but merely a contrary or paradoxical perspective on the same facts.

The difference between naive and arcane knowledge in such cases is not quantitative but qualitative. In an objective scientific enterprise, the expert has more empirical and theoretical capital than the layperson. In cases such as I am describing, the expert has the same coin as the layperson and is contemplating the other side of it.

A very rich and detailed ethnographic example of this qualitative contrast from elsewhere in New Guinea may illustrate the point. Among the Baktaman, Barth (1975) was able to isolate no fewer than seven levels of arcane knowledge, each new level achieved by a deeper initiation. With each successive ceremony, initiates are taught that the rules of conduct and avoidance (including many food rules of the sort described here), rules that were introduced at a previous ceremony as absolute, are incomplete or simply false. With their entrance to the third degree of enlightenment, male initiates learn that the meat of the despised *eiraram* marsupial mouse is in fact the most sacred food and scent of all. Some of the secrets of Baktaman ritual thus are not new facts but a different perspective on the old facts.

The ideology in regard to female reproductivity among Hua males, discussed in chapters 1 through 4, illustrates a corresponding but radically simplified contrast between levels of knowledge. The naive conception is that female sexual organs and substances are not only disgusting but also dangerous to the development and maintenance of masculinity. The arcane knowledge, however, is that female substances, dangerous and repugnant though they may be, are necessary to the growth of the male and to the maintenance of his vitality. In fact, female substances are the most awesome and powerful known to men. This arcane perception is kept secret from women for obvious reasons.

Although many interesting and useful comments could be made about the structural and functional reasons for which Hua males entertain a system of ideas of this nature, I choose in this book to forego this etic perspective and confine myself to the emic. It is my goal to describe an ideology as it is remembered, and to a lesser extent still practiced, by a group whose culture is now in decline.

ACKNOWLEDGMENTS

This book is a revised and expanded version of a Ph.D. dissertation written while I was a student at the University of Pennsylvania. I would like to thank that institution for its support and the use of its facilities. Among its faculty I am especially grateful to Sandra Barnes, Peggy Sanday, and Bill Davenport for their comments and criticisms on the manuscript. I thank Ward Goodenough for encouragement, stimulation, and support from my first year as a graduate student to the present time. I am indebted to the National Science Foundation for a doctoral research grant and to the University of Pennsylvania for an additional grant.

I would also like to thank the University of Pittsburgh Press for allowing me to use portions of my own work: "Male Pregnancy and the Reduction of Sexual Opposition in a New Guinea Highland Society," *Ethnology* 15 (1976): 393–406 in chapter 3; and to the Royal Anthropological Institute of Great Britain and Ireland for the same permission in regard to my "A Papuan Perspective on Pollution," *Man* 13 (1978): 304–318 in chapter 6.

I would like to thank Roger Keesing for welcoming me as a visiting scholar to the Australian National University at Canberra while I wrote up part of my research. The Department of Anthropology at the University of Manitoba generously granted me status as an adjunct professor during the period in which I was preparing the manuscript for publication.

In Papua New Guinea I owe a debt for hospitality extended by Rod Donovan and Alan McNeill, assistant district commissioners at Lufa, and to Roslyn and Peter Tarplee, who took me and my family in for Christmas and other exotic festivals. The government herbarium at Lae provided me with plant identifications.

I owe a great debt to the residents of Kemerake and Sara villages. Not only did they give us a warm welcome and steady support, but they were enthusiastic, generous informants, who were tolerant of our occasional inability to meet their very high standard of neighborliness. Their courtesy and emotional health continue to inspire my admiration. I want especially to thank Bomena Biru and Kiomu Kutani for the loving care they gave our daughter, Claire; Ronson Kevao for his help around the house; and Buro Kutani for the house site. Claire spent the first months of her life in the field. The memory grows sweeter as it fades, till now I recall her as our neighbors fondly knew her: *kigi abade* "the laughing girl."

My greatest debt is to my teachers and I thank them heartily for enduring the long, rambling, confused, and confusing conversations into which I dragged them. For me these discussions were tremendously exciting and enlightening. In Kemerake village I thank in particular Norope Rekupe and Momoti Iremuto, with whom I worked on a fairly regular basis; both of them had a quiet and well-organized style of teaching. Bandi Famuti, an older woman, gave me much of my introduction to the women's conception of their own bodies. Amamo Kenekenea and Forapi Maunori also occasionally provided me with information. In Sara village I want to thank Roko Kevao and Fitome Kusri for their regular assistance. Rohakvi Zakafo, Havagova Kevao, Kusri'eva Kevao, Kiomu Kutani, Unga Roko, and Frisuvi Furimo all provided me with some important information. Many other Hua people helped me along my mental road—I thank them all and apologize for not naming them individually.

Now, however, I want to sing the praises of the two men with whom I talked daily and who provided me with the basic design of Hua mental culture as I know it. They are Aza Kevao and Busa Hagaiteme, both of Sara village. In the early stages of my fieldwork I spent whole days with Aza, who agreed to my determination to speak Hua (however badly) and with infinite patience, ingenious pantomime, and sometimes hilarious models explained the ins and outs of Hua food rules by the hour. He was a born teacher and gave me confidence in myself as a fieldworker. Busa, father of seven children, avid gardener, and lineage leader (Aza had four children, disliked gardening, and abstained from all political activity) was a busier and more impatient man and I was able to work successfully with him only after I had "mastered" the Hua language. Once I could talk to him, he was tremendous fun; witty, sophisticated, and urbane, he was the undisputed leader of left bank (Tua River) intellectual life. Having received an extremely thorough education in the beliefs and rituals of traditional life from his father, he was an absolute storehouse of arcane information. These two men were my intellectual partners at Lufa; it has been hard going on without them.

Readers may wonder at my heavy use of male informants. I want to emphasize that my interest in food rules developed in the field and that initially I had little idea of where such a study would lead. Nor did I have any idea about who observed food rules. My original assumption was that both males and females were heavily involved and, therefore, that both would serve as informants. I found instead that food rules are understood by males and females alike as essentially belonging to males. In their most complex and elaborate forms, food rules are followed exclusively by males. Females, though observing abbreviated and relatively simple rules, claim relative lack of knowledge and consistently referred me back to males. Consequently, for better or for worse, my choice of food rules as a research topic involved me in the study of what appears to be primarily a male ideology. My apologies, therefore, to Hua women, especially to my friends, whose conceptions of their own bodies are underrepresented in this work. Ultimately, I hope to be able to redress this imbalance.

Last but not least, I would like to thank my husband, John Haiman. In addition to hewing wood, drawing water, changing diapers, and washing dishes, he taught me the Hua language and gave me encouragement and criticism at every stage.

INTRODUCTION

The highlands of New Guinea may be described as a chain of valleys lying at altitudes of four to seven thousand feet. To the west the valleys are relatively open but elsewhere they are small and separated by ranges that vary in height from twelve to fourteen thousand feet. Although many populations live and garden on mountain slopes, the heaviest population concentrations are in the valleys and on the lower slopes of the surrounding foothills. Over the course of time large stretches of the indigenous forest, a rich source of food and innumerable essential materials, have been replaced by comparatively impoverished grasslands. Today the brilliant high grasses of denuded mountainsides, ridges, and valleys are a common sight in populated areas.

The Hua live on the slopes of Mount Michael (Hua *Roko*) near the Lufa District Office about forty miles southeast of Goroka, capital of the Eastern Highlands Province.[1] The eleven Hua villages are located at an altitude of 6,050 feet at the intersection of two ecosystems: montane forest stretches from the villages up the slopes of Mount Michael, while grasslands fall away from them to the Tua River several thousand feet below. Annual rainfall is approximately a hundred inches, with a wet season from November to April. As is to be expected from the proximity to the equator, there is little seasonal variation in temperature, though diurnal variation is considerable as a consequence of the altitude.

Settlement of the mountainous interior of New Guinea

---

1. *Lufa* is probably a corruption of *Ruva*, the Siane word for *Hua*. *Ruva* may mean something like "origin, base, foundation," its meaning in some Hua compounds (Haiman 1980a:xxix). The reference may be to the Siane (Hua *Kma*) practice of taking Hua brides.

dates back only ten thousand years (S. Bulmer 1964). An initial hunting and gathering economy gradually gave way to a seminomadic agriculture based on a stone age technology and the cultivation of taro, bananas, yams, and sugarcane. Production of these crops restricted the population to altitudes below 6,900 feet (Brookfield 1964). The final stage in the development of agriculture in the highlands began with the introduction of the sweet potato approximately three hundred fifty years ago (Conklin 1963). This crop allowed the development of considerably larger communities and settlement up to altitudes of 8,800 feet.

Throughout the highlands, as among the Hua at Lufa, slash and burn or shifting agriculture is the norm. Gardens are formed in forested areas, cultivated for a number of years, and then fallowed. Because of the leaching effect of heavy rains and the rapid invasion of insects and weeds, the productivity of slash and burn gardens declines rapidly after two to three years. Fallow periods ideally last from ten to twenty years, allowing sufficient time for the regeneration of substantial secondary growth of large trees but insufficient time for trees to revert to climax forest size, when they become extremely difficult to cut down. Slash and burn agriculture is successful only where the population is limited in size and the forest reserves are abundant. Otherwise, the population ultimately destroys the forest by shortening the fallow period to the point where only grasses and weeds replace trees. This has already occurred in the lower reaches of the Hua lands.

Clearing the forest is an arduous task, undertaken by males and made easier since contact by the replacement of the stone axe with a steel one. Prior to planting, the felled trees and undergrowth are burned, producing wood-ash fertilizer. To keep out marauding pigs, the garden must be fenced, an extremely laborious and time-consuming task performed by males. Planting, weeding, and harvesting were traditionally female work, but today these tasks are in many cases performed by husband and wife together.

Although sweet potato is the year-round staple of the

Hua diet, taro, yams, *pitpit* (a vegetable), bananas, sugar-cane, and a variety of leafy greens are also important, though on a more seasonal basis. European contact has led to the cultivation of potatoes, corn, peanuts, cucumbers, beans, tomatoes, and cabbage. The Hua have pig herds, traditionally raised by women, and consume large quantities of pork during exchange ceremonies, but pork is a minor food source in terms of overall dietary intake. An extended study of Hua nutrition found—despite the apparently inadequate diet, particularly in regard to protein—only relatively minor and infrequent signs of malnutrition (Norgan, Ferro-Luzzi, and Durnin 1974, Hornabrook, Crane, and Stanhope 1977). The Hua exhibit, as is typical of a population with an imperfect diet, a slow rate of growth, delayed attainment of maturity, and marked decreases in body weight with aging. Otherwise, they are not only extremely fit but very healthy (Sinnett 1977). Chronic respiratory disease is the only sign of ill health and, remarkably, there are no signs of the degenerative diseases common to our culture (Hornabrook, Crane, and Stanhope 1974).

The first patrol post was established at Lufa in 1954. By the 1970s Lufa Station included a district office, school, jail, medical aid post, and two trade stores. Adult males are required to pay an annual head tax and strongly encouraged to aid in road and school construction projects. Despite a mass baptism, mission influence among the Hua has been negligible. The Australian officers departed in 1975; the station is now staffed exclusively by New Guineans, most of whom come from coastal areas. They are, as one Hua told me, "our white men," an indigenous elite.

The Hua are subsistence gardeners who, through the techniques and resources of their traditional culture, can produce literally everything they need, with the exception of cash for the head tax and for the purchase of the steel axe. For this, they must either grow coffee for sale, work on a local government project, seek employment in Goroka, or receive money from a kinsman. Few adult males or females are involved in any kind of wage labor, but young unmarried males commonly leave Lufa for several years to seek employment in Goroka or Port Moresby, Papua New Guinea's capital city. On their return (and very few do not return to take up the traditional gardening life), whatever money they may have accumulated is soon dispersed throughout the community, through bride price payments, gambling at cards, and other means. Purchases at the local trade stores are sporadic and confined to nonessential items, such as tobacco, matches, salt, clothes, lard, canned fish, and kerosene.

SOCIAL ORGANIZATION

The eleven villages in the area around Lufa Station constitute the *Hua vede* "Hua people," a population of approximately thirty-one hundred. The residents of Korova, Auno, Rapiva, Roseve, and their respective offshoot villages of Sara, Himamu, Degi, and Kemerake are thought of as the descendants of four original brothers. Welded together by an idiom of common patrilineal descent, marriage within this eight-village unit was traditionally prohibited. The three remaining villages of the Hua people (Duto, Kiosa, and Havakeve'da) are conceived as a separate but more truly indigenous line and are bound to the first eight through ties of marriage. The idiom in which the Hua express the relationship between these two groups is "The Duto, Kiosa, Havakeve'da people live inside the Hua people." Rather than describing them as two opposed and relatively equal halves, as is typical of exogamous moieties, the Hua express the idea of a larger outer circle of population intermarrying a smaller inner circle.[2]

2. This kind of endogamous structure is attributed by the Hua to many peoples. The Siane people has Bi and Fo "inside" it, the Gono (a Gimi-speaking people) has Zanoto, Fusa, Maneve, and Ainsi "inside," the Hairo people (speaking a dialect of the Zagaria language family closely related to Hua) have Nana and Kumuhava on the "inside."

The Hua origin myth sanctions this division of the Hua people into two exogamous and unequal parts:

> A small fire had been lit in Bgukaiga [in the grasslands below Lufa]. On one side of this fire sat an old woman. On the other, a young one.
>
> Two wandering men saw the smoke of this fire. One of these men was a Duto man; the other a Hua. They went to the fire. The Duto man slept with the old woman and the Hua man with the young. The old woman, being old, had few children, and her descendants, to this day, are few [Duto, Kiosa, Havakeve'da]. The young woman had many children. Her sons, Rapiva, Auno, Korova, and Roseve, were the founders of the villages by those names.[3]

(Note that this myth accords to females the superior status of original inhabitants while allocating to males the inferior status of immigrants.)

Informants claim that in the past the eight common-descent villages married almost exclusively into the three "inside" ones. Examination of genealogies reveals that though many marriages were of this type, such marriages do not constitute the majority of cases in remembered history. The disproportion in population between the two groups alone would make exclusive intermarriage impossible. In any case it is clear from informant statements that such marriages represent one kind of ideal marriage choice.

A second important feature of the myth is its attribu-

---

3. Other versions of this myth use different names for the young woman's sons. Kemerakians, for example, name Kemerake as one of the original brothers. There is, in addition, considerable variation in the identity of the two males. In one version the male who sleeps with the old woman is an *u'be de* "original times man" and the man who sleeps with the young woman is an outsider. In another version the fire is imagined to have been located in Duto itself. Three people were sitting around it: an old man, his wife, and their daughter. A male stranger arrives and sleeps with the daughter. Their offspring are the ancestors of the common-descent villages, and the offspring of the old couple are the ancestors of the spouse villages.

tion of seniority to Duto (the Duto man married the old woman). Informants from the common-descent villages often defer in matters of history to residents of Duto. They say that other Hua people have not lived here always and do not know the proper answers to such questions; the people of Duto, who are the original inhabitants of this place, know its history well.

Until recently the Hua people were divided into two hostile camps: *aunoga vede* "upper inhabitants" and *ki'viga vede* "lower inhabitants." Members of the *aunoga vede* were the four brother villages of Korova, Sara, Roseve, and Kemerake, and of the *ki'viga vede* the four brother villages of Degi, Auno, Rapiva, and Himamu. Informants differed as to the position of the three remaining villages, Duto, Kiosa, and Havakeve'da, with respect to these two warring camps. Some claimed they were allied with the upper, others with the lower, and still others said that they remained neutral.

In their protracted civil war both sides formed alliances outside the Hua area. At the time of contact in the early 1950s the upper inhabitants were living as refugees with their Gimi-speaking allies at Gono, though they have now returned to their homes. While some drunken brawls, sorcery accusations, and competition in the local government council attest to a continuing upper-lower enmity, I get the impression it is growing stale. Cooperation in pig feasts and initiations is now common, though this presumably was not the case immediately after the repatriation of the upper inhabitants, which occurred shortly after pacification. In 1972 the upper inhabitants attended funeral ceremonies for a renowned lower man. Everyone arrived armed with bows and arrows amid rumors of impending conflict, but the event came off smoothly, suggesting that old antagonisms are dying.

In the late 1960s the upper and lower inhabitants added a new dimension to their already complicated relationship by "opening the gate for intermarriage" within what had previously been considered an exogamous patrilineal descent group. In a formal ceremony a pearl shell was ritually broken to satisfy the spirits of dead ancestors and women were exchanged.

Hua villages, which range from eighty to three hundred persons in size, contain two to six *aita* "patrilineages." These lineages exhibit the usual solidarity and notions of collective ownership and responsibility. Land, although held and inherited individually, cannot be alienated from the lineage without the permission of its leaders. Genealogical information seems to be considered the lineage's private property as well. (Any comment on another lineage's genealogy may be interpreted by that lineage as interference in its internal affairs and as a potential challenge of its legitimacy.) Traditionally males of a lineage live together in a single men's house and are united in their association with one of its doors and with the special tune of a single pair of flutes. A person collecting food, goods, or money for a bride price, a head payment, a funeral, a party for visiting affines, or any other payment or party common to Hua life relies most heavily on his lineage mates for assistance. This pattern of solidarity extends to fights between village members as well. Finally, each lineage fields a leader, and it is from these men that the village leaders are selected.

The official fiction is that each village member is a descendant of the village founder, but the proliferation of small lineages suggests a more complex reality. One Sara man told me, with a great show of secrecy, that in truth Sara lineages were not comprised of descendants of the original Hua ancestors but rather were all descendants of immigrants. Their claim of common patrilineal descent was, he said, "decoration." Other informants, when asked about the possibility that their own or other lineages were of immigrant status, were enraged. Further, they were determined to discover who had made this outrageous suggestion. In the end, however, most informants privately acknowledged that many lineages—their own excluded— were composed of descendants of an individual or group that had immigrated at least three generations in the past. The public attribution of such a status, however, was tantamount to a challenge of legitimacy.

Nonagnatic composition of patrilineal groups has been widely reported in the highlands starting with Barnes (1962), and the only respect in which the Hua seem different from other reported groups is that there is no evidence of current immigration. In Sara and Kemerake villages, for example, only one nonagnate is a permanent resident.

The idiom of patrilineal descent organizes the Hua conception of social structure at the largest (*vede* "people") and smallest (*aita* "lineage") levels. Intermediate levels are described in terms of the (*rafuri* "men's house") idiom. Traditionally each village had one, two, or rarely three centrally located, palisaded, and exceptionally large houses that were the exclusive residence of initiated males (and postmenopausal initiated females). Set on an east-west axis, each men's house ideally housed two lineages, each identified with a door over which it had the exclusive right of use.

The Hua conception of intermediate levels of group structure derives from this men's house model. Each people is imagined to have originated from the two doors of a single men's house, these two doors producing the four doors of two separate men's houses, and those four doors producing the eight doors of four separate men's houses.

As a consequence of this men's house idiom, duality pervades the Hua conception of the internal structure of all people, their own included. Each village is paired with a second (Kemerake with Roseve, Sara with Korova, and so on) with which it is supposed to have formerly shared a men's house and to which it provides extra loyalty and support. Further, the villages that comprise each people are divided into two groups representing the descendants of opposite doors of the original men's house. One can say of such a people, "They are people of one men's house." For example, the Chuave-speaking Irava group, with whose

members the Hua intermarry, has Kemaragu and Ruka-
movi villages at one door, Aunaporikaiga and Kifekonaro
at the other; the Gono group has Oritikevatoa, Frauvina,
and Nimihaipina villages at one door, Akuihaipina, Masa-
vikaiga, and Nimiaipi at the other; and the Kma group (a
Siane people) has Kitiro and Kuamo villages at one door,
Kione and Bi at the other.

This men's house idiom is intimately related to the Hua
form of genealogical reckoning known as *kivuro kia ri'di'*
"to trace out the vine of the sweet potato." Typical *kivuro kia ri'di'* involves tracing connections through mother,
mother's mother, father's mother, mother's mother's father,
or through sister, sister's daughter, sister's son's daughter,
sister's daughter's daughter's son, and so on—that is, tracing connections along paths made available by in-marrying
and out-marrying women. Such reckoning is particularly
important in compensation payments.

Nuria'bo ri- "to take a head" refers to the custom whereby
a real or classificatory mother's brother (*nono'*) or a group
of mother's brothers receives payment (one to three pigs,
substantial sums of money, shells, feathers, and so forth)
for "the head" of a sister's child, usually at the time of initiation for boys and menarche for girls. The general assumption has been that payment is made exclusively to
real or classificatory brothers of the mother's patrilineage
(A. Strathern 1972:97, Wagner 1967:68), an assumption
that undoubtedly has played a role in the characterization
of these payments as compensation to the matrilateral kin
for their inability to recruit the child. In the Hua case, however, payment may be made by a woman to any same-
generation male (*sa'* "sibling of opposite sex") who is a
member or descendant of the "door" of her father's father
(I recorded sixty-three remembered cases), father's mother
(four remembered cases), mother's father (nine cases), or
mother's mother (five cases). "Door" here may be interpreted narrowly to mean lineage or widely to mean village
or even village pair when convenient. Thus, for example,
a woman from Kma (Siane) married into Lufa whose

mother's mother came from Irava (Chuave), mother's father from Zobga (Siane), and father's mother from Gono (Gimi) could give the head of her child to men of her own generation from Kma, Irava, Zobga, and Gono.

Accordingly to some but not all of my Hua consultants, a real brother is specifically excluded as a possible recipient of the head payment. One's sister's son, they say, is analogous to one's child, and to profit from either through any kind of payment would be inappropriate. Parents, for example, do not themselves receive any of the bride price sent for their daughter.

Which of the numerous men eligible to receive payment actually does is determined by a gift-giving behavior called *kapito hurmi'bai-* "to wander at the door." Only the man (or men) who wanders at the door of his classificatory sister making regular prestations over a period of years will be favored by the woman to receive the head of her child.

Aumo sgo'di na "burning feast thing" refers to a second custom involving compensation of real or classificatory mother's brothers (*nono'*) or sister's sons (*nogu'*) who have wandered at ego's door. It takes place on the occasion of a physical injury to a male ego in which blood is drawn, especially from his head, or of a moral injury in which ego's genitals are exposed or his person is made the butt of an obscene joke. In the particular *aumo sgo'di na* that I observed, the mother's brothers and sisters' sons assembled before dawn at the injured party's house, their bodies smeared with white mud and decorated with branches of dead trees. While doing a shuffling dance, the men chanted the names of men of Kemerake, the injured man's village, and called to them mockingly that they were like a *hitura* ("mite") alleged to live only on female bodies, particularly in the pubic area; like thresholds that are filthy from being constantly stepped over; like a small bird called *kirigita*; or like pigs. In between their abuse of the males present, the dancers singled out the women in the crowd for praise as beautiful birds normally associated only with males.

The stated objective of the abuse is to shame the males into quick payment; the dance and chant continue without pause until this goal is achieved. In the observed instance, it took three and one-half hours for the men of Kemerake to come up with twenty-two Australian dollars, which they spread on the backs of two still dying pigs. The dancers immediately took the money and carried off the pigs shouting in unison *Dmine! Dmine!* "You have given me! You have given me!" To this the injured party's village replied loudly *Kmue! Kmue!* "I have given you! I have given you!"

Nine of the dancers came from Auno (a Hua village) but were eligible to dance because they were descended from women who came from Kma, as did the injured man's mother. Another party of four dancers actually had come for the event directly from Kma itself. Two dancers from Sara village also had Kma mothers. All of these people were related to the injured party through his mother's father's door, but informants insisted that any person who could reckon himself as mother's brother or sister's son through any of the injured person's three other doors (father's father, mother's mother, father's mother), and, of course, who had made the necessary prestations would have been eligible to dance and receive payment. Several days after the events, compensation was also made to some men and women residing in Kemerake whose mothers also had been born in Kma.

The *aumo sgo'di na*, which initially appears to be a custom that provides for the maintenance of active relationships with distant kin, in fact turns out to be a custom in which the nonpatrilineal connections between people living together in patrilineal communities are exploited; matrilateral kin and descendants of sisters living abroad are virtually excluded.

The Hua say that they marry their friends, never their enemies, but the fact that the upper and lower inhabitants, although still in some senses enemies, are cautiously beginning to intermarry suggests some complications. Under Hua marriage rules, cross-cousin marriage, either matrilateral or patrilateral, is preferred. The only limitations on cross-cousin marriage are, in the Hua idiom, that in a matrilateral marriage ego cannot take a woman from ego's mother's door and that in a patrilateral marriage ego cannot marry the daughter of a woman of ego's own door. A minimal version of this rule, and the one preferred by the younger generation, is that ego cannot marry a woman of his mother's lineage or of his own. A second, stricter interpretation is that ego cannot marry a woman of his mother's village or of his own (that is, the daughter of a woman born in his village but married elsewhere). The strictest interpretation of all, one that is suggested only occasionally, is that the rule applies to the village pairs. In other words, ego cannot marry a woman from his mother's village or the village with which it is paired, or a woman born to a woman whose natal village was ego's or the one with which ego's is paired.

In whichever case, Hua males say they like to marry from the opposite door of one of their own men's houses, which may be reckoned back to the fourth generation in exceptional cases. Such a marriage may be staged as an exchange between the two doors of the same men's house, two segments of the same community—in other words, as endogamy. Furthermore, a woman may say (and presumably feel) at marriage that she "is entering the gate of her father's mother's community," that is, that she is returning to the home of her ancestors. I witnessed such a marriage in which the two doors of the original Kemerake men's house each played a separate role: one the role of wife giver with the bride's people and the other the role of wife receiver. The bride, descended through one of her ancestors from Kemerake, was perceived as marrying a relative.

These rules seem, however, mysteriously inapplicable to marriages with the inside villages of Duto, Kiosa, and Havakeve'da, which informants tell me have no doors and with which marriage is not only frequent but indiscriminate. When asked why outside villages so often marry into Duto, Kiosa, and Havakeve'da, informants often say either that they do not want to waste their sisters' offspring on another people or that they do not want to isolate their sisters in groups with which they might fight in some future war. Clearly these are reasons only for marrying one's sisters to Duto, Kiosa, and Havakeve'da, not for taking wives from them. Hua males say that while they like to marry their sisters into the immediate vicinity and thus keep them close at hand, they themselves do not like to marry women from nearby for fear of the scrutiny and demands of their kin. Marriage with a woman from Duto, Kiosa, or Havakeve'da is clearly marriage within the immediate vicinity and thus violates this stated preference.

Because of the Hua custom of concentrating their marriages both as bride givers and as bride receivers, each Hua village contains pools of women who originated from the same people, if not lineage, who speak the same language, and who are real or classificatory kin. The older generation of in-marrying women is called *ku' a'* "first women" and the younger *i' a'* "later women." The first women are under an obligation—they receive a portion of the bride price for this purpose—to provide extensive physical and emotional support to the later women. In fact, women maintain that they refuse marriage offers from areas that do not contain kinswomen. The children of these women are called X *none*, where X refers to the women's natal community. These shadow communities also recruit women married to sons of their village who have never lived in the original community but who are born to a woman who lived there prior to her marriage. To the first women these women are mother's sister's daughters. The sons of the first women call them siblings of the opposite sex and extend to them the hospitality and support appropriate to a consanguine but totally inappropriate to an opposite-sex affine, who is the object of suspicion and avoidance.

Many of the head payments and most of the injury compensation payments at Lufa are negotiated not with "true" mother's brothers or sister's sons residing abroad but with their surrogates, fellow members of Lufa's shadow community. This shadow group phenomenon is, I believe, related to the previous Hua geopolitical situation. In a war with their immediate neighbors (the "civil war" at Lufa and alienation from the Yagaria speakers immediately to the north), the Hua were forced to make their alliances in the far distance. The upper inhabitants, for example, were allies with the Gimi (a half-day walk away) and the Siane and Chuave (two full days away).

(This alliance pattern results in a quite unusual degree of multilingualism among the Hua. In a 1974 survey of 359 adult speakers of Hua, 305 were fluent in Gimi, 287 in Siane, and 103 in Chuave. At least half a dozen other languages were also spoken. Only 2 people claimed to be totally monolingual, and only 11 knew just one other language besides Hua. Many people were fluent in four or five languages [Haiman 1979:36].)

The *kivuro kia ri'di'* mode of genealogical reckoning and the institution of shadow communities provide the Hua with the means of fulfilling the personnel requirements for compensation customs that are traditional throughout the highlands without necessitating the inconveniences and dangers of travel. They also provide the new bride, unable to make frequent visits home as in other areas (M. Strathern 1972:96), with a surrogate family.

MALE AND FEMALE

From the beginning ethnographers reported what seemed to be an exceptional state of sexual affairs in the New Guinea highlands (Read 1952, 1954, Meggitt 1964, Langness 1967). Men lived in strict residential segregation and indulged in frequent rites of expulsion of dreaded female substances, such as nose or penis bleeding, vomiting, tongue scraping, sweating, and eye washing. Male initiates were forbidden to eat substances that had been touched by women, and innumerable foods were tabooed because of their alleged resemblances to abhorred aspects of female anatomy or physiology. Contact with menstrual blood could destroy a boy's growth or a man's health, bring defeat in war or the failure of a hunt. Sexual intercourse was thought to occasion debilitating losses of life-sustaining semen.

Women were confined to the nonmale sections of village and garden, required to perform numerous onerous tasks, regulated into submission, and denied knowledge of the religious truths of Hua culture. The sacred flutes were paraded openly, but men reserved the right to kill a woman who looked at them. Marriages were arranged by males, and if women ran away they were allegedly trussed up on poles like pigs and returned to their husbands.

The first generalization drawn from these data was that male-female relations in the highlands of New Guinea were antagonistic. The data were used as a diagnostic of the emotional contents of social relationships. The problem then became one of explaining the origins or correlates of that hostility. Meggitt (1964) pointed to the affinal relationship: where people marry those whom they also fight in battle, he predicted a fear by "prudes" of female pollution, as among the Mae; where people confine their marriages to their friends, he predicted an absence of pollution fears and instead the struggle of "lechers" to assert their control over women, as among the Kuma. Lindenbaum (1972: 247), on the other hand, saw pollution fears as a "cultural whip in societies where available resources are endangered by further population increase." Pollution, she alleged, is of less concern in the Eastern and Central Highlands, where population expansion is not an environmental threat.

Langness (1967) suggested that the antagonism between the sexes is intimately related to the warfare endemic to the highlands. A small population faced with almost constant threat of annihilation urgently needs a powerful and dedicated army. To achieve the necessary solidarity, males need to be separate, physically and emotionally, from women. The ideology of female pollution and danger motivates this segregation and thus provides the conditions necessary for male solidarity, but it simultaneously leads to sexual frustrations and antagonisms. Langness's theory seems to me particularly relevant to the Hua.

The next generation of anthropologists eschewed functional formulations and concentrated on the description of previously overlooked facts. Hogbin (1970) and Meigs (1976) inferred male envy of female procreative powers from male imitation of menstruation and pregnancy; A. Strathern (1970) reported all-male fertility cults and male worship of female deities, which reinforced the growing impression of male feelings of sexual inferiority. It was discovered that men as well as women could pollute (M. Strathern 1972, Faithorn 1976) and, furthermore, that the female substances of pollution might also serve as powerful stimulants of growth and health. Sexual intercourse was not only feared but also enjoyed, and in many societies initiates were given a double message: sex is dangerous and debilitating but sexual success is a source of pride and prestige. The power implicit in the female role as the provider of food was finally recognized, and the denigration of women was seen in a new light as the male response to their dependence on females (Lindenbaum 1976).[4]

4. Throughout the highlands men find themselves dependent on women not only for their daily food but also for the pigs important to exchange. See Buchbinder and Rappaport (1976) and Lindenbaum (1976).

Chapter One

EATING AS A
SYMBOLIC ACTIVITY

Most, perhaps all, distinctively human institutions—art, myth, ritual, language, society, and law—are essentially symbolic inasmuch as they are conceived as meaningful representations rather than as things in themselves. Anything can stand as a sign for anything else, given the appropriate interpretive conventions. For the Hua, as for many other Melanesian peoples, food and its consumption are also symbolic representations of another reality. The values food assumes in Hua thinking are illustrated by the constraints on its consumption.

In principle, food values fall into two categories: values intrinsic to the food (the nutritional, repletive, homeopathic, and aesthetic values) and values extrinsic to the food (the contagious or consubstantial values), which depend on the status of the person who produced or prepared it.

Roughly corresponding to these two kinds of values are two kinds of rules, which I shall characterize as absolute and relative. Absolute rules define a relation between the consumer and a certain kind of food: prototypically, "X may not eat Y." The relationship between "X" and "Y" is determined largely by properties intrinsic to the food that may be injurious to the consumer. Relative rules define a relationship between a consumer, a food, and a source: prototypically, "X may not eat Y from Z." Here the relationship between "X" and "Y" is determined principally by the social relationship that exists between the consumer and the producer; it is relatively independent of the nature of the food itself. Both types of rules reflect biological and social conceptions.

The following are typical examples of the many absolute rules among the Hua (see appendix A for a complete list of these rules and their motivation):

1. A male undergoing initiation may not eat foods that are red or that release a reddish juice. (The redness is explicitly associated with menstrual blood.)
2. A male undergoing initiation may not eat foods that smell *be' ftu*. (*Be' ftu* is the smell of a menstruating woman and of a number of rotting substances.)
3. A male undergoing initiation must eat soups made of *kosidi' zasa* "leaves for growing." (Males in general are preoccupied with the male rate of growth. Fathers compare their sons to determine who is growing faster and boys make frequently painful comparisons.)

The following are examples of relative rules, of which there are fewer (see appendix B for a complete list):

1. A mature initiated male may not eat leafy green vegetables picked by his real or classificatory wife or first-born child. (These vegetables carry some of the *nu* "vital essence" of the wife or child and are therefore dangerous to the eater.)
2. An adult must not eat a pig raised by, wild animal shot by, or the prize garden produce cultivated by his or her firstborn child or agemates, or her co-wives. (These substances are suffused with the *nu* of the producer, inasmuch as the labor involved in raising, cultivating, or killing these foods transfers *nu* to the food itself.)

Analogs to rules of these two types have been reported— without comment—by ethnographers from elsewhere as well. For example:

Havik Brahmin, South India (Harper 1964:155–158)
   Absolute: A pregnant woman may not eat any food from the sea.

Relative: A pregnant woman may not eat any food from a woman who has just had, or is likely to have, sexual intercourse.

Baktaman, New Guinea (Barth 1975:162–172)

Absolute: Male initiates may not eat dogs, lizards, snakes, and so forth.

Relative: Male initiates may not eat pigs that they themselves have tended.

Baan Phraan Muan, Thailand (Tambiah 1969:431)

Absolute: A pregnant woman may not eat a civet cat.

Relative: A village member may not eat an animal from his own village at a village ritual; similarly, a household member may not eat an animal from his own household at a household ritual.

The Hua, like anthropologists in general, do not comment on this absolute-relative distinction. They do not have different names for the two kinds of rules (indeed, they may be said to have no word for rule, other than the Pidgin borrowing *ro* "law"), but the distinction need not be dismissed as an artifact of the ethnographer's taxonomy, because behavioral distinctions correspond with the two types of rules.

Absolute rules were clearly uppermost in people's minds as the subject of ceremonial injunctions or sermons at initiations. Both the inception and the termination of absolute rules were the focus of ceremonial rites of passage. Ironically, these rules are the ones that tend to survive chiefly in the recollection of informants. Relative rules were much more casual, imparted without ceremony and terminated without undue fanfare. Although somewhat more difficult to elicit than absolute rules, they are mostly still observed. Very broadly speaking, then, the absolute rules were a part of ceremonial life, while the relative rules were and continue to be much more securely embedded in the daily round.

Young (1971:146) wrote, "It is a truism that Melanesian peoples in general value food in ways which transcend its value for them as a necessity of life." What he and most Melanesian ethnographers have meant in speaking of the symbolic value of food is that its transfer and consumption symbolize a variety of social relationships. In the general theoretical literature, this point has been made repeatedly by Lévi-Strauss (1963, 1966, 1967), Leach (1964), Douglas (1966), and Tambiah (1969).

Unquestionably Hua food rules do mirror distinctions of age, sex, and ritual and reproductive status, because food has social value attributed to it. According to the Hua, food carries some of the *nu* and therefore some of the power of the persons who cultivated or prepared it for eating. This notion, which corresponds roughly to the Western idea of germs, may be called the contagious social value of food.

In addition to carrying *nu*, food is also in some sense congealed *nu*. Food, like blood, breath, hair, sweat, fingernails, feces, urine, footprints, and shadows, is viewed as an effusion of the body, more specifically of its labor. I call the resulting social value of food its consubstantial social value.

The changing relative rules that affect consumers when the producer is a woman neatly reflect the changing status of the woman throughout her life. It is worth tracing a woman's biography as reflected in the food rules to demonstrate how pervasive the metaphor is.

In the community of her birth, an *abade* "girl" may produce or prepare food for all but the newest *kakora* "initiates." Her food, like the girl herself, is fully accepted in her natal village. After marriage, the girl is a *hauva a'* "new woman" in the community of her husband, where her stock plummets. No initiated person of this community, including her husband, can eat any food that she has produced, prepared, or served. Nor may any initiate eat from an earth oven into which she has placed leafy green vegetables. Once the new woman has borne a child, her alienation from her husband's community diminishes; it continues to diminish with every subsequent child she bears. So too does the danger of pollution from her hands. By the time she has had three children, she may assume the honorable status of a *ropa a'* "mature or venerable woman." Leafy green vegetables that she has picked may then be freely eaten by an older initiate, though still not by new initiates or her own husband. After about fifteen years of marriage, the proscriptions on eating leafy green vegetables picked by the wife are informally terminated. The wife gives her husband some leafy greens, and his classificatory elder brother (that is, any older man from his village) tells him to eat them freely, as if they came from the hand of his own mother, who is not only a woman he has always trusted but also a totally desexed being to him. The final transfiguration of a woman occurs after menopause. If she has had more than three children, she is formally initiated, and like male initiates, must obey all the food rules to which this most pure and vulnerable class is subject.

As the female's danger index changes throughout her life, so does the male's vulnerability. As a young *figapa* "noninitiate," a young boy may eat food produced or prepared by anyone except a menstruating woman. After his initiation, which occurs between the ages of seven and twelve, he enters his period of greatest vulnerability: consumption of any food produced or prepared by a menstruating or postparturient woman, by a "new woman," or by anyone of either sex who has recently had intercourse could permanently stunt his growth. Gradually, the vulnerability of the initiate and his subjection to food proscriptions diminishes, so that by the time a man has had several children, as a *ropa de* "mature man," he is required to obey relatively few restrictions. In extreme old age, a man reassumes the role of noninitiate and with it total invulnerability to female pollution and nearly total freedom from constraints on what he may or may not eat.

It is easy to infer from examples like these the extent to which the contagious and consubstantial values of foods—that is, their extrinsic values—limit and define social status and relationships. More striking than the delineation of these relationships, however, is the definition that food rules provide for the intrinsic values of various foods.

Intrinsic to a given food are its nutritional, repletive, homeopathic, and possibly aesthetic values. In a Western social order where the relationship between consumer and producer is in most cases an entirely impersonal one, these intrinsic values are presumably the only ones that may determine the attitude of a consumer to the food he or she eats.

The nutritional value of a food is its nonsymbolic value *in itself*, whether as a source of protein, roughage, or whatever, for growth, work, and vital processes. The Hua express no opinions on the nutritional value of food, and it is tempting to infer that the concept is unknown to them. Yet any observer must realize rather that it is taken for granted, for the sweet potato, the recognized staff of life, is subject to exactly two intrinsic restrictions, neither of which affects intake: initiates are enjoined not to eat the ends of sweet potatoes because they resemble the ends of feces and not to eat insufficiently cooked sweet potato because its persistent rawness indicates it has been contaminated by menstrual blood. The absolute rules, which in many cases do interfere with consumption, are restricted to the numerous peripheral items in the diet, such as peripheral species of vegetable greens and nonmeat portions of pig. The relative rules prohibit consumption of pork, vegetable greens, and sweet potato produced or prepared by specific persons, but again these restrictions do not appreciably limit overall consumption.

Although the distribution of food rules suggests that the Hua are aware on some unspoken level of nutritional value, their explicit comments indicate that foods have no powers to nourish other than those provided by their homeopathic or social values. One grows fast, they say, if one eats a fast-growing food. One's vitality and general health are enhanced by eating a food produced or prepared by a trusted friend or relative, that is, by receiving good *nu*. The same food produced or prepared by a distrusted individual can cause weakness, ill health, malnourishment.

Some Eastern Highlands populations recognize a repletive value of food in contrast to a nutritive one. For example, to the Daribi of Karimui, bananas and sugarcane, among other foods, serve merely to stave off the pangs of hunger and pass through the alimentary system entirely as urine and feces (Wagner 1972:40). It is possible that the Hua recognize such a repletive function for some foods, but I was able to gather no data that confirmed this.

It seems safe to say that for the Hua, the intrinsic value of a food is almost entirely homeopathic, a value that a peripheral food acquires by virtue of being a symbol (or more accurately, an icon) of something else.[1] Certain analogs to the homeopathic evaluation of food are familiar to Western readers. American children generally find okra and certain kinds of cheese repulsive because of their tactile and olfactory similarities to spittle and excrement. Though for some people this revulsion may last a lifetime, it is not a culturally approved response.

Matters are different among the Hua. Two closely related homeopathic principles motivate a large number of restrictions on the consumption of food. The first is that a substance develops effects similar to the qualities that it contains. A slimy food causes the consumer to become slimy, a fast-growing food causes him to grow quickly, and so forth. The second principle is that where a substance causes a specific effect, a similar-looking substance will cause a similar effect. For example, the Hua believe that contact with menstrual blood causes males to degenerate physically. Consequently there are constraints on the consumption of pandanus, whose redness is reminiscent of that of menstrual blood. Contact with female pubic hair is viewed as a threat to male growth and strength. Consequently there are constraints on the ingestion of hairy foods. The homeopathic value of a food, then, is its power

1. An icon is any sign that resembles its referent; an index, a sign that bears a relationship of contiguity with its referent; and a symbol, a sign whose connection with its referent is arbitrary and determined by convention.

to make the consumer develop the qualities of the food itself or to produce in the consumer effects similar to those of some dangerous or beneficent substance that the food resembles.

The extent to which the nutritional values of peripheral foods are ignored may be inferred from traditional responses to malnutrition. Kwashiorkor is not unknown, and the distended belly that is characteristic of the condition is not unreasonably attributed to the consumption of some forbidden foods rather than to a deficiency in protein. The traditional Hua response to this disease is to limit or proscribe many of the peripheral foods whose consumption could partially redress the deficiencies of a diet that is largely based on the sweet potato.

A few words should be said about the aesthetic value of food. Differences in taste are certainly appreciated. Not only may foods be identified as either *haga* "sweet, good tasting" or *ta* "bitter, spicy hot," but there are foods that are generally identified as desirable in taste: pork is a prized *deke'na* "delicacy," and the manufacture of native salt, which was recognized to have no nutritive or repletive value and only minimal homeopathic value, seems to have been the most technologically complex element of traditional Hua culture. The aesthetic properties of various foods, however, seem to have been the occasion for no dietary restrictions.

Food as a symbol and the functions served by the constraints on its consumption may be viewed from an etic or an emic perspective. The etic perspective is that of the Western ethnographer, the emic, that of the local resident. Because this book is an account of an indigenous ideology, it focuses on the emic perspective. Objectively (or etically) speaking, food is no more a symbol than is anything else. Whether or not an object is viewed symbolically and the nature of any symbolic value are purely matters of convention, and thus emic. Etically, objects exist not as symbols of something else, but as objects in themselves.

From the (emic) perspective of the Hua, food is an indexical symbol of its producer or preparer by virtue of its association with that person, and an icon (albeit a conventionalized one) of objects perceived to be similar. Food may thus symbolize an individual (whose value relative to ego is defined by a culturally specific theory of social relationships) or another object (whose value is determined by a culturally specific theory of biology).

The functional value of a food rule or of the set of dietary restrictions depends on our evaluation of these indigenous theories. To the functionalist ethnographer, the etic social functions of many constraints, and not only those that relate to food, are to define and reinforce the social categories of a culture and to heighten the individual's sense of participation within it. It does not matter if these functions are not recognized by the local person him or herself. For Radcliffe-Brown (1964:271), for example, food proscriptions served to remind the individual of his dependence not only on food, but also on society, and thus "to awaken in him day after day the feeling of his relation to his fellows."

To such an ethnographer, the function of the Hua food proscriptions is to enhance the individual's participation in or alienation from groups and subgroups in the Hua community. The vast complex of prohibitions to which initiates are subject creates among them an esprit de corps as each initiate is reminded at every meal not only of what relates him to some of his fellows, but of what sets him apart from others.

Although these rules probably do intensify local perceptions of social categories, my Hua consultants never mentioned this function. I doubt whether it exists in their conscious thinking at all. In fact, I suggest that if we were to survey the accounts of dietary restrictions in world ethnography, we should encounter few cases where the social functionalist explanation for such restrictions is recognized by the person who obeys them. I can think of only one whose *original* motivation is a social one, an example which by its familiarity may serve as a kind of yardstick by which to evaluate the others.[2] When American liberals in 1968 refused to eat California grapes, their avowed purposes were to express not only their social solidarity with the grape pickers but also their hostility to agribusiness giants and to cause the conglomerates economic hardship. The function of this food constraint was transparently social.

Contrast this case with the food avoidance practice reported by McKnight (1973:205) among the Wid-Mungkan of Australia that prohibits a man from eating food directly from his mother-in-law: "If I am ill, even my mother-in-law may give me *ngaintja* [tabooed] food, but she must give it to me indirectly by giving it to my wife to cook for me. The cooking will remove the sweat, smell, or presence of my mother-in-law from the food."

In both cases, ego is enjoined to avoid food from an alter who is defined as socially inimical to him. In the American case, the refusal is made on principle, to give expression to social hostility. The Wid-Mungkan, however, obeys the taboos to protect his health. The rejected food is the symbol of a hostile alter, but the rejection has a biological rather than a social function. Though the worldwide ethnographic literature on dietary restrictions is not extensive, it suggests that the Wid-Mungkan, rather than the American liberal, represents the more common case.

It has often been observed that the producer of a food is identified with the food he or she cultivates, kills, or cooks. (See, for example, Richards 1948:170, Tuzin 1972:233–234.) It has less frequently been observed, though it is even more apparent, that we are what we eat: the consumer is identified with the food he or she consumes and thus absorbs. (Bell [1948–1949:51] points out that in Tanga, as well as in other Oceanic languages, one's food is classified grammatically with one's body parts and kindred, as an inalienable possession.)

2. A number of rules such as the Jewish and Muslim dietary restrictions on pork probably *originated* as biological in intent but acquired a life of their own, continuing as an index of the religious affiliation of their adherents even after the original motivation was lost.

Clearly, the value of a food may depend on the relationship between its producer and its consumer. That is, food is a social symbol. Crawley (1960,1:196–199) lists some examples of resulting prohibitions on ingestion:

> In New Zealand, one can be "bewitched" by eating or drinking from the calabash of the ill-wisher or by smoking his pipe. . . . in ancient India, a Brahmin might not eat the food of an enemy or an ungrateful man, or that offered by a sick, angry or intoxicated person. . . . Cardiak whalers are considered "unclean," and no one will eat out of the same dish with them, or even approach them, for that reason. . . . in the Am Islands, a menstruous woman may not plant, cook, or prepare any food.

In all of these cases, what motivates the abstainer is not principle but biological self-interest.

Certainly, it is to this motive that the Hua give frequent and vehement expression. Consider, for example, the following two absolute rules and the explanations for their existence:

1. Initiates must eat soups of *kosidi' zasa* "leaves for growing" (all of which are *korogo* "soft, juicy, fast-growing").
2. A menstruating woman should not eat *kito'* "leafy green vegetables," *pitpit*, or sugarcane (all *korogo* substances). She should instead eat substances that are *hakeri'a* "hard, dry, slow-growing."

What motivates these and many other rules ultimately is a native theory of health deriving from the notion of the proper distribution of *nu* between the sexes.

The male, having a relatively small amount of *nu*, has difficulty in growing in his adolescent years and in maintaining adequate vitality in his adult years. The female, because of her inherently greater endowment of *nu*, grows fast, ages slowly, and maintains her vitality, but because of an excess of *nu*, she suffers from a disturbing and unattractive moistness and smelliness of her body.

The explicit motivation of the first absolute rule is that it releases to the male extra supplies of *nu*, which is stored in *korogo* substances, to compensate for his inherent deficiency. The second rule is an attempt to compensate for an excess of *nu* in females by reducing the intake of *nu*.

The biological function of relative rules is no less evident:

1. Certain egos must not eat leafy greens picked by certain alters.
2. Certain egos must not allow their bodies, food, or implements to be crossed by the body or the shadow of certain alters.
3. Certain egos must not eat the deceased body of, deceased child of, blood of, pig of, or wild animal shot by certain alters.

In all of these cases, the social relationship between ego and alter may be characterized as ambivalent if not hostile. But the given function of the rule is to provide biological protection against substances inimical to good health.

The first of these relative rules provides protection to Hua individuals from bodily emissions in general and from sexual fluids in particular, of which the hand is thought to be the predominant transmitter. (Consultants pointed out that matter accumulates under the fingernails of infrequently washed hands.) These emissions represent hostile *nu*, the absorption of which damages or destroys growth and health.

The second relative rule is directed to the avoidance of *nu* in the form of excretions, as well as sexual fluids that may drop from alter's genitals onto ego's food. (The Hua wear only loincloths.) This rule is also directed to the avoidance of the shadow, which represents an immaterial manifestation of a person's essence and is thus as dangerous as *nu* itself.

The third rule, unlike the others, is meant as a protection of the individual against the consubstantial rather than the contagious social value of food. Like the others, however, the rule is motivated by purely biological self-interest. Hostile *nu* in any form can cause ill health and is thus to be avoided.

These rules are thus not only, perhaps not even primarily, signs of social categories and relationships. They are a significant expression of the Hua theory of growth and health. In terms of that theory, a strong and healthy body and a proper rate of growth are dependent on the regulation of the vital essence or *nu* in a food by virtue of its resemblance to another object, its own properties, or the person who prepared it for consumption. The indigenous explanations for most Hua dietary restrictions allow us to infer from these rules the outlines of an ideology of life.

Chapter Two

FOOD RULES
AND THE TRADITIONAL
SEXUAL IDEOLOGY

To talk with a Hua male about why he does not eat a food is ultimately to talk with him about the nature of sexual differences. Most foods stand for sexual states, organs, and processes, and indigenous explanations of food rules are rife with sexual references. A question about a food rule immediately embroils ethnographer and consultant in the details of a complicated, multifaceted sexual ideology.

Here I shall examine only one facet of this ideology: the naive or common knowledge that males are superior, powerful, and pure, that females are inferior, malevolent, weak, and polluted. This general portrait of the sexual stereotypes was drawn by the first generation of New Guinea highlands ethnographers and continues to dominate the literature today. It was based on a relatively standard set of data: the residential segregation of the sexes, the existence of men's cults, the males' fear of menstrual and parturitional fluids, the various rituals to expel symbolically such substances from the bodies of men, and the rules of female avoidance in general.

These phenomena do exist among the Hua, and the eating rules and the metaphors associated with them provide strong new support for the description of New Guinea sexual ideology as one of overwhelming male superiority and power. But beneath the arrogant male ideological stance, the ground is soft. Careful study reveals a second facet to male thinking—an attitude of reproductive impotence and sexual inferiority.

The analysis presented in this chapter, although applicable to the entire set of food rules, derives from a detailed study of only one class of prohibitions, those enjoined upon a male initiate, the most vulnerable class of persons, and, therefore, the one most in need of protection through isolation from dangerous foods. These prohibitions may last a week, a month, a year, or until extreme old age. The following simplified catalog groups the prohibitions into eight main categories, which are summarized in table 1 (see appendix A for a complete list):

1. Things that are red. This prohibition includes all the reddish spinachlike vegetables, the two reddish taros (*koraiziziya* and *kai atve*), the reddish banana (*opne*), the red birds, the two reddish mushrooms (*arerua* and *kuhara*), and most important, the red pandanus. The oil of the pandanus is identified by male informants with menstrual blood (see also Lindenbaum 1976). The original pandanus is said to have been created out of refuse at the site of an abandoned menstrual hut.

The identification between the pandanus and menstrual blood is paralleled by that between the color red and the vagina. The insult "Your mother's red bird burns!" refers to her vagina. Male informants say that the vagina is like the red impatiens flower (Balsaminaceae *Impatiens hawkeri*). One man, who occasionally wore a blossom pasted to his nose, told me he did so because he liked women and sex.

2. Items that smell *be' ftu*. *Be' ftu*, the smell of a menstruating woman, is said by males to be like the smell of a number of rotting substances. (Buchbinder and Rappaport 1976 report a similar association between female sexuality and decay among the Maring of the Central Highlands.) Included in this class of prohibitions are certain species of possum, one mushroom (*zokoni*) that resembles the commonly eaten North American one, and two species of yam (*fanu hgu* and *ame'*).

3. Foods that male informants associate with a hole. Included are the birds and possums that live in holes in trees, a species of fish (*dgopo'*) that lives under rock overhangs, the mouse, and the possum species that live in holes in the

Table 1
CATEGORIES OF PROHIBITED FOODS

Foods that are	Because of identification with
Red	Menstrual blood and vagina
Be' ftu in smell	Smell of menstruating woman
Associated with holes	Vagina
Hairy	Pubic hair
Possum (or foods associated with)	Female sexuality and fertility in general
Associated with the ground	Uncleanness and subordination in general and of women in particular
Dark on the interior	Ill health and fertility
Wild	Things inimical to males and their projects

ground. In addition, one mushroom (*dkugea'*) is forbidden because it grows in holes in trees.

Some informants identified the mouse holes with the vagina. My inference—that holes have vaginal connotations in certain eating contexts—receives confirmation in insults that play on the vaginal origin of the insulted person: "Are you something that came from an earth overhang? from a hole in the ground? from a hole in a tree? from a hole in the rocks?"

4. Things that informants claim are hairy. This prohibition includes all the furred animals with the exception of the pig, the birds that have particularly profuse facial plumage, and a vegetable (*fera okani*) that is said to be hairy.

Informants say that possum fur is like female pubic hair and that bird faces in which the mouth is surrounded by heavy plumage are like the female pudenda.

5. Possum. So potent is this taboo that a number of foods are forbidden simply because of their resemblance to possum. For example, insufficiently cooked sweet potato is prohibited because its whiteness resembles that of possum eyes, traditional salt because the cake was curved like

a possum tail, pork from the bone because pig bones resemble possum bones, and a ground-growing mushroom
(knegu) plus all water from the jungle because possums
have polluted both with their urine and feces.

Male informants, when asked why they do not eat possum, usually answer, "Because I might become pregnant."
One informant, however, answered, "Possum is the counterpart of women." Other informants confirmed this statement and some, when asked how possum was the female
counterpart, volunteered that possum fur is like female
pubic hair, that the holes in which possums live are like vaginas, that possums smell like menstruating women, or that
the way one species of possum, the hazubre', creeps out of
trees is like the infant's emergence from the vagina.

6. Substances that informants associate with the ground.
They include short sugarcanes, ground-growing mushrooms, birds that live or feed on the ground, pig feet,
mouse, dog, and ground possums. What was taboo about
the ground was difficult to elicit in reference to the food prohibitions themselves and emerged only in other contexts.

The ground is associated with uncleanness. The Hua,
who have no latrines and undergarments for humans and
stalls or pens for animals, maintain that the ground is
heavily contaminated by human and animal waste. The
ground-feeding animals, with which women are identified, are said to have interiors darkened by this waste,
while the tree-feeding animals, with which men are identified, remain pure and white. In the residentially segre-
gated past, the dirt floor of a woman's house was alleged to
be especially contaminated. When crawling around inside
these very low structures, males supported their hands
with sticks to avoid contamination, according to informants. (A similar identification of the ground with pollution and of the arboreal heights and sky with purity has
been reported in numerous New Guinea societies. See
R. Bulmer 1967, Barth 1975.)

The ground is also associated with subordination. The
relevant features are the uncleanness and the lowness of
the ground. Women traditionally were compelled to hide

their eyes and bend their bodies to the ground in an attitude of submission when men paraded the cult flutes. Female sleeping platforms were low, barely off the ground, in contrast to the greater elevation of the male platforms—a difference that male informants claim as a significant contrast between the sexes. (Barth 1975:20 reports a similar low-high contrast between the houses belonging to females and those belonging to males among the Baktaman of New Guinea's Western District.) A standard response to a question about why a man should not eat a prohibited food is "Lest I be on the ground." Informants explain this statement as meaning "Lest I fail in my subsequent efforts and battles," in other words, "Lest I become subordinate."

Finally, the ground is associated with women indirectly because of their allegedly unclean and subordinate qualities and directly through various metaphors. Women are said to be like the ground-living toads while men are like birds. Nearly all female names are drawn from the ground-hugging plants, while male names are taken from the tall trees, birds, and mountains.

7. Substances that informants say are dangerous to eat because they have dark interiors. This class includes two species of taro (*ekremu'* and *kinarikogu*), mouse, dog, possum, the large birds, and the heart, liver, and intestines of the pig. (Possum, mouse, and dog appear in many of the prohibition classes. Being multiply prohibited, they are highly taboo.)

Informants were unable or unwilling to specify the dangerous characteristics of foods with dark interiors. I think it is fair to infer that their conception of this danger is related to their ideas about food and fertility. Darkness of blood is said to be a sign of bad health: blood darkens, thickens, and consequently begins to smell only with sickness and old age. The awesome state of fertility is associated by males with rotting, putrid, dark, and heavy matter. The interior of a woman's body, like a fertile soil, is said to exhibit these qualities. (The Maenge of New Britain also associate fertility with blackness, liquid, coolness, and rot, and infertility with whiteness, dryness, and hardness. See Pan-

off 1970b:242.) These associations undoubtedly derive
from observation of relative soil fertilities.

8. Wild things. In this class informants include the wild
yams and taros, wild bananas, wild green vegetables, and
wild red pandanuses, the white pandanus (of which all
species are considered wild), and, again, the possum and
mouse.

In all of the prohibited types discussed so far, informants
made, or I was able to infer, an association between the
prohibited aspect of the food and some aspect of the female body or social status. In the case of the prohibition on
things that are wild, the association with women is secondary. The primary characteristics that the Hua attribute
to wild biota in general are that they are unknown to and
uncontrolled by humans. As such, they constitute a danger. Female reproductive powers fall into this class of mysterious, dangerous, and uncontrollable phenomena.

The assumption that female reproductive powers are essentially wild is implicit in the male view that the mere
presence of certain categories of women destroys many
cultural projects. A man making a bow, arrow, axe, or flute
must do so at a distance from women. If a male makes an
earth oven, he has to keep women away, for their presence
would prevent the food from cooking. Similarly, butchered
or cooked pork must be isolated from women, as their
presence causes it to rot. This conception of the effect of
women on cultural processes in general and on meat in
particular is widespread. De Beauvoir (1964:149), for example, quotes the British Medical Journal in 1878: "It is an
undoubted fact that meat spoils when touched by menstruating women."

ASSOCIATION OF ALIMENTARY
AND SEXUAL SYSTEMS

These eight prohibition types suggest an intense male
preoccupation with and anxiety about female fertility and
sexuality and, in addition, a masculine insistence on the

notion of feminine inferiority. Men deny women a political voice, rights in land, and authority over the products of their labor. They seek to impress their superiority on women through a number of symbolic devices. Significant among them are the well-known secret flutes, common throughout the highlands as one of the main cult items of the secret society of the men's house. Hua males claim that they traditionally killed women who so much as dared to look at these flutes, which men paraded openly through the community. Women and children were taught to believe that their sound came from weird birds.

A second symbolic device whereby men seek to reinforce their position of sexual superiority and political dominance is based on the reciprocal association of alimentary and sexual organs and processes, two body systems that are universally associated but whose mutual identification receives here an unusual degree of publicity. The identification of foods with sexual organs and substances has been demonstrated. The reverse identification, of sexual organs and substances with foods, receives considerable public elaboration in folktales, expressions of endearment, and insults.

In one tale a man cuts off one of his testicles, wraps it in vegetable leaves, and asks his wife to cook it. She cannot resist the delicious smells emanating from the packet and in his absence eats it. In a second tale a small bird discovers a house full of sleeping girls. He plays a trick on them by pasting an edible mushroom (*zokoni*) to their vaginas.

The expression "I will eat your blood" is one of the means by which a man indicates he would like to have intercourse with a woman. Certain insults play on the identification of stolen food with a part of the owner's anatomy, which the thief is then ordered to eat. Where the thief takes a wide range of items from a woman's garden, it is appropriate for her to say, "Burst open my pregnant womb and eat it." Where the thief steals the white pandanus, a woman can say, "Eat the fruit at the center of a woman's vagina." Where he takes the red pandanus, she can say, "Since you like pandanus, drink the clotted blood from my vagina." When the owner is male, the insults differ. For example, if the thief steals sugarcane, which is identified with semen in many contexts, the male can say, "Eat the semen in my penis."

Parallel to the identification between foods and sexual substances is that between the mouth and the vagina, which is allowed considerable public expression in Hua culture. A woman observing my naked two-year-old daughter eating an ear of corn said to her, fondly and laughingly, "Eat it with your vagina." A prohibition on males eating pork that has been formally given to a woman hinges on the identification of her vagina with her mouth. Men say that at the announcement of the woman's name before she receives the pork, her vagina answers, *ve* "yes?" Other informants say, *Kaumu'bo bu' bo bre* "Her vagina expresses its appreciation."

Consider the following two stories about facial hair. According to one, the Hua males originally had no facial hair. One day, however, they blew into the mouths of flutes into which women had stuffed their pubic hair. That pubic hair became the male beard. According to the second story, the variation in the density of men's beards is accounted for by a similar variation in the density of their mother's pubic hair.

Where facial hair is publicly associated with pubic hair, one would expect that the mouth might also be publicly associated with the vagina. A rule forbids initiates to eat any bird that has a very feathery face—in particular, three owllike birds (*hazuifi'a*, *bume*, and *ktrupe*). These faces, in which a heavy plumage surrounds a mouth, are publicly said to resemble the female pudenda.

Where one finds public or semipublic association of the orifices of the upper and lower halves of the body and of the substances taken in at both, it is not surprising to find open and reciprocal association of feeding and sexual intercourse. The equation of these to acts comes from a transfer of two substances that males say occurs during intercourse. The first is *nu* (Pidgin English *gris*), which is for the Hua the essence of life and vitality. Men claim that the transfers of *nu* (semen and sweat) occurring in intercourse result in female gains in weight and vitality and corresponding male losses. The second substance is *vza bu'* "mouth steam, breath, air," conceived as the gaseous form of *nu*. So essential is *vza bu'* to growth and strength that initiates must undergo a period of silence to prevent its loss through speaking. During intercourse females take in the *vza bu'* that males breathe out; thus, according to male informants, the female's strength is increased while the male's is reduced.

In describing these transfers, my informants did not specifically say that sexual intercourse is like feeding. However, given the common association between the mouth and the vagina, between foods and sexual substances, and the attribution of a nutritive effect to sexual intercourse, it seems reasonable to claim an implicit association between feeding and sexual intercourse. This association is also implicit in the belief in oral conception. At least two of the most important male food taboos (the prohibitions on eating possum and on eating leafy green vegetables picked by certain categories of women) are obeyed in order to avoid oral conception.[1]

VALUES OF MALE AND
FEMALE BODIES

Hua males use the association of the sexual and alimentary systems to make a particular statement about the relative value of male and female bodies.

Loss of *nu* causes the stunting of growth, aging, impo-

---

1. The Umeda of the New Guinea Sepik see eating, violence (hunting), and sexuality as alternative modes of a single basic activity, which is represented by one verb, *tadv* (Gell 1977:32). In dreams these modes are switched around. An instance of love-making in a dream has implications for the dreamer's real-life hunting. A man dreaming of his sister coming and giving him food prefigures his success in a real-life love affair.

tence, and weakness in general. The many manifestations of a person's *nu* include his or her blood, lymph, sweat, body oil, sexual or reproductive fluids, and any living thing that the person has invested great effort into growing, for example, children, pigs, and special garden produce. It is important to note that all *nu* substances are readily transferred between persons. Each act of *nu* transfer, whether through the medium of pig, garden produce, blood (which the Hua let from their veins and drank), sweat or body oil (both of which they rubbed on one another's bodies), or actual flesh (the Hua traditionally were cannibals) has two possible effects. It can cause the recipient's body *kosi-* "to grow, increase in weight, strength, and vitality" or *keva ro-* "to become stunted, dry out, wither, decrease in weight, strength, and health."

Whether a positive or negative value is attributed to any act of *nu* transfer is determined by the social relationship of the parties to the act. Where the social relationship is positive, the value attributed to the act is also positive. Where the social relationship is negative, the value attributed is also negative. For example, a man may eat or otherwise permit his body to come in contact with the *nu* substances of his real and classificatory fathers, mothers, grandparents, aunts, uncles, and siblings as long as he is enjoying the relationship of support and warmth that is expected to exist between them. A man may not eat or otherwise permit his body to come in contact with certain of the *nu* substances of his agemates or his real or classificatory cross-cousins (his relationships with both agemates and cross-cousins are typically competitive), or with any person of any category with whom he has a relationship of enmity.

The effects attributable to any act of *nu* transfer suggest that the Hua like to have physiological or body relationships mirror social ones. They like to express the expected or experienced emotional quality of a social relationship through a physical metaphor. To make that metaphor work, each body act must be represented as having an ambiguous value. The fact that the same act can have positive and negative physical effects permits it to reflect both the trust and the hostility common to social relationships.

The public and explicit identification of the alimentary and sexual acts, both of which are prototypical acts of *nu* transfer, allows the Hua to attribute to them the dual value posited for other acts of *nu* transfer. The value normally attributed to each act may be changed, enabling Hua males to perceive the act associated with their bodies as superior to the act associated with females bodies—at least within those contexts where these associations are made.

VALUES OF SEXUAL
INTERCOURSE AND FEEDING

Although sexual intercourse and feeding are viewed as the prototypical acts of *nu* transfer, they are not normally assigned a dual value. Sexual intercourse is viewed as a negative act. According to males the sex act, although it increases the female's vitality, decreases the male's. Each act depletes the finite quantity of a man's *nu* and thus increases the rate at which he ages. Balding, which Hua males hide with small woven caps, is thought to be a direct result of sexual excess because semen is believed to originate in the head. Females deny that they profit from the receipt of semen and maintain instead that sexual intercourse increases menstrual flow, which women (but not men) think involves potentially dangerous losses of *nu*. Both sexes commonly express enthusiasm for the sexual and reproductive inactivity of old age.

Feeding is viewed as the opposite of sex. It is the quintessentially positive act, the one that best produces strength and health. In fact, feeding is the most morally positive act. A good person is, almost by definition, one who feeds others generously.

Sexual intercourse and feeding are associated not only with moral values but also with gender identifications. Sexual intercourse is viewed as a male act, as males in the "publicly prescribed" Hua view take the active part in it. Feeding, on the other hand, is viewed as a female act, as women are the feeders, and children and men are fed.

Where the male act of intercourse is the morally negative act and the female act of feeding is the morally positive act, the implication that females are, at least in this respect, morally superior is unavoidable. Reinterpretation of the male sexual act as similar to the female feeding act, and the female feeding act as similar to the male sexual act, achieves the usual duality in matters of *nu* transfer. The values usually attributed to these two acts in a daily context are reversed in this specialized context of male ritual and taboo.

My argument depends on a careful delineation of contexts. Certain kinds of comments and statements about a topic are appropriate in some contexts but not in others. For example, in North American society uninhibited and chauvinistic comments about the sexuality and status of females are appropriate, at least in some males' perspectives, in barracks, pubs, locker rooms, all-male card games, and so on. Similar comments are inappropriate in other all-male contexts, like board meetings, planning sessions, and church vestry meetings, where discussions of sex, if they occur at all, are inhibited and blatant chauvinism is avoided. Hua males also have a variety of attitudes and styles for talking about females and sex, each appropriate to certain contexts. If a stranger entered a Hua village and wanted to talk publicly about sex and feeding in an appropriate fashion in the normal course of the day, it would be correct for him or her to assume that sexual intercourse is a negative act in which the male has the initiative and that feeding is a positive act in which the female has the initiative. The Hua context in which these assumptions are not appropriate is the men's house. If this same stranger wanted to talk about these topics with the men in the men's house, he or she could talk about how males nourish females in the act of having sex with them, and about how females pollute and in some extreme cases impregnate males in the process of feeding them.

By reversing the functions normally attributed to the sexual and feeding acts—by making sex a feeding act and feeding a sexual act—the males reverse the values normally associated with each act, at least within the men's house context. In the process they make it possible to allocate to themselves, at least for the duration of the context, the role of moral superiority. It is a role that conforms with their preferred image of themselves as social benefactors, protectors of the community, supporters of its people. It also conforms with the much promoted image of females (other than consanguineal ones) as hostile and threatening to the community. This image makes some sense in a community that draws most of its wives from foreign groups, groups with whom there may now be a peaceful relationship but with whom wars were fought in the past and may be fought again in the future.

This reversal of the functions and values normally attributed to the alimentary and sexual acts is comparable to the role Buchbinder and Rappaport (1976) report for a Maring ritual in which males plant cultigens over a special earth oven that is identified with the vagina and its fertility. The ethnographers interpret this planting as a male attempt to assert authority and control not only over the vagina and its powers but also over the earth and its fruits, normally considered a female preserve. Lindenbaum (1976) reports a similar concern among Fore males to achieve a semblance of control over female fertility through ritual devices.

The Hua reversal enables males to say in the appropriate contexts that the female physical act of feeding is a negative act, just as female social acts are negative, and that the male act of copulation is a positive act, just as male social acts are positive. Body acts and relationships are made to mirror the preferred male conception of social acts and relationships. The physical or natural order has been reversed to bring it in line with the social order (or the preferred male conception of that order) and thus to strengthen this particular male conception or theory about social relations. Such a reversal and linking of different orders is not uncommon.

confuse the neat male-superior/female-inferior opposition outlined in much of the literature. An extreme opposition between the sexes and the allocation of superiority to males and inferiority to females represent only one perspective among several that Hua males take on the complex issue of male-female relations.

Four facts are disconcerting given our preconception of New Guinea highland societies as ones in which males feel loathing and disgust at the processes of menstruation and childbirth, express abhorrence for female organs and fluids, and insist on extreme distance from and domination of women in everyday life.

First, Hua males imitate menstruation. Such imitation has been reported elsewhere in New Guinea (Read 1952, Allen 1967, Hogbin 1970, Lindenbaum 1972, Tuzin 1980). The Wogeo custom is the most explicit:

> [The man] goes to a lonely beach . . . removes his clothing and wades out until the water is up to his knees. He stands there with legs apart and induces an erection. . . . When ready he pushes back the foreskin and hacks at the glans. . . . A menstruating woman and a menstruating man are alike *rekareka* [polluted]. They go into retirement, keep warm, and observe food taboos. (Hogbin 1970:88)

Although Wogeo men are not required to menstruate every month, they are supposed to do so regularly. "The majority, however, delay until sickness reminds them of the need to act" (ibid., p. 91). The men claim that the salutary effects of penile surgery are immediately apparent: "The man's body loses its tiredness, his muscles harden, his step quickens, his eyes grow bright, and his skin and hair develop a luster" (ibid.).

Second, Hua males believe that they can become pregnant, a condition they supposedly abhor in women. A similar belief has been reported by Hayano (1974) for the Tauna Awa, also of the Eastern Highlands, who explain a distended stomach by claiming that a fetus has entered it through the penis. Glick (1963:117) reports for the Gimi, close neighbors of the Hua, a disease called *amusa kio* "pregnant disease" in which victims exhibit extreme swelling of the abdomen. A concern about extreme abdominal swelling and its attribution to a condition of male pregnancy is also reported for the Keraki of the Trans-Fly area of New Guinea:

> The express purpose of this [lime-eating] ceremony is to neutralize the effects of the homosexual intercourse; in fact, to ensure that the young men do not become pregnant. At first I could not credit this; but the existence of the implied belief was amply verified. Among a lean and often scraggy people a corpulent or pot-bellied native is a comparative rarity. His condition is possibly due to disease of the spleen. By the natives it is put down to pregnancy. I have recorded the names of five such individuals, well remembered, who were thought to be with child. One of them, Sosopa of Wekamara, whom I knew as a sorcerer and marked because of his protuberant stomach—an extreme case—died prior to my last visit. The theory was that he had become pregnant because the lime had not gone down his throat properly and that he had died because he could not deliver the child. We must not examine native theories of gestation too critically: it is not thought impossible that a man should go pregnant for years. Cases of what appears to be *prolapsus ani* have been described to me in awed breath and put down to the unavailing effort of the male mother at delivery. The native indeed fears that such unduly corpulent men may actually succeed in delivering their children and thus betray the secret of sodomy to their womenfolk—a revelation which, they say, would cause extreme shame to every man. (Williams 1969:201–202)

The status of the Hua belief in male pregnancy is difficult to describe. Most informants if asked directly, "Can a male become pregnant?" answer, "No." Many add, "Our pregnancy claim is just talk." Nevertheless, this belief is implicit in informants' discussions of many of the food prohibitions and sexual avoidances. In these contexts male pregnancy is presented without excuse or qualification as a dangerous outcome of improper practice. Some informants even claim to have seen fetuses after their removal from men's bodies, an operation performed by non-Hua specialists. (A cut is allegedly made in the abdomen, often in the area of the navel, and a bamboo tube held to the wound. The fetus is said to be carried by the blood into the tube.)

Leach (1966) mentions the importance of context to statements of belief in his discussion of the alleged aboriginal Australian ignorance of the causal connection between copulation and pregnancy. He cites Meggitt's (1962:273) observation that the answers a Walbiri gives to questions about conception depend on who asks and in what circumstances: "In ritual contexts, men speak of the action of the *guruwari* [spirit entities] as the significant factor; in secular contexts they nominate both the *guruwari* and sexual intercourse" (cited in Leach 1966:40). Hua enunciation of the male pregnancy belief is conditioned by similar contextual factors, as are, for example, protestations of belief in God in Western culture.

The third disconcerting fact is that Hua males secretly eat foods identified with the supposedly loathsome *korogo* "juicy, soft, fertile, fast-growing, cool" qualities of women. Women, on the other hand, eat food identified with the *hakeri'a* "dry, hard, infertile, slow-growing, hot" qualities of men.

Finally, despite the apparently extreme opposition of the sexes, postmenopausal women are initiated into the secret male society and take on the ritual status of male vulnerability. They become *kakora*, a term usually reserved for the initiated male who is, because of his purity, vulnerable to the pollution of others. Old men, on the other hand, lose their vulnerability and, like women, become able to eat anything and need to avoid nothing. They become *figapa*, a term usually reserved for the uninitiated and for polluted women and children.

The image of male-female relations provided in chapter 2

suggests that male and female among the Hua at Lufa, as elsewhere in the highlands of New Guinea, are strongly opposed categories. That is one perspective on male-female relations. The four disconcerting facts presented here suggest a second perspective, an attempt to neutralize or obscure the male-female opposition through a sharing of characteristics and flow of membership between the categories of male and female. Neutralizing phenomena include imitation of the behavior or states of members of the opposite sex and a reclassification that scrambles the membership of the original categories and draws new lines of opposition.

ETHNOANATOMY AND PHYSIOLOGY

It was relatively easy to involve male and female informants alike in discussions about reproduction, although male informants frequently pointed out that such talk, even such knowledge, was traditionally taboo. Several informants maintained that their fathers had died believing, or claiming to believe, that children are born through the navel. Schieffelin (1976:125) reports a similar situation among the Kaluli men of the Southern Highlands, who claim that they do not know where babies come from. Many Maring men of the Western Highlands claim to be unaware that their wives menstruate (Buchbinder and Rappaport 1976:21). For Hua men even to speak the word "womb" was polluting. The reproductive information given to me was frequently accompanied by disclaimers of uncertainty and confusion. In the face of my incredulity at this self-proclaimed ignorance, male informants emphasized that they were unable to observe copulation or birth among animals other than the pig and that women bore their children in hiding.

Interest in and knowledge of anatomy and physiology are generally slight among the Hua and neighboring groups. Glick (1963:105–107), an anthropologist and physician working among the nearby Gimi, reported a lack of knowledge of the functions of the heart, lungs, kidneys, and blood. He claimed, in addition, that the Gimi had not observed the pulse. Hua and Gimi ignorance seems less unbelievable when put into a comparative perspective. According to Ackerknecht (1971:90), there is a remarkable ignorance of anatomical and physiological knowledge among many native peoples. Where an organ is recognized and named, there is very often no inkling of its real function. Leach (1966) maintains that some of this so-called ignorance is a reflection not of actual absence of knowledge but of theological dogma, as in the case of Virgin Birth in Christian belief. The role of dogma in Hua thinking should not be minimized, as informants frequently distinguished between permissible and impermissible items of reproductive knowledge.

According to Hua belief, all creatures except the possum bear their young through either the *kau* "vagina/urethra" (dog, pig, mouse, and human) or the rectum (snakes, birds, fish, and frogs). The possum is thought to reproduce from leaves left to rot in the marsupial pouch. Bothered by this one exception, I asked one informant, "Well, what about the possum's penis?" He acknowledged that the male possum had one but said that he did not know if it produced semen and suggested that he might catch one to find out. Such a search for information through observation seemed alien to the usual Hua way of thinking about reproduction. I never heard the theory of possum reproduction through rotten leaves questioned or doubted.

The Hua recognize no specifically genital orifice, as opposed to passage. The *kau* is thought by male and female informants alike to open into a single passage that then bifurcates, forming the *bademo brodi kibo* "childbearing path" and the *vimo rodi kibo* "urine-making path." The former leads directly into the *aipa* "intestine" and the latter into the *vinobo* "bladder." The intestine is thought to bifurcate, leading both into the rectum and into the *fgagetava*

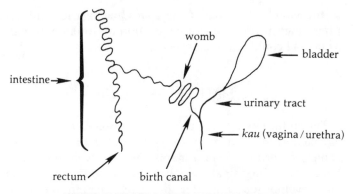

ETHNOGYNECOLOGICAL REPRESENTATION

A composite of sketches made by informants. As the Hua are unpracticed in drawing and in physiological representation, it is out of proportion and fails to show, among other things, the relatively large size and the correct position of the intestine, though the Hua are aware of both. It does show the Hua conception of the relationship between the intestine and the womb (diverging off the same channel), between the womb and the bladder (two organs feeding into the same channel), and the convergence, in Hua thinking, of the vagina and urethra.

"womb," which is thought to be an enlargement at the end of this channel of the intestine. The exit from the womb is into the childbearing path, which leads into the *kau*.

The Hua maintain that the birth canal of a premenarcheal girl is shut. The moon, which is likened to the girl's first husband, opens the passage at the onset of menstruation. The girl's actual husband opens the passage further through intercourse. At menopause the passage shuts and, according to some informants, disappears. It is, incidentally, because the passage is so nearly shut that many acts of intercourse are thought to be necessary to conceive the first child. Subsequent children require fewer acts, the passage becoming each year more open.

The Hua theory of conception is based on the externally visible substances of sex and reproduction, namely, menstrual blood and semen. Conception is said to occur whenever sufficient semen mixes with sufficient menstrual blood in the womb. The role of the testes and ovaries and the physiological processes of conception are unknown and, as far as I could tell, unsuspected.

MALE PREGNANCY

The condition of being pregnant but unable to give birth is called *kupa*. In a male the abdomen of the victim becomes, according to informants, progressively more distended as the initial *kora haugepa* "blood clot" grows and develops fetal characteristics. Unless countermeasures are taken, the abdomen ultimately bursts, causing death. (Countermeasures include bloodletting and the consumption of the eldest brother's wife's feces. A small fragment, it is said, is removed by the woman from her anus and added to a soup that the victim, ignorant of its contents, eats while his kinsmen, aware that he is eating feces, cry.) This abdominal bursting is supposed to coincide, according to one informant, with the eruption of the still unborn baby's teeth, suggesting that the Hua, like the Keraki, believe that the pregnancy can go on well beyond nine months.

The Hua recognize three possible causes of *kupa* in males. The first is eating a food that has been touched or stepped over by a menstruating woman or a woman newly married into the community. This prohibition on eating foods contacted by women falls with particular emphasis on *kito'*, leafy vegetables picked by snapping the stalks between the fingernails. Because of contact between the hands and genitals, the fingernails become, according to informants, contaminated by menstrual blood. Young initiated males traditionally ate no *kito'* other than that which had been picked by prepubescent and postmenopausal females.

The second cause of *kupa* in males is eating possum, which males publicly maintain is permitted only to uninitiated and very old males, although I could not initially find any old men who would admit to eating possum. Possum is publicly abhorred by males because it is considered the counterpart of women. The following comparisons of possum and women were made by male informants:

1. Possum fur is like female pubic hair. Either, if touched, will cause stunting to the adolescent and premature aging to the adult male.
2. The holes in trees, rocks, and most particularly the ground in which possums live are like women's vagina/urethras.
3. Possum and women, plus several mushrooms and two yams, are *be' ftu*, that is, have a particular rotting smell that is associated with menstrual blood.
4. The way in which one possum, the *hazubre'*, jumps out of trees is like the child's slipping out of its mother's vagina/urethra. The Melpa of the Western Highlands draw a similar analogy and make it the basis of a spell to quicken delivery (A. Strathern and M. Strathern 1968:185).

The final cause of *kupa* is a type of sorcery, called *kembige*, which is effected by introducing into the prospective victim's food a fragment that has been soaked in menstrual blood. Sorcery and possum eating are supposed always to bring on the *kupa* condition, while ingesting menstrual blood often results merely in physical degeneration.

Although informants say *kupa* is not a rare condition, I observed only one case, an initiated boy of about fourteen. Members of his village suggested one or more of the following theories to account for his extreme abdominal distension and general debilitation: that he had secretly eaten some *vare'*, a kind of grasslands wallaby classified as possum; that he had recently eaten food prepared by a menstruating woman; or that he was the victim of sorcery that had used strings from a woman's genital apron to knot his intestine. People were uncertain as to whether the boy was *kupa* but thought it likely. In the hospital he was diagnosed as having kwashiorkor. His condition did improve when his diet was enriched.

The Hua admit to a belief in oral conception. There are, however, strong suggestions of an additional belief in anal conception. A direct connection between anal intercourse and pregnancy was suggested independently by two informants, who, in denying the existence of anal intercourse, said it would result in pregnancy and for this reason, among others, was not practiced (the Keraki beliefs about the relationship between homosexual intercourse and male pregnancy are similar).

Although it is difficult to be precise about the various beliefs about conception, it is possible to describe the condition of body viewed as necessary for the onset of *kupa*. That condition is the absence of a properly functioning passage for the birth of a child. A key phrase in all discussions of *kupa* and one that was delivered always in the same mildly exasperated and bewildered manner was *Aiga kipiti vis*? "Through what passage can it go?" Because men have no passage, conception always results in *kupa*. Women are more fortunate. When conception occurs in the normal moist womb, birth is possible and *kupa* does not ensue, unless the birth canal has become blocked through efforts at contraception. When conception occurs in an abnormal womb, or in the intestine or in the abdominal tissue, both of which are reckoned by the Hua as possible (perhaps in recognition of ectopic pregnancies), women are in the unfortunate position of men. Lacking an exit adequate for the birth of the child, the woman becomes a *kupa* victim.

I observed one case of *kupa* in a female and many were described to me. In the observed case the woman had missed several menstrual periods yet claimed, with the support of her husband, not to have had sufficient acts of intercourse to be pregnant. Some people feared that a rotten mass of blood was developing inside her and soon would be too large to expel. Others suggested privately that the woman was simply pregnant by another man and was trying to hide the fact.

A second woman was alleged to have developed *kupa* after having a contraceptive device (perhaps an intrauterine device) placed inside her in the Goroka hospital. According to informants, such devices are not completely effective; if an unlucky user becomes pregnant, the device, they say, makes delivery of the baby impossible. A third *kupa* victim had eaten numerous *hakeri'a* leaves in an effort at contraception. These leaves were alleged to have changed the condition of her womb so that when she did become pregnant, she could not deliver the child and so died.

Infertile women are normally judged to be susceptible to *kupa* because the opening to their wombs is thought to be wrinkled and shut, not enough to prevent a very occasional entrance of semen but sufficient to prevent the exit of the fetus. Postmenopausal women are liable to *kupa*, which they can contract, as men do, from eating foods contaminated by menstrual blood. They too have no adequate birth canal. When menstrual periods cease, older women are alleged to suffer considerable anxiety wondering whether the cessation betokens the arrival of the welcomed menopause or the dreaded *kupa*.

It should be emphasized that *kupa* is a feared and an abhorred condition. Yet one cannot resist suggesting that it is also desired. All the facts deny the premise that males can become pregnant. I submit that the reason males believe they can become pregnant, and believe in the fake fetuses provided by the curers, is that they have strong psychological reasons to do so. They have a will to believe that they are fertile.[1]

IMITATION OF MENSTRUATION

Menstrual blood, although considered disgusting and dangerous, is also thought to be the source of the female's

1. Male pregnancy fantasies and their counterpart, female fantasies of possessing male sexual organs, are psychological phenomena documented by Western psychiatrists (Freud 1909, 1925, Eisler 1921, Silberer 1925, Boehm 1930, Evans 1951, Jacobsen 1950, Bettelheim 1962). Dundes (1976) discusses the prevalence of customs of male envy of women, including envy of pregnancy in secret initiation ceremonies.

more rapid rate of growth and her greater general health. Males comment that it is immediately after menarche that the female child has her growth spurt. The view that the release of blood, through either bloodletting or menstruation, purifies the body has been reported for many different ethnographic areas (see, for New Guinea, Mead 1940, Whiting 1941:63–64, Hogbin 1970:88, Lewis 1975:36).

Hua men have two techniques of menstrual imitation, neither of them as explicit as that described for the Wogeo. The first is bloodletting, which is currently used by the Hua as treatment for headache, toothache, and pain or swelling of limbs or joints, and was used before prohibition by Australian patrol officers for pain in the torso. Speculations as to the cause of internal pains dwell on the probable presence of a growing and hardening clot of blood. Such a clot, called in all these cases *kora haugepa* "blood clot," is precisely what develops in cases of *kupa*, one of the cures for which, as for the other clots, is letting blood. A surprisingly similar understanding of pain is reported among the Maenge of New Britain (Panoff 1970a). A Hua *kupa* victim's blood was let from his stomach (sometimes directly from the navel), lower back, and buttocks. One male informant volunteered that *kupa* victims would not need to let blood if they could menstruate.

It is interesting that the reason women give for the traditional prohibition on the use of menstrual padding (internal padding was the only feasible type given the scanty traditional dress) is fear of a blockage of blood and the development and subsequent putrefaction of a clot. When a woman's flow of menstrual blood is blocked, she develops a blood clot like that which males fear and seek to avoid by letting their blood.[2]

2. Paul (1974:291) reports a similar belief among Indian women of a highland Guatemalan village: at menarche a girl may be told "that if she stops menstruating she might swell up and die." Skultans (1970:642) reports that some women of South Wales believe that menstruation purges the body of "badness" and "excess." Women who hold this belief welcome the loss of blood as purifying and invigorating.

These beliefs, in addition to suggesting a functional equivalence between bloodletting and menstruation, also indicate an equivalence in substance between the blood released in lettings and that in menstruation. Normal blood and menstrual blood are not differentiated lexically. Blood let from the limbs of middle-aged men was eaten by other males to enhance growth and strength. Informants report that an occasional male would refuse to eat the blood, saying, "They are eating the counterpart of women's menstruation and I don't like it." Most males, however, ate the blood, although no male ate blood during the new moon, which is "women's time," the time when—for purposes of ritual simplification—it is assumed that all women menstruate and therefore are dangerous. I conclude that while Hua males make only a vague and partial identification between bloodletting and menstruation, the bloodletting that they administer to the *kupa* victim is a specific imitation of menstruation.

A second form of menstrual imitation is achieved through eating plants that have reddish juice.[3] These juices are reported to have the power to break up a clot of blood and force its evacuation through the intestine. Males eat these juices (squeezed onto sweet potatoes) when they have *kupa* or have eaten something that could cause its development. Women, who also identify the juices of these plants with blood, eat none of them for fear of excessive menstrual flow.

The identification between bloodletting and the evacuation produced by red-juiced diarrhetics on the one hand

3. Plants with reddish juice include *visge* (Gesneriaceae *Cyrtandra*), a purplish red flower; *dekma'* (Rubiaceae *Gardenia*), the fruits of which are reported to have a red interior; *rihima* (Podocarpaceae *Podocarpus*), the inner bark of which has a coppery color; *kogiva* (Saurauiaceae *Saurauia*), in which the underside of the mature leaves and the whole surface of the immature ones have a silvery, pinkish cast; *fitupa* (Compositae *Souchus asper*), the fruits of which are reported to have a red interior; *kovrena'*, a lurid plant with maroon leaves and pink flowers; and all the red *kito'* (leafy vegetables), including *ruarokorarome*, *hgerua*, *bokome*, and *sagrekre*, all of which are dull to lurid red in color.

and female menstruation on the other is sufficiently far-fetched to reaffirm a strong motivation on the part of males to imitate females. We see also an ambivalent attitude toward female reproduction. Female menstruation is considered repugnant and dangerous for males and at the same time enviable in its contribution to growth and health.

MALE IMITATION OF FEMALE

The beliefs in male pregnancy and menstruation certainly suggest male imitation of female. So also do a number of the secret and semisecret male eating habits. At the time of initiation and later in initiationlike rejuvenation ceremonies called *pauge zubo* "body oil house," males eat a soup made from various kinds of forest leaves, each of which is characterized as *korogo* "soft, juicy, fast-growing, fertile." It is by means of daily consumption of this soup that male strength, health, youth, and virility are regenerated. It is a truism among the Hua of both sexes that women are *korogo*. They grow quickly, have soft, juicy interiors, and reproduce rapidly and abundantly. They are, as informants never grow tired of repeating, like *pitpit*, a fast-growing, rapidly reproducing edible that has a soft, wet interior. The *korogo* quality of women is contrasted by males and females alike with the *hakeri'a* "hard, dry, slow-growing, infertile" quality of men. Informants say men are like the *kimi* "black palm," an extremely slow-growing, hardwood tree used by Hua men in making their bows.

The attempt to stimulate growth through eating substances associated with the *korogo* characteristic of women is another example of male imitation of female, in this case of her more rapid rate of growth. Males openly admire what they consider to be the rapid rate of female growth and, like their counterparts elsewhere in the highlands (see Glasse 1965, Salisbury 1965, Barth 1975), they are anxious about what they perceive as their own retardation.

According to Hua males, almost all of the food prohibitions are designed to provide, among other things, protection from the stunting of growth. Males who are smaller than their agemates are derided for having eaten *siro na* "pollution" and traditionally were forced to undergo purification, which took the form of vomiting, nose bleeding, and consumption of red-juiced diarrhetics. Male initiations feature a marked emphasis on growth. In addition to being fed the growth stimulating *korogo* leaves, the initiate is repeatedly raised up into the air by his father, who chants:

U hauo, u hauo, u hauo.	Grow tall, grow tall, grow tall.
Za kurekare zao.	The Kure tree.
U hauo, u hauo.	Grow tall, grow tall.

The growth rate of female children, on the other hand, is not regarded with anxiety by either males or females. Smallness in comparison with agemates does not provide cause even for comment, much less accusations or purifications. Female puberty ceremonies contain little emphasis on growth.

Possum eating is another behavior suggesting male imitation of female. Possum, which is identified with women, is the most dramatically tabooed of all foods. A male who eats possum becomes pregnant. His abdomen becomes enormously distended and, unless countermeasures are taken, bursts, causing death.

During fourteen months of fieldwork I never encountered a male informant who admitted to eating possum flesh, although many claimed that other males whom I knew had eaten it since mission and government contact. It therefore came as a considerable surprise when one male informant, shortly before my departure, told me that all males, except the newly initiated, traditionally ate and still eat possum in secret. Far from being dangerous to the male eater, it increases his growth and provides him with protection from sorcery, enemy arrows, and female pollution.

Consumption of possum was traditionally considered so important that any initiate who died during the brief period of actual prohibition was "fed" it posthumously: a small bit of possum fur (which was actually eaten in small amounts on ritual occasions if a hunt was impossible or unsuccessful) was placed between the deceased's lips.[4] The ceremony by which the prohibition on possum is terminated, called zgama' zubo "possum house," occurs several years after initiation and, like initiation and rejuvenation ceremonies, involves several weeks of seclusion, carefully regulated eating and sleeping, and heavily coating the skin with black soot and body oils. Traditionally, women, on pain of death, were supposed to have no knowledge of male possum eating.

Most male informants confirmed the existence of possum house and its role in releasing males from the possum prohibition. A few subsequently did admit to eating possum but most did not, claiming either that they had not participated in the possum house ceremony or that even after the ceremony they still did not have the confidence to eat possum. Women informants maintained, as my male informants initially had, that it was only since contact that initiated males had eaten possum secretly in the forest. They appeared to have no knowledge of the possum house.

Possums, incidentally, are important ritual items not only among the Hua but also among the Baktaman, who identify them with the sacred ancestors (Barth 1975:69); the Karam, who identify the terrestrial cuscus with the ghosts of the dead and the striped possum with witchcraft (R. Bulmer 1967:23); and the Maring, who consider marsupials to be the pigs of the red spirits (Rappaport 1968:39–40).

Possum had the public status of an extremely dangerous

4. Hair and fur are seen as suffused with the individual's essence. As such they may serve the Hua, as they do the Baktaman (Barth 1975: 92–93), as more powerful symbols or carriers of individual essence than the flesh itself—more powerful because more condensed.

food because of its identification with women; yet it was also secretly regarded, presumably also because of this identification, as beneficial. A similar status was accorded human blood, which was eaten openly by women and children but only secretly by men.[5] Again, women were supposedly killed for the discovery of this secret, and even today no female informant admits publicly to the knowledge that males eat blood. The only males who did not eat blood were the new initiates, to whom possum was also forbidden. All other classes of adult males ate their real and classificatory fathers' blood, which was thought to stimulate growth and strength.

Blood, like possum, is associated with women. In fact, male informants state that all blood is female. The fetus is formed, they say, from a large amount of menstrual blood and a small amount of semen. All the blood in the newborn, as in the adult, is the mother's and is therefore female. Older males recount the kind of comments typically made by old women who, when initiated, saw men eating blood for the first time: "I don't like it. You are eating pollution. . . . The blood which you let from your bodies is like our menstrual blood. . . . You are in effect eating menstrual blood." Eating the blood even of a male involves, in the Hua reckoning, eating what is essentially female. Hua men ate blood, possum, and leaves identified as *korogo* in an attempt to induce in themselves the faster rate of growth and greater invulnerability that they consider to be characteristic of women.

Conversely, women, through their consumption of food associated with the *hakeri'a* qualities of men, attempt to

5. A comparable duality in status appears to be attributed to the color *nupa* "black." Initiates are prohibited from eating foods with black or dark interiors because of their alleged resemblance to the dark, putrid interior of the female body. Yet a deep blackness of skin is a highly sought sign of strength (a white man is known as *havade* "nothing man, weak man"), and blackness is associated with newness and freshness of life (the new shoot of a plant is called *nupa*).

achieve some male characteristics. At menstruation, after childbirth, and in efforts at contraception, women eat small bits of *hakeri'a* leaves.[6] The one most commonly used is brown, dried out, and extremely hard. The women's stated intention is to induce a dryness and hardness in the womb so that the menstrual or postparturitional flow will be reduced and fertility inhibited. Women who achieve such a condition of the womb, according to the Hua, neither menstruate nor conceive. Such women proudly claim to be like men. In fact, Hua women pride themselves as a group on the small quantity of their menstrual flow and the infrequency of their periods. (Menarche is late among the Hua. Given that women are frequently pregnant and lactate for very extended periods, it may well be that menstruation is not frequent.) Hua women claim to welcome menopause because it brings to a close the uncleanliness, embarrassment, and degradation of menstruation and childbirth and marks the beginning of a period when a woman can claim to be "like a man."[7]

It should be clear from the eating habits of males and females and the male imitation of female menstruation and pregnancy that the Hua are not content, at least in some respects, with the rigid sexual boundaries imposed by their culture. Males are warned that women are dangerous and should be avoided. Nevertheless, in spite of (and perhaps because of) this hostility and distance between the sexes, attempts to eradicate the differences and to blur the boundaries persist.

6. *Hakeri'a* plants include *kure* (Sapotaceae *Planchonella*), an enormous hardwood tree; *hrretre* (Barringtoniaceae *Barringtonia*), a nondistinctive hardwood tree of which the edible portions, the new shoots, are red; *rokeva* (Ericaceae *Rhododendron*), a small tree with silverish bark and white, trumpet-shaped flowers; and *hakrua'* (Symplocaceae *Symplocos*), a hardwood tree.

7. Skultans (1970:648) reports a similar attitude among village women of South Wales. One seventy-year-old woman told her that at menopause women turn into men inside. Skultans writes that doctors in this area perform many hysterectomies for psychosocial rather than medical reasons.

THE NATURE OF POLLUTION

Given the intensity of Hua male efforts to imitate females, and given the less intense but still abundantly attested female efforts to imitate males, it is less than surprising that there is a common alternative pair of sexual categories in which the traditional male-female opposition is eliminated.

This alternative classification is based on the concept of *siro na* "dirty thing, pollution," which includes a wide variety of things from menstrual blood and parturitional fluids to sweat, hair, and body odors. In this chapter I discuss menstrual blood and parturitional fluids, the two polluting substances about which Hua males express the greatest anxiety. Unlike the other polluting substances, these two are exclusively female, and they retain their female identity even when they move outside the female body. Moreover, female pollution is permanently transferable and thus feared. (Most discussions of female pollution in the New Guinea highlands have drawn attention only to temporary transfers, that is, to pollution states whose duration can be terminated by special rites. Temporary transfers and temporary states of pollution do exist among the Hua, but they are not the ones with which I am here concerned.) Because the Hua believe that the quantity of female pollution in any single woman is finite, transfers can result in its complete removal. A body originally full of female pollution can become empty (the female pattern), and one that was empty can become full (the male pattern).

There are three mechanisms by which pollution is transferred out of the female body: childbirth, sexual intercourse, and menstruation (the purifying effect of which has been discussed above). Pollution transfers occur most dramatically through childbirth. The newly married woman is so polluted that no initiated person in her husband's community may eat anything she has produced, prepared, or served, but with the birth of each child, she becomes less polluting and less subject to taboo. Although informants do not directly say so, it is fair to infer from the reduction of prohibitions that the passage of the child through the birth canal is considered purifying to the mother. It is consistent with this interpretation that Hua males find barren women particularly repugnant.

Given that the child is the literal instrument of the mother's purification, it is not surprising to find that the child is considered polluted. (The pollution does not initially endanger the child personally but does endanger others through him or her as its vehicle.) The degree of pollution corresponds to the degree of pollution of the mother. The most dramatic decrease of her pollution, reflected in the subsequent sharp reduction in eating prohibitions and avoidance rules directed toward her, occurs after a woman has borne her first child (male or female). And this firstborn child, called *baru*, is the most polluted of all her children. Leafy green vegetables that the firstborn has picked, pork that the child has cut, and food that he or she has stepped over or that his or her shadow has touched can cause physical degeneration if not *kupa* in other persons. The second child, born at a period of reduced pollution in the mother, is less polluted than the first but more than the third, who is of course born at a period of even further reduced pollution. The decreases in the pollution of the child are reflected in, among other things, the rule prohibiting any father, real or classificatory, from touching his newborn infant. Informants say that traditionally a father never touched his firstborn but only poked at it playfully with a small stick. This prohibition was sometimes applied to the second child but never to subsequent ones.[8]

8. Labby (1976:74–78) reports an almost identical theory of the diminution of female pollution through menstruation and childbirth on the Micronesian Island of Yap. Among the Gnau of the Sepik there is a similar notion, although without the connotation of pollution (Lewis 1975:37, 138–139). Full maturity is achieved around the time a person's first child is born, when the individual is considered to be complete. "From this

Just as childbirth is conceived as purifying for the mother but polluting for the child, so also sexual intercourse is viewed as purifying for the female while polluting for the male. This aspect of the Hua male theory of pollution may be inferred from eating prohibitions. An unmarried man cannot share his sugarcane or water with a married man, nor can he eat leafy green vegetables picked by or pork cut by a married man (although the last two rules are often relaxed to apply only when the married man has recently had sexual intercourse). Similarly a married man who has recently had intercourse is prohibited from entering a new garden or a yard in which salt is being made.

The fact that pollution can be transferred at childbirth and in acts of sexual intercourse means that by old age a woman is nearly or completely drained of her female pollution. Her original pollution, created by her body, is now mixed with the soil over which she has moved or concentrated in the bodies of her children and the men with whom she has had sexual relationships.

THE ALTERNATIVE CATEGORIES

Kakora "initiated person," described by Hua men as the pure class of person, includes preadolescent, adolescent, and mature males plus postmenopausal women who have borne three or more children. The contrasting category, *figapa* "uninitiated person," identified by male informants as polluted, includes women of reproductive age, old men, children, and postmenopausal women who have borne one or two children.

Is my description of pollution transfer consistent with this categorization of persons by pollution? The inclusion

---

whole and untried state, the person does things like having children, planting gardens, shooting pigs. Gradually his wholeness is diminished. The firstborn child is said to be *nemblisa* 'the child of his wholeness,' or his whole blood, and each subsequent child is relatively less the child of his whole blood than the one before" (ibid., p. 139).

of children in the polluted *figapa* class fits my statements about the pollution transfers occurring at birth. What, however, justifies the inclusion of the preadolescent male in the pure class of *kakora*?

For the male there are two main sources of female pollution: mother and sexual partners. The preadolescent male has not yet experienced pollution from sexual partners, and pollution from his mother is at its lowest point in the developmental cycle. In the course of maturation, as a boy's contact with his mother decreases, so also does her pollution in him. Although male informants do not themselves correlate maturation with pollution, such a correlation can be inferred from the gradual increase in the boy's vulnerability accompanying maturation. Hua men consistently associate vulnerability with purity and invulnerability with pollution. What maternal pollution does remain in him is deliberately removed at initiation through the induction of vomiting, sweating, and bleeding. The preadolescent boy whose relations with his mother have been terminated through residential segregation at initiation and who has not yet entered a sexual relationship is in a position of maximum purity and therefore maximum vulnerability. He is, in fact, the epitome of *kakora*.

Once the male initiates a sexual relationship with a woman, he has embarked on the road to pollution. The steady increase of his pollution during the course of his married life can be measured by, among other things, the steady decrease of his vulnerability as indicated in the gradual relaxation of restrictions on his contact with women. His pollution does not become so great as to remove him from the *kakora* class until old age, by which time he is so polluted as to be nearly invulnerable. This pattern of increasing male invulnerability to pollution with age has also been reported by Buchbinder and Rappaport (1976:20) for the Maring and by Lowman-Vayda for the Jimi, another Maring group (cited ibid., p. 20). It is interesting that the pollution of old men among the Hua, like that of old women, which we shall come to in a moment, can be measured not through its danger, because it presents none, but only through the invulnerability that it provides. I suggest that the Hua distinguish, in the case of sexually inactive people, a degree of pollution in old men and old women that protects without being dangerous from a degree in children that protects and is dangerous.

In terms of the pollution concepts presented so far, the only problematical members of the *kakora-figapa* classes are the postmenopausal women. Why is there the distinction between those who have had three or more children and those who have had fewer? Traditionally, this distinction resulted in a dramatic contrast in the lives and status of the two categories of women. The postmenopausal woman with three or more children was formally initiated; took up residence in the men's house, where she was shown the secrets of male society, previously hidden from her on pain of death; and adopted most of the male avoidances and prohibitions. For example, she did not eat possum or leafy green vegetables picked by the prohibited categories of women, nor did she eat food that had been stepped over by noninitiated women. The postmenopausal women with one or two children, on the other hand, retained her status of *figapa*, uninitiated outsider.[9]

Clearly, nothing about genitals in themselves accounts for this dramatic differentiation. Both classes of postmenopausal women are thought to be without a functioning birth canal. One must infer they are differentiated only through the amount of their pollution, which depends di-

9. Sexual category crossovers in old age are widely reported. Gururumba women of the New Guinea highlands may be made the guardians of the flutes, and old men are allowed once more to eat the formerly tabooed frogs, lizards, and snakes (Newman 1965:81). Hershman (1977:275) reports for the North Indian Punjab: "With the shedding of her shameful sexuality a woman becomes more like a man and she has the ability to exercise power according to the strength of her own personal character. Meanwhile for a man, old age is symbolized in his physical and sexual decline." Reichel-Dolmatoff (1971:168) reports that postmenopausal Desana women of the Amazon basin are allowed to see the cult flutes.

rectly on the number of children they have borne. Women with fewer children and thus more pollution remain uninitiated, while women who have borne more children and whose bodies therefore contain less pollution are admitted to the society of the pure. This distinction in pollution reflects not a difference in dangerousness, as neither class is dangerous in comparison with the class of sexually active women, but rather a difference in vulnerability. The woman without pollution, that is, the woman who has borne at least three children, is vulnerable to inadvertent eating of menstrual blood or possum. If she were to eat either food, she would, like a male, suffer physical degeneration and could develop *kupa*. The woman who has borne only one or two children has, on the other hand, held onto some pollution, similar in quantity to that which old men have gained, which is adequate to protect against the dread possibilities of physical degeneration and *kupa* but not sufficient in itself to be an active polluting agent.

KAKORA-FIGAPA AND MALE-FEMALE

Although it has been consistently assumed that female pollution is located exclusively in adult females, the situation among the Hua is not so simple. Although adult females are the most polluted class, in that they are the origin of female pollution, it is not only adult women who are polluted and dangerous. Nor are all adult women polluted. Female pollution, being transmittable, flows across both age and sex boundaries, emptying itself from one category into another. Thus both the dangerous, polluting category of *figapa* and the vulnerable, nonpolluted category of *kakora* include various age and sex classes. The *kakora* and *figapa* categories sort persons on the basis of female pollution, while the more usual distinction of *vi-a'* "male-female" sorts on the basis of genitalia. Each pair of categories has its own contexts of relevance. The male-female classification is relevant to the division of labor, the allotment of authority, and the modes of dress, sitting, sleeping, and carrying a load, to mention only a few. The *kakora-figapa* classification, however, is restricted to the following contexts:

1. Rules specifying vulnerability and danger in relation to eating. For example, possum is publicly prohibited not to a male but to a *kakora*.
2. Rules specifying vulnerability and danger in relation to contact between persons. The male avoidance of food or implements that have been stepped over by a woman, which has been widely reported in the New Guinea highlands, applies among the Hua not to male in relation to female, but to *kakora* in relation to *figapa*.
3. Eligibility for initiation, residence in the men's house, and knowledge of the secrets of the flutes and of male consumption of possum and blood. Only members of the *kakora* class, regardless of sex and age, who qualify as unpolluted, are eligible.

We see then that *kakora* and *figapa* are the categories relevant to pollution, avoidance, eating prohibitions, and residential segregation. Hua ethnography seems to contradict other highland ethnographies that assume that male-female is the only relevant opposition. Anthropologists have generally agreed that pollution lies primarily in menstrual and sexual fluids and that it can be transferred (Read 1954, Meggitt 1964, Langness 1967); they have thus emphasized purification rituals and rules of avoidance. However, it has also been assumed that the polluted class of persons includes only adult women, though recently M. Strathern (1972), Buchbinder and Rappaport (1976), Faithorn (1976), and Kelly (1976) have noted polluters other than females. If pollution is a substance that can travel, then perhaps elsewhere in the highlands, as among the Hua, the polluted class of persons cannot be defined in terms of the genitalia, which are not in and of themselves polluting, at least among the Hua. It would be interesting to know whether reexamination of other New Guinea highland societies would yield additional forms of classification, and whether one of these new forms would be relevant to sexual avoidance, female pollution, eating taboos, and residential segregation.

NEUTRALIZING THE
MALE-FEMALE OPPOSITION

Kakora-figapa and male-female represent two variations of the same kind or type of opposition, namely, the sexual one. Any member of the polluted class, *figapa*, who is not in fact female is said by informants to be "like a woman," and those women who are members of the *kakora* class, that is, the postmenopausal women with three or more children, are said to be "like men." Given the Hua conception of female pollution as originating in the reproductive processes of the female body, it is not surprising that the presence of pollution is given a female sexual identification and its absence a male one.

Ethnographers tend to assume that sex is genital. Where the genitals are male, the sex is male, and where the genitals are female, so is the sex. Theoretically, sexual classification can be based on a number of different criteria. Most common, of course, are the genitals. Another common, although less salient basis for classification is behavior. Certain behaviors are marked male and others female, so that a person who is genitally male can, in certain contexts, be classified as female on account of his behavior and vice-versa.[10] A third mode of classification is through the substances associated with sexuality, namely, menstrual blood, vaginal secretions, parturitional fluids, and semen. As these substances are transferable between the two genital classes, this classification permits crossovers: a genitally male person may be classified as female through his con-

10. Wikan (1977) describes a system among the Omani in which the sexual act rather than the organs defines gender.

tamination by female substances, and a genitally female person may be classified as male through the transfer of pollution out of her body. In the Hua case, the critical substances are female. A male can achieve and maintain his masculine identity only through laborious purifications of female substances, first of his mother and then of his wife. As one male informant commented,

> Today we do not induce vomiting or nose bleeding and so we are no longer like birds [white and clean on the inside], or like the flying fox [which the Hua maintain vomits after any ingestion]. Now we are like women [black and putrid on the inside]. Really we are only women now. In the past we stayed *kakora* for longer [by virtue of following the food rules and purification rituals].

There is an idea here that the residual sexual form is female.

The Hua clearly make heavy use of this mode of classification through the substances associated with sexuality. The reason they do so is related to the reason they perform the imitative behaviors described earlier in this chapter. The Hua identify with, perhaps envy, members of the opposite sex and attempt to induce in themselves physical states typical of the opposite sex (pregnancy, menstruation, and a soft, juicy interior in the case of males, and absence of menstruation, infertility, and a dry, hard interior in the case of females). Reclassification permits the same kind of cross-sex identification on the social level. Women who satisfy the *kakora* criteria socially approximate males. They reside in the men's house, gain access to secret male knowledge, and observe the rules normally observed by males. When men are old enough to satisfy the *figapa* criteria of pollution, they take on, at least in certain limited contexts, the social status of females. At weddings, for example, old men eat with women and children in a section of the wedding ground reserved for *figapa*.

Any opposition sets up tensions, and the male-female opposition is no exception. Individuals find the categories to which they are assigned restrictive. They try to reduce the distance and differences between categories in the interest of reducing the discomfort of being consigned to only one category. It is in this light that the Hua male's rather unusual interpretation of kwashiorkor as male pregnancy and bloodletting as male menstruation is to be understood.

The *kakora-figapa* distinction, being an alternative to the male-female opposition, provides release from confinement and tensions. Implicit in the *kakora-figapa* distinction is a theory of sex as transmittable. A person's gender does not lie locked in his or her genitals but can flow and change with contact as substances seep into and out of his or her body. Gender is not an immutable state but a dynamic flow. Such a view permits most persons to experience both genders before they die.

All ethnographies of the New Guinea highlands describe societies in which an extreme opposition is made between male and female. In the Hua case, however, this extreme opposition can be shown to be only one of several perspectives taken on male-female relations. In this chapter a second perspective, one that attempts to neutralize the opposition and reduce the distance between male and female, has been presented. The first perspective necessitates the second. It is precisely because the male-female opposition is made with such force that the rather extreme attempt to eliminate physiological differences and reverse social position exist. My prediction is that the more dramatically or rigidly a categorical distinction is drawn, the more we can expect to find alternative distinctions through which the tensions and dissatisfactions set up by the original distinctions are released.

Chapter Four

REDUCTION OF
SEXUAL OPPOSITION
AND AMBIVALENCE

Hua males are not only preoccupied with the facts of sexual differentiation but also ambivalent about them. Males label female organs and fluids as disgusting and dangerous, and yet also view them as the awesome sources of life itself. Female sexuality is not something, like the sun, moon, and stars, that Hua men take for granted and can comfortably leave unexplained. Instead, they fuss continually over the details of female anatomy and physiology, evaluating them first one way, and then another.

The Hua men have a third perspective, one in which sexual features receive neither the positive nor the negative ratings described in chapters 2 and 3. Differences between the sexes are instead integrated into a larger theory, the *korogo-hakeri'a* classification of all natural phenomena. Female sexual features are not bad or good: they are examples of the female's *korogo* nature. Male sexual features are similarly neutral in value: they are examples of the male's *hakeri'a* nature. Male and female bodies are not only classified as *korogo* or *hakeri'a* but are also manipulated within the terms of this distinction.

Korogo is that which is soft, juicy, fast-growing, fertile, and cool; *hakeri'a* that which is hard, dry, slow-growing, infertile, and hot. Not only all plants, but also all animals and humans, each in their entirety and in their several parts, are classified as either *korogo* or *hakeri'a*. The distinction is central to the entire Hua conception of life. The evidence from a number of Melanesian ethnographies suggests that a similar distinction is widespread. According to Buchbinder and Rappaport (1976), among the Maring of

the Central Highlands the opposition between *rombanda*
"hot, dry, hard, and strong" and *kinim* "cold, wet, soft, and
tending to rot" is the organizing principle behind the conception of the two basic classes of Maring spirits and the
two sexes, and the conflation of the notions of fertility and
death, both of which are *kinim*. Panoff (1970a:74) describes
for the Maenge of New Britain a concept nearly identical to
the Hua *korogo*:

> "Cold" plants are those species which have abundant latex,
> rich foliage, and a nutritive effect on the soil so that taro or
> other cultivated plants grow well in their vicinity. . . .
> rapid-growing trees . . . are also considered "cold."

The distinctions between hot and cold and between dry
and wet are, of course, common to many cultures. The
Hippocratic treatise *On the Nature of Man* specifies that hot,
cold, dry, and wet are the four primary elements or components from which all is created. Many diseases are attributed to an imbalance in either the temperature or moisture dimension (Lloyd 1964). In Spanish-American folk
medicine hot is identified with ease of digestion, aliveness,
affection, support, fertility, potency, activity, and pregnancy, and cold with relative indigestibility, inactivity, bar-
renness, and withdrawal (Currier 1966). The South American hot as described by Currier is the Hua *korogo* and the
South American cold is the Hua *hakeri'a*; the heat values of
the dry-wet distinction are reversed. Beck (1969), describing a South Indian variation of the hot-cool polarization,
identifies cool with inactivity, well-being, and purity, and
heat with activity, illness, and pollution.

Pitpit and impatiens are the two plants cited in all Hua
explanations of the *korogo* concept. Informants point to the
pitpit's soft, juicy interior and to the multiplicity of its stalks
as evidence of its *korogo* qualities. Impatiens, a plant with a
red flower commonly used to decorate gardens and house
sites, has shiny, succulent leaves and a soft, pliable stalk.
As evidence of the *korogo* qualities of this plant, one male

informant snapped a shoot from a healthy plant, shoved it into some soil, and said almost contemptuously, "Now watch. It will grow. Nothing can kill these *korogo* plants."

The species most commonly cited in a discussion of the *hakeri'a* quality is the *kimi* "black palm," a tree whose extremely hard wood is used by the Hua in the manufacture of bows and arrows. Any of the massive, single-trunk, hardwood trees of the jungle may also be cited by the Hua as *hakeri'a*. Their barks are hard and dry and their trunks difficult to cut. These trees grow slowly but to tremendous height, in marked contrast to the rapidly growing but squat and soft *korogo* trees and plants.

The pig, with its vast quantities of soft, juicy fat, receives a *korogo* rating, although pig meat is rated as *hakeri'a*. The wild animals, on the other hand, are *hakeri'a*—birds, because of their relative lack of fat and blood, being the most *hakeri'a* of all. Possums, which shed only a small amount of blood when shot and whose meat is tough when eaten, receive a *hakeri'a* rating, though the tree-dwelling possums are rated as more *hakeri'a* than the ground-living ones.[1] Mice, rats, and dogs, like the ground-living possums, are *hakeri'a* but not as *hakeri'a* as the animals that live in the trees.

The *korogo-hakeri'a* distinction is also relevant in many ways to humans. It is the feature most commonly used in discussion of an individual's physical condition or the general pattern of his or her development. Thus, a newborn is *korogo*, an old person *hakeri'a*, an adolescent boy *korogo*, a mature male *hakeri'a*, a menstruating or postparturient woman *korogo*, and so on. Lineages are also rated as *korogo* or *hakeri'a*. A *korogo* lineage is one whose members grow fast and develop a full musculature, a *hakeri'a* lineage is one marked by slow growth and insufficiently developed musculature.

Whether an object is labeled *korogo* or *hakeri'a* is deter-

---

1. Given the Hua identification of possum with women, it is surprising that possum is thought of as *hakeri'a*, though women are *korogo*.

mined by the amount of its *nu*. A plant's *nu* is its sap. The earth's *nu* is its moisture. The amount of an object's *nu* determines the degree of its pliability, durability, fertility, longevity, and of course the rate of its growth.

Variation in the quantity of *nu* is also used to account for differences between the sexes. Women are short because *korogo* things are short. Like all *korogo* things, they also grow fast and reproduce quickly. It is part of their *korogo* nature to be full of fluids that they release frequently and without subsequent loss of strength, as in menstruation and lactation.

Males are tall because *hakeri'a* things are tall. Like other *hakeri'a* things, they grow slowly but become tough and hard. Like the *hakeri'a* plants and animals, they are relatively infertile. Because of their small amount of *nu*, any loss of blood comparable to the female loss in menstruation is dangerous. Even very small *nu* losses are viewed as damaging. For example, the Hua believe that balding is the consequence of sexual excess, that semen is stored in the head and travels to the penis via the spinal column.

Males never tire of saying that women are like *pitpit*, fast-growing but short, quick to reproduce, and difficult to injure. Men, on the other hand, are like the black palm tree, strong but marked by slow growth, relative infertility, and vulnerability to *nu* losses.

The *korogo-hakeri'a* description of male-female differences makes these differences consistent with a larger pattern. Why this division exists, why some things have more *nu* than others—specifically, why females have more *nu* than males—remains mysterious, despite a few tentative efforts at explanation. Males maintain that females have more *nu* in part because in sexual intercourse males give *nu* and females receive it. Moreover, the Hua consistently associate the quantity of *nu* with the size of passages and orifices. The very small pores of hardwood trees are contrasted with the larger pores of the soft and succulent plants. Where passages or orifices are small, as is alleged to be the case with males, the quantity of *nu* must be small.

Where passages or orifices are large, as is claimed to be the case for females, the quantity of *nu* is correspondingly great. Frequent loss of blood, as in menstruation, is thought by males to stimulate further production of blood and to increase its fluidity (*nu*). If blood is not periodically lost, as in the case of males, it begins to clot and its *nu* content begins to decrease, necessitating bloodletting. But despite these attempts at explanation, the higher *nu* content of the female body remains for males an enigma—for the most part attributed to mysterious and awesome inner fountains.

The Hua male ambivalence about specific features of sexuality, particularly female sexuality, is resolved through the theory of *korogo-hakeri'a* states, which constitutes a third perspective on sex. It is worked out in customs in which both males and females manipulate the *nu* content of their bodies in accordance with desired adjustments in their *korogo* or *hakeri'a* states.

MALE EFFORTS TO
INCREASE *KOROGO* CONTENT

The prepubescent initiate is enjoined not to eat any of the following foods because they are *hakeri'a* and consumption of them might inhibit growth by increasing the dryness of the body: seven varieties of banana, one variety of pandanus, and two species of yam.[2] Drinking and washing with water paradoxically are prohibited to preserve the internal *korogo* quality because water dilutes and washes away internal and external juices and fluids.

In addition to avoiding *hakeri'a* substances, initiates must eat soups made of *kosi'di zasa* "leaves to make you grow," which are *korogo*.[3] These leaves exhibit one or more of the

2. The seven varieties of banana are the ones the Hua call the *hzapa*, *vugeta*, *airvia*, *mnimniva*, *opne*, *figa*, and *kta*. The single variety of the red pandanus is the *trua'*. The two species of yam are the *minava* and *vai*.

3. These leaves include *kugume* (Euphobiaceae *Acalypha*), *rasuza* (Com-

following qualities: they grow in water or at the water's edge, they are shiny or satiny, their stems are soft and juicy, they exude larger than average quantities of sap, or they grow fast. From eating these juicy leaves a *kotu bro* "lake/puddle develops" inside the initiate. In other words, his *nu* content is increased.

The purpose of these "injections" of *korogo* substances and avoidance of *hakeri'a* ones is to increase the boy's rate of growth. The persistent effort on the part of New Guinea males to stimulate their growth demonstrates their need to intervene in a biological process about which they feel considerable insecurity.

A. Strathern (1970:581) reports an apparently related ritual use among the Melpa of the Western Highlands for one of the growth-stimulating leaves, the Hua *bupa* (Melpa *kengena*):

> *Kengena* is a cool thing, it grows in watery forest places, and stays fresh when it is picked. If we place it with the pork our crops will grow well and we men will live long lives. In the ovens the grease from the pork will be as plentiful as water, and so crops and men will be healthy.

Through the rejuvenation ceremonies of the body oil house and through diet the adult male periodically seeks to increase his *korogo* content in order to recover his strength, heighten his sexual potency, increase his weight (weight loss in middle age is common), and replenish his hair. Each day a soup is prepared from large quantities of *korogo* leaves, most of which have one or more of the same qualities found in leaves eaten by initiates: they grow in water or at the water's edge, they are shiny or satiny, their stems are soft and juicy, they exude larger than average

---

positae *Blumea*), *aimeza* (Eleaocarpaceae *Elaeocarpus*), *maita'* (Amarantaceae *Amaranthus*), *hevia'* (Acantaceae *Rungia blossii*), *nanameza* (Melastomataceae *?Medimilla*), *kogiva* (Saurauiaceae *Saurauia*), *ktupa* (?Saurauiaceae), and *bupa* (Urticaceae *Elatostema*).

quantities of sap, or they grow fast.[4] In addition to eating
this soup, males bake their bodies at the fire to increase the
output of oils and rub themselves and each other with pig
fat and soot to create a rich, black coating called *kumurimo
faie*. This coating is understood to be an external manifestation of an internal *korogo* state, a state indicating virility
and strength. In order to protect this highly valued coating
against the day they emerge from their seclusion in the
body oil house, males sleep on special raised boards and sit
nearly motionless during the day.

Further evidence of male attention to the *korogo-hakeri'a*
content of their bodies is seen in the ideology behind the
custom of bloodletting. It is by the periodic releasing of
their blood that males seek to increase its *nu* content. The
male circulatory system, left to itself, will gradually slow
down and the blood will begin to clot. Letting the blood
eases this circulation problem and generates "new blood,"
in which the ratio of *nu* to *haugepa* is high. In Hua thinking
old blood leads to aging; frequent rejuvenation of the
blood maintains youth, strength, and virility.

Sexual intercourse reduces the male's already short
supply of *nu*. Stunting of growth, balding, headaches,
weight loss, impotence, and weakness may result. The first
act of intercourse is particularly feared. Against its dangers
the male wears a packet of charms in his hair and, more
significantly, eats some of the profuse sap of the casuarina,
a tree that the Hua identify as fast-growing. Consumption
of the sap, in which is supposed to lie the essence of the
casuarina's superb rate of growth, is said to provide protection for the young man's as yet incomplete growth.

The semen lost in acts of intercourse can be replenished,
at least in part, by eating sugarcane. Males traditionally

4. The following plants were mentioned by informants: *kopu* (Be-
goniaceae *Symbegonia*), *nanameza* (Melastomataceae *?Medimilla*), *fnuko'*
(Gesneriaceae *Cyrtandra*), *zavarigmi'a* (Myrsinaceae *Maesa verrusosa Scheff*),
remuza (Loganiaceae *Geniostoma* or Acanthaceae *?Graptophyllum*), *visge*
(Gesneriaceae *Cyrtandra*), *bavoni* (Urticaceae *Elatostema*), and *zavavaroga
biguva'* (Pandanaceae *Freyanetia* or Orchidaceae *Phreatria*).

had their own sugarcane gardens and their cultivation was viewed as essential. Tea and coffee, which the Hua drink with enormous amounts of sugar, are viewed as the white man's way of overcoming semen loss and as more than acceptable substitutes for sugarcane.

MALE EFFORTS TO
INCREASE *HAKERI'A* CONTENT

Although males eat great quantities of *korogo* substances, they traditionally did so primarily in the protected environments of the initiation house or the body oil house. When not in these special environments, males traditionally avoided any but the most modest consumption of *korogo* foods. Even such items of the everyday diet as *pitpit*, leafy vegetables, and red pandanus oil are said to have been eaten only sparingly. Abstinence was motivated by a fear of becoming flabby and overweight. Males mention that superfluous *nu* collects in the joints and stomach, which has bad effects on strength and speed. Abstinence from *korogo* foods intensifies before battle.

The rules exhibit a mixed pattern: males try to make themselves both more *korogo* and more *hakeri'a*. The rules of female *korogo* and *hakeri'a* consumption show the same confusing mix.

FEMALE EFFORTS TO
INCREASE *HAKERI'A* CONTENT

For the female, increases in the *korogo* content of the body are, in normal conditions, to be avoided. At menarche, the girl's diet is strictly controlled. Of the fourteen prohibited foods, eight are tabooed precisely because they are *korogo*. Hua women believe that increases in the intake of *korogo* substances lead to increases in the quantity of the menstrual flow and thus to losses of *nu* and body vitality

Table 2
PROSCRIPTIONS AND PRESCRIPTIONS FOR GIRLS
AT MENARCHE

Proscribed Food	Effect
Water, sugarcane, *kito'* (leafy vegetables), *hevia'* (Acanthaceae *Rungia blossii*; a leafy green vegetable), *pitpit*, pig fat, and cucumber	Heavy menstrual flow
Red pandanus	Makes water in the girl, who will menstruate like a stream
Snails	Vagina will become slimy like a snail
Zokoni (a mushroom that resembles the European one)	Breath will smell bad and boys will not want to kiss the girl
Mouse	The hair will fall out (from the way in which a mouse is said to pull up grass to make his nest)
Ekremu taro (a species of taro in which the inside exhibits dark discoloration)	Girl's inside will become dark and her nose will lose its oiliness
Banana, *bupa* and *kta* varieties (skins are used to wash the body of menstruating female)	Causes contamination through the association with menstrual blood and loss of strength

Prescribed Food	Effect
Zau (small pinelike bush that grows on the higher slopes of Mount Michael)	Tough, dry needles reduce menstrual flow
Hakrua' (Symplocaceae *Symplocos*; a hardwood tree)	Leaves reduce menstrual flow
Rka' (Fagaceae *Nothofagus*; a hardwood tree)	Hard brown pod is used as a contraceptive
Venevene' (a kind of fern)	Reduces menstrual flow
Finmu (Melastomataceae *Memecylon*; a tree used in fence building because of its exceptionally hard wood)	Leaves reduce menstrual flow; leaves may also be placed over wounds to reduce blood flow

and potency, as table 2 shows. Women, incidentally, *never* complained to me about menstrual cramps and pains. All of their anxiety in relation to menstruation focused on the loss of blood. The foods that are prescribed at menarche are, without exception, characterized as *hakeri'a*. If the girl eats sufficient amounts of *hakeri'a* leaves, her flow will be reduced and the onset of her next period delayed. Schieffelin (1976:67) reports similar thinking among the Kaluli of the Southern Highlands: women, said to be in a "sort of sickly or runny state since they menstruate," are forbidden to eat juicy foods lest their flow "drastically increase" and they bleed to death.

Table 3 shows the prescriptions and proscriptions on the mature menstruating woman, which are very like those for menarche. The usual *korogo* substances are prohibited for fear of excessive bleeding, while *hakeri'a* leaves are eaten to reduce bleeding. All women possess some of these leaves, but the favorite is the *kauare*, a hard brown pod shot by boys from the top of the *rka'* (Fagaceae *Nothofagus*) trees on Mount Michael. The Hua associate height—in this case, the tops of trees and the mountain—with infertility, cleanliness, hardness and dominance. In eating these *kauare*, women are eating a substance imported from the male *hakeri'a* world of hardness, height, and sterility. Once the menstrual period is over, women are supposed to drink large quantities of water and eat other *korogo* substances in order to replace the lost *nu*.

After the birth of a child, considerable effort is devoted to decreasing the woman's *korogo* content. The stems and seed pods of *rike* (Cruciferae *Rorippa*) are mixed and rubbed on the abdomen to make the womb *kreki* "wrinkle and dry up." *Rike* and *kizo*, another unidentified leaf that the woman is supposed to eat, are *hakeri'a*. Women are also advised to sit on the leaf of another very *hakeri'a* tree called *koripa*. This leaf is supposed to assist the birth canal in closing and drying up.

Approximately four weeks after the birth, there is a ceremony called the *zaumo vaima'na* "*zaumo* [a leaf reckoned as extremely *hakeri'a*] drying-out thing." Many *hakeri'a* foods

Table 3
PROSCRIPTIONS AND PRESCRIPTIONS FOR
MENSTRUATING WOMEN

Proscribed Food	Effect
Water and sugarcane	Heavy menstrual flow
Pitpit	The way in which water collects in the fork of its branches and then runs down its base encourages a similar flow of blood in the woman (not all women subscribe to this idea or this prohibition)
Kito' (leafy vegetables) picked by the woman herself	Heavy menstrual flow from self-contamination
Ginger	Menstrual flow reduced through a long period of fasting on ginger, which has the power to open passages

Prescribed Food	Effect
Kimi (black palm)	Bark scrapings reduce bleeding
Rka' (Fagaceae *Nothofagus*), *vazaninike*, *korezasi*, and *hrgava'*	Leaves or pods are *hakeri'a* and reduce bleeding

are prescribed, including the leaves of the *hakrua'* tree
(Symplocaceae *Symplocos*); possum and pig bones; the
brittle, hard *zau*, which grows on the higher slopes of
Mount Michael and from which the ceremony receives its
name; the roots of the *hzapa* species of banana, which are
renowned for their toughness and strength; and the leaves
of the hardwood *dekema'* tree, which are also eaten by warriors before battle.

FEMALE EFFORTS TO
INCREASE *KOROGO* CONTENT

The woman's desire to increase her *korogo* content is not
continual but related to particular contexts: pregnancy, lactation, childbirth, and infertility.

Table 4
PROSCRIPTIONS AND PRESCRIPTIONS FOR
PREGNANT WOMEN

Proscribed Food	Effect
Hakeri'a varieties of taro, yam, and banana	May cause the womb and birth canal to dry out, leading to a difficult birth
Possum bones (*hakeri'a*)	Cause a long and difficult labor
Burned tubers	Burned substance will cause the fetus to stick to the womb just as it causes the tuber to stick to the cooking rocks or pot
Food from either end of bamboo cooking tube (some informants say just from the lower end)	Causes a difficult birth. Food at the ends of the tube, where it is packed more tightly, tends to stick
Food from a small bamboo tube	Prevents the birth canal from opening sufficiently for the birth
Tree grubs	May cause a difficult birth. They live in passages in the tree that lack exits.
Mouse	May cause a difficult birth. It crawls into places from which there is no apparent exit.
Flying fox	Because its anus is said to be sealed shut, the child's might be similarly formed
Cat, dog, and possum	Because these animals are capable only of *dri dri ke* "babble, confused stutterings," the child may never be capable of more
Food given by present or former enemies	Might cause the fetus to die because it may carry evil intent
Pork butchered in another village	Might cause the fetus to sicken because it may carry negatively charged *nu*

Prescribed Food	Effect
Pig fat, frog, *kva kito'* (a vegetable green), *maita'* (Amaranthaceae *Amaranthus*; a particularly juicy vegetable green), and *trgu'*, *zokoni*, and *zagi* (three kinds of mushrooms)	Speed up delivery; each is a *hrupo'di na* "slippery thing"

Table 4 demonstrates the importance of the consumption of *korogo* substances and the avoidance of *hakeri'a* ones for the pregnant woman. The pregnant woman's need to avoid *hakeri'a* foods is the exact opposite of that of the menstruating woman. The taboo on *hakeri'a* foods extends, at the discretion of the woman, beyond possum bones and *hakeri'a* varieties of taro, yam, and banana. If she fears or has experienced a difficult birth, she will probably avoid many other *hakeri'a* items. This avoidance is intended to insure, in addition to an easy birth, a sufficiently wet placental environment for the fetus. According to the Hua, the greater the fluidity of this environment, the greater the ease of delivery and health of the newborn.

The proscriptions on burned tubers and food from the ends of a cooking tube or a small tube are on *bzgo'di na* "things that stick." By avoiding them, women hope to avoid a difficult and protracted labor. The proscriptions on tree grubs and mouse reflect an anxiety about the vagina's capabilities as an exit for the child. The remaining proscriptions reflect other themes that have no relevance to the discussion of *korogo* and *hakeri'a*.

Every prescribed food is a *hrupo'di na* "thing that is slippery." Eating them is said to ease the passage of the child out of the body.

The concern to increase *korogo* content at the time of birth is also obvious in the following cure. A woman in an advanced state of pregnancy is fed a meal of extremely *korogo* (and delicious) foods that have been cooked in a single bamboo tube. The foods are *kva kito'* (the juiciest of the leafy vegetables), *higo'* (unidentified), *hevia'* (a leafy green vegetable), *ktrgu'* (a soft and somewhat slimy mushroom), canned fish (which is packed in a profusion of oil), and salt. Later, at the onset of labor, the woman is sat naked in water while a spell is said over her. According to my informant, the water goes inside the woman's vagina and up into her womb, making the child wet, slippery, and therefore easier to deliver. The greasy foods that the mother eats are supposed to have a similar effect, working through the entrance that the Hua believe connects the intestine to the womb.

For the lactating woman, *korogo* substances (water, pig fat, sugarcane, cucumber, *kito'*, and *pitpit*) are prescribed; *hakeri'a* varieties of taro, yam, and bananas are proscribed. The proscriptions, however, are not viewed as compulsory. Where the milk is coming in abundance, no taboos need be observed. On the other hand, where there is a shortage, these taboos plus others at the woman's discretion are thought to help. The idea behind the prescribed foods is obvious: the lactating woman should consume liquid in the form of either water or vegetable matter. Sugarcane is thought to be the most effective food in replacing breast milk. As mentioned earlier, it is also used to replenish lost semen, providing further indirect evidence for the association of breast milk with semen and for the woman's role in feeding with the male's role in sexual intercourse.

The Hua have several cures for a barren woman. In one cure, two holes are dug, one large and one small, and connected by means of an underground tunnel. In the large hole an earth oven is made; its steam escapes through the underground tunnel into the smaller hole, from which it rises into the air. The barren woman places her naked genitals directly over this small hole, exposing them to the steam. Informants say the steam rises through the vagina into the womb, softens it, and thus prepares it for conception. In addition, the woman's abdomen may be rubbed with leaves classified as *korogo*.

The barren woman and her husband may also be questioned about their dreams. In the case reported to me, the wife said that she frequently dreamed of herself either looking at or walking on Mount Michael, which is associated with maleness and with the *hakeri'a* quality because the plants that grow on its heights are renowned for their dry, tough hardness. She said she never dreamed of water. Her husband, on the other hand, admitted that he always dreamed of himself up in trees, which have male and *hakeri'a* associations, and never of himself on the ground, which has female, fertile, and *korogo* associations.

THE THIRD PERSPECTIVE ON
MALE AND FEMALE

Male and female efforts to manipulate the *nu* content of their bodies reveal significant information on their attitudes toward their own sexuality. Male and female are considered extremes of the same continuum. Being extremes, each sex experiences problems and each sex is therefore in need of balance. Nonetheless, the extreme characteristic of each sex is accepted and affirmed.

In most of the public and official contexts of Hua culture, males maintain that males and females are categories in total opposition, creatures of a different order. Males are like birds, females like frogs. Males and females sleep in different positions and on different kinds of beds, sit differently (males squat on the ground, females sit), carry loads differently (men on their shoulders, women on their heads), know different things (males have secret knowledge), and live in different houses (the men's house is surounded by female residences). A whole section of Hua culture, including the eating rules, is devoted to upholding the proposition that males are radically different from females.

The *korogo-hakeri'a* theory reveals another perspective on males and females: they are creatures of the same kind but differ in the quantity of their *nu*. They represent two extremes of a continuum whose underlying identity is explicitly acknowledged. The male, because of his relatively small amount of *nu*, has difficulty insuring adequate growth in the adolescent years and maintaining adequate vitality in the adult. The female, because of her relatively large amount of *nu*, grows fast and remains full of vitality, but her excess of *nu* results in an unattractive moistness and unpleasant smell to her body—according to both male and female informants. Furthermore, a woman's *nu* excess handicaps her for action. How can she run fast and fight or work hard when nursing an infant or menstruating, or after childbirth?

The male has too little *nu* for the maintenance of vitality, the female too much for action. Because each is an extreme, each is deficient. There is a clear assertion of equality of value between the two sexes.

The best balance would be if each sex could modify itself in the direction of its opposite. The ideal male would still be sufficiently *hakeri'a* to run quickly, grow tall, and fight long and hard, but sufficiently *korogo* to grow fast, age slowly, lose blood without losing strength, and lose semen without losing hair. Men's efforts to increase their *nu* content represent their attempts to achieve this ideal. The ideal female would still be sufficiently *korogo* to grow fast and produce and nurse a child, but sufficiently *hakeri'a* to reduce her menstrual and postparturitional flows, decrease her vaginal secretions, limit the size of her breasts and pregnant womb, limit the duration of her fertility, and thus be better adapted to a life of continued action. Women's efforts to decrease their *nu* content represent their attempts to achieve this goal.

Although the balanced middle is the ideal, both males and females recognize the need for males to make themselves even more *hakeri'a* than usual in some situations and for females to make themselves even more *korogo* than usual in others. These extremes of *korogo* and *hakeri'a* states are required by the opposed needs of human populations for reproduction and defense. For the female to reproduce, she must be extremely *korogo*; for the male to defend himself and her, he must be extremely *hakeri'a*. These extremes, although presenting problems, are affirmed as necessary to the varied needs of social life.

Chapter Five

CONTEXT AND THE CONCEPTUALIZATION OF MALE AND FEMALE

The public expression of attitudes and opinions is constrained by cultural rules. In other words, the culture provides patterns and individuals talk about topics in accordance with them. No single attitude or style of expression is necessarily prescribed, but rather a variety of alternative attitudes and styles exists, each tied in with a system of appropriate contexts of expression. An attitude or style appropriate in one context will be inappropriate in a second. Contradictory attitudes do not feel contradictory because they are expressed in separate contexts.

ATTITUDES

The male attitude of contempt for females receives its most explicit expression in the eating rules, the rites of expulsion of female substance (such as nose bleeding, cane swallowing, and sweating), and the cult of the flutes. Each of these customs is specifically associated with the men's house. For example, the eating rules, which connect the female reproductive anatomy and physiology with bad odors and unattractive textures, and which encourage an attitude of mockery toward the female body, are taught with considerable flourish and chauvinistic pride to initiates during their seclusion in the men's house. Full adherence to all the rules is required only during this relatively brief period of seclusion.

The rites of expulsion (sweating, vomiting, and nose bleeding) also occur in isolation from females, either in the men's house or in an all-male ceremony at the banks of a stream. The stated purpose of these initiatory rites is to remove female influence in order to enhance the processes of growth and maturation.

The flutes are also intimately associated with the men's house and with its ceremonies and general atmosphere. Like flags, the flutes serve as the symbols of the component lineages of a men's house and of male solidarity and pride. Their musical function is more social than aesthetic. The flutes are stored in the men's house, hidden from the sight of women and children. The revelation of the true origin of their mysterious sound is one of the central ceremonies of the male (and of the postmenopausal female) initiations.

The men's house is the physical locus of one particular male perspective on females. Its role is analogous to that of the Western church, which is the physical locus of another set of beliefs and moral perspectives. Just as those beliefs and moral perspectives have limited relevance outside the church context, so also the Hua male attitude of loathing and contempt for females has limited application outside the men's house. Observations of male-female interactions reveal little of the disgust and contempt that these men's house rites lead us to expect.

The opposite perspective on females, the attitude of envy, is appropriate in the same context. The male eating of possum and human blood, the association of bloodletting with menstruation, and the knowledge that women were the first possessors of the flutes and the original rulers of the society are secrets belonging to the exclusive men's society. They are part of a hidden body of special ceremonies that have limited relevance outside the specialized context of that society.

In contrast to the attitudes of contempt for females on the one hand and envy of them on the other, the attitude of acceptance of sexuality, one's own and others', is the predominant attitude in the normal contexts of Hua everyday life. Women do not claim to understand male efforts to make themselves more *korogo* at initiation and in the re-juvenation ceremonies, but they are aware of the general outlines of these procedures and appreciate them. Males do not attempt to hide from females their need to become more *korogo*, and their efforts to achieve a more *korogo* state often occur outside the men's house. The same is true of their efforts in the opposite direction, their efforts to decrease their amount of *nu*. Increasing and decreasing *nu* quantity are practical maneuvers in the everyday management of the male body and are carried out in the usual nonspecialized contexts of Hua life. Implicit in these maneuvers is male and female acceptance of the male body as overly *hakeri'a* but necessarily so, given the requirements of defense and to a lesser extent of labor.

Women's efforts to make themselves more *hakeri'a* at menstruation and after childbirth, and their counterefforts to make themselves more *korogo* prior to childbirth, during lactation, and in the event of infertility, are similarly public procedures about which there is little embarrassment and no secrecy. Males and females alike accept them as practical procedures for alleviating the problems connected with reproduction.

Very few cultures provide monolithic attitudes toward important issues. Ambivalence, contradiction, diversity, and complexity are far more common, particularly on an issue like sex. This complexity is simplified, the awareness of contradiction avoided, by assigning different attitudes to different contexts. As a result divergent points of view are rarely expressed side by side within the same context.

STYLES

New Guinea highland cultures have usually been characterized as prudish, and there is clear evidence of some prudery or inhibition among the Hua. Males traditionally refused to use the words *fgagetava* "womb" and *kau* "vagina/urethra." There is, even among females, no non-euphemistic word for menstruation, which is referred to only as *a'di kuna* "women's time," *kaimo haie* "the moon hits her," *zu'bo havie* "she has gone up into the house," or *korogo na'a* "her soft, juicy, fertile thing."

In addition to word taboos, there was, and to a lesser extent still is, a male cult of ignorance in regard to female anatomy and physiology. Informants claim that their fathers died believing the Hua version of the stork story, namely, that infants were born through the navel. Even today males never witness childbirth and claim not to touch the vaginas of their sexual partners. There is a prudery about observing the female sexual parts (initiates are cautioned that they will get sores if they look at the female pudenda) and about gaining intellectual knowledge of them. These things properly remain unseen, untouched, and unknown. Female infants and children, unlike their male counterparts, are required to keep their genitals covered.

During conversations in which I probed male knowledge of female reproductive anatomy and physiology, it occasionally happened that an informant would mention how inappropriate such a discussion would have been in the past and how his fathers would have berated him for his *siro ge* "dirty talk." Discussions of sexual issues as they are embedded in and attached to food rules, however, never elicited this response. For example, there was no embarrassment or shame about saying males cannot eat snails because their slime is like vaginal secretions. It is my impression that Hua males are prudish about sexual curiosity, about any attempt to observe and explore the female body, but not in the least embarrassed about repeating the standard correspondences between foods and sexual items or enunciating the body beliefs that underlie them. These beliefs constitute the reason why males may eat some things and may not eat others; as such they represent information of a practical and nonprurient nature. That is certainly the tone in which they were taught to me.

The prudery about sexual and reproductive curiosity

contrasts rather dramatically not only with the explicitly sexual references made in the food rules but also with the conversations of everyday life. In these conversations individual sexual proclivities and characteristics are discussed without inhibition by both males and females. Gossips delight in prurient facts and events, and the folktales are full of sexual details. Individual sex organs and proclivities are known and discussed. For example, one man in late middle age was alleged "always to have semen dripping from his penis," the implication being that he was an adulterer. Two younger men, both childless, suffered from a condition known as *hosa'a vai'di* "foreskin shriveled and dry." One of them was additionally alleged to have an abnormally small penis. A much remarked feature of an older woman was the exceptional size of her clitoris.

Much attention and laughter were devoted to the following account of the sexual stubbornness of a man known to all as unusually soft-spoken and mild. One day a woman was down at the river, bent over on its bank washing her clothes. The mild-mannered man managed to sneak up on her from behind and enter her. She screamed for help and people came running, but when they tried to pull the man off her, he would not let go. It was only after much pushing and pulling that they succeeded in separating him from her.

While I was at Lufa two women from Irava, a Chuave community from which the Hua traditionally take brides, were visiting their classificatory older sisters married into a Lufa village. It was well known that one of the women was looking for a husband. Suddenly, these two women disappeared and with them a teenaged Hua girl. People who gathered to gossip and speculate concluded that they were heading for Lae, a large town on the coast, and a life of prostitution. It was thought that they would hitchhike to Lae, paying for their rides with sexual favors. The disappearance of these women was discovered in the late afternoon. By evening a search party of young and middle-aged males had been organized. They set out with lanterns, proudly boasting that when they found the three females, they would force themselves on the two who came from Irava. Members of the search party later reported that they found the women and the girl hiding in the fields that surround the village. They described with great gusto the high grasses, the night, the flaming torches, the final discovery, and then how each member of the party had sex with the two Irava women.

The folktales provide the most conclusive evidence of an uninhibited style. These tales were and are told by parents to children in a cosy, giggly, bedtime atmosphere. They are presented as innocent and amusing stories and destroy any theory of the Hua as a generally prudish culture, at least on the verbal level. The following are somewhat abbreviated versions of the most uninhibited.

> An old man and his wife were working together in their garden at the bottom of a hill. A crowd of little boys came tumbling down the hill shouting.
> The old man called out to them, "Hey, little boys, what's going on?"
> The little boys shouted back, "Fuck, you two, fuck, fuck, fuck, fuck."
> The old man replied, "We're working. What's the matter with you?"
> "Don't work," the little boys shouted. "Fuck, fuck, fuck."
> Then the little boys started to slide down the hill on big leaves, and while sliding they shouted, "Hey, old man, hey old woman."
> "What is it?" the old man asked impatiently.
> "Fuck, you two fuck, fuck," the children replied.
> The old couple didn't know how to respond to the boys' teasing. But then they got an idea. They dug a big hole at the bottom of the hill and collected ripe bananas. The old man took a needle and stitched the woman's anus shut, and the old woman took a needle and stitched the man's shut. Then they began to eat bananas. They ate, and they ate, and they ate, until they were so stuffed that banana was oozing out their mouths.
> The children were still sliding down the hill and shout-

ing, "Fuck, fuck, fuck." The old couple called the children down to see them. While they were coming, the old man cut the stitch out of the old woman's anus and the old woman cut it out of the man's. They hung their buttocks over the hole which they had dug and defecated. The hole was filled.

The children slid down the hill and disappeared into the banana-feces one after the other.

The children's parents came looking for them. They rescued the children and asked the old couple why they did this. The old couple told the parents that the children were saying *vare'ke*, "strange talk." And so it was.

An old man, out watering his sugar cane, comes up with an idea. He chops off his testicle, wraps it in leaves, and puts it in the house to cook. When he thinks it is cooked, he calls to his wife to take it off the fire and give it to him.

In removing it from the fire, she can't resist tasting a little bit of the juice which has dripped out on her hand. She finds it delicious and says "Mmmmmm, this is my favorite juice." She can't resist, eats the whole packet, and then runs away.

After running for a while she meets an enormous squat old man built like a drum. She asks him, "Which way is my path?"

He replies, "There is no other path but this, my rectum." Then he opens his enormous anus, as in a yawn, and she climbs in, leaving no trace of herself except a tiny end of her string bag which she neglected to pull all the way inside.

Meanwhile, the husband is becoming more and more impatient. Finally, he goes to the house and looks in the fireplace, but the packet is not there. The woman's feces (which she has left behind to talk for her) direct him to look in the yard, but it's not there. Then the feces direct him to look on the rafters, but it's not there. Then they direct him to look in the bamboo cooking tube, but it's not there. They direct him to look in the cooking drum, but it's not there.

Finally, the old man realizes that his wife has made off with it and he follows her tracks until he comes upon the old drum-shaped man.

"Old man, has a woman come by here?" he asks.

"No," replies the drum-shaped man.

"But I've followed her tracks directly to here. Are you sure you're not hiding her?"

The drum-shaped man replies, "There are lots of paths here. You'll find her on one of them."

"All right," says the husband but he asks the drum-shaped man if he will let him test the sharpness of the axe which he has been sharpening during this conversation. While testing the axe, he catches a glimpse of the bit of his wife's string bag hanging out of the drum-shaped man's anus. He turns on the drum-shaped man and gives him a tremendous whack with the axe at the base of the spine. Suddenly animals begin to come out from between his buttocks.

First comes a frog [identified with females in many contexts] saying, "*tioko tioko hugu hugu.*" He comes down and jumps into the water and is carried away.

Then comes a toad going "*u′u′u′u′″*" and goes into the mud.

Then a black pig which begins to root with his snout, a white pig, a mouse which builds his nest and sleeps, a wallaby, and a possum saying, "*tiri tiri tiri.*" (Haiman n.d.)

While the simultaneous existence of inhibited and uninhibited styles of talking about sex is undoubtedly universal, the distribution of these styles to various contexts in cultures varies. In North American culture the uninhibited style of expression is most obviously appropriate in such all-male contexts as locker rooms, barracks, and bars. By contrast, the comparable context in Hua culture, the men's house, is consonant only with a relatively inhibited style, or so I was told. Talk about sex that Westerners would regard as uninhibited is permitted in Hua informal social groups including both males and females. In Western society "mixed company" represents precisely the context in which talk about sex is generally more inhibited.

Day-to-day relationships between males and females are marked by little of the avoidance and antagonism on the one hand and envy on the other that the rules and attitudes described in the preceding chapters would lead us to expect. These relations are strikingly similar to relations between the sexes in our own society. Although Hua males disparage women, beat them up, deny them a political voice more frequently and to a greater extent than in our own society, the difference seems to be one of degree, not of kind. Moreover, informants are not loathe to speak of sex as fun, and children are born as soon as the nursing needs of elder siblings permit.

Although the consciously cultivated male attitude toward females is one of hostility combined with envy, that attitude and the behaviors and customs that reflect it appear only in a limited number of contexts. The usual attitude toward females, like the usual style of talk about sex, is casual, accepting, "normal" in our terms. The hostility and inhibition commonly associated with highland cultures occupy a narrow, highly organized, consciously cultivated niche.

Chapter Six

VITAL ESSENCE
AND POLLUTION

M ost of the transactions of social life, among them the acts of sexual and alimentary intercourse, involve the sharing of vital essence, or *nu*, between otherwise discrete individuals. As such, they are subject to a network of rules and prohibitions. In a sense, these prohibitions may be interpreted as a mechanism for regulating the transfer of *nu* in the Hua community.

Two propositions are axiomatic in Hua thinking about the nature and function of *nu*. First, whatever can be eaten or otherwise ingested is a source of *nu* and, conversely, whatever is a source of *nu* (however wildly unlikely) can be thought of as nourishing. Second, all *nu* may be either good or bad for a person, depending on the social source.

The Hua conception of *siro na* "pollution" therefore does not correspond exactly to the Western one. Not all substances that we regard as food are invariably edible to the Hua. Conversely, not all substances that we regard as filth are invariably inedible. The first difference, which restricts Hua eating practices, is far more significant, although far less spectacular, than the second.

SOURCES OF *NU* AND *SIRO NA*

The substances thought of as *nu* include sexual fluids, feces and urine, breath and body odors, sweat, body oil, hair, saliva, fingernails, and flesh and blood. Many of the food restrictions are motivated by the need to avoid ingestion of these substances.

The rule that prohibits certain persons from eating leafy green vegetables picked by or any food from the hand of certain other people is explicitly meant as a protection against sexual fluids. Men point out that women wash their hands infrequently and that dried clots of menstrual blood and other sexual exuviae remain under their fingernails. Presumably, women should be motivated by a similar horror of dried semen under the fingernails of men, but I never heard of any such fear.

A rule that enjoins ego to prohibit various others from crossing over his or her body, food, or implements is a protection against both sexual fluids and excreta. So too is a rule that specifies that certain people may not eat pork from villages other than their own. This pork is alleged to be contaminated by the *nu* substances of the alien villagers.

Several prohibitions are motivated by the need to avoid the ingestion of certain smells or breath, the potency of which in Hua folklore is considerable. Some smells are aphrodisiacs; others are thought to stimulate the growth of infants, while the *rga'* odor of parturition is thought to stunt it.

Certain categories of ego must vigorously expel air from their nostrils after inhaling in the vicinity of a menstruating woman, or they may not eat any food cooked over a fire into which a menstruating woman has blown. Another rule prohibits infants from being held by either a man or a woman who has had sexual intercourse within the last day: otherwise the "foul smell" from the skin and mouth of the sexually active person would go into the infant's body and cause him or her to cease nursing.

A rule that prohibits wearing the clothes or the string bags of certain others is a protection against their sweat and body oil. A rule that prohibits touching the hair of specific alters may be intended for the protection of ego or of the person he or she may not touch; not only is hair itself *nu*, but it contains sweat and body oils.

Many rules are intended as protection against the ingestion of prohibited saliva. An example is the rule that ego may not eat any tuber that has been partially eaten by certain others, nor may he or she share a knife with them or drink from the same bamboo tube or cup.

No food rules relate specifically to fingernails, the polluting power of which is feared largely in sorcery. It is thought that a woman may ensorcell a man by putting her fingernail parings into his food. As a result, he will waste away and ultimately die.

The Hua were traditionally cannibals. A traditional prohibition, which has now gone the way of cannibalism, prohibited the consumption of the deceased body of certain hostile alters, together with a surprising variety of other possible foods that were as closely related to that alter as were his or her own flesh and blood: these included his or her pigs, the largest and best produce from his or her garden, and any wild animals he had shot.

It is fairly clear that most of the prohibited substances not only contain *nu* but are intimately identified with the person from whose body they originated. Hair is perceived as being nourished by liquid *nu* in the scalp, the relationship between the two being analogous to that between plants and moisture in the ground wherein they grow. Breath, literally *vza bu'* "mouth steam," is related to liquid *nu* as steam is to water. It is in order to conserve this vital resource that young male initiates are enjoined to refrain from talking. The connection between a person and his or her child, pig, or garden produce is a consubstantial one (see chapter 1). The identification of a person with the prey he has shot is, I think, the most problematic, although analogous beliefs are widely reported in New Guinea. The most graphic expression of this consubstantiality is reported by Lewis (1975:37) for the Gnau of the Sepik, who believe that the hunter's blood invisibly enters the body of the prey when the hunter's arrow does.

SOCIAL RELATIONS AND *SIRO NA*

Whether or not *siro na* substances, which seem to be intrinsically foul, are actually perceived as such, however, depends on social relationships. The system of Hua food prohibitions outlined in appendix B characterizes three relationships in which *nu* transfer is to be avoided: where the relationship between the two parties is marked by jealousy, distrust, competition, or hostility; where the genealogical distance between two parties is inappropriate to an eating or sexual relationship; and where the direction of transfer of *nu* is somehow felt to be unnatural.

The major class distinction in the Hua social universe is between one's consanguines, who are *bgotva' auva* "one skin," and one's affines, who are labeled *kta vede* "heavy or difficult people." A male may eat foods freely from most of his consanguines, but not from his affines.

The Hua, like other New Guinea highlanders, are not always able to take their brides from peoples with whom they enjoy a secure and stable alliance. The resulting tension and hostility between affines is sufficiently well established to require no further description here.

Three surprising cases of distrust are classes of kin whom ego is constrained to avoid although two of them are consanguines and the third, although an affine, is the one toward whom we would expect the greatest expression of friendship and trust. The consanguines are the *baru'* "firstborn child" and *varu'* "agemate, fellow graduate of initiation ceremony"; the affine is the *naru'* "wife or classificatory female cross-cousin" (that is, potential wife).[1]

The food proscriptions mark the relationship with the firstborn as one of the highest degree of avoidance. A Hua parent cannot eat any food from his or her male or female firstborn or from the children of his or her firstborn: it will be *siro na* by contagion. Nor can he or she eat any food cultivated, bred, or killed by his or her firstborn: such food will be *siro na* by consubstantiality with the firstborn. Finally, the parent cannot allow his or her body, food, or implements to be crossed by either the body or the shadow of the firstborn; to do so would incur the risk of catching *nu* in

---

1. The phonetic similarity of these three kin labels suggests the possibility of a common root *-aru'*, for which, unfortunately, there is no evidence (John Haiman, personal communication).

the form of sexual fluids dropping from the firstborn's genitals, or the certainty of catching *nu* in its immaterial manifestation as shadow.

Three further avoidance rules apply to body contact and do not involve food. First, the firstborn may not tend his or her parents' hair. For the Hua, as for Samson, hair is a form of vital essence. Premature baldness is explained as the consequence of excessive copulation or child begetting, a prodigal waste of one's limited lifetime supply of *nu*.

Second, the firstborn may not pass close behind his or her parent's back. Such movement, it is said, may cause the parent to bend his or her back and bow his or her head, thus assuming the posture of a sick elderly person. If this is the only motivation for the prohibition, it protects the parents not from actual loss of *nu* but from the appearance, however temporary, of such loss. Steiner (1956:45–46), however, reports a similar prohibition among the Polynesians, motivated by the belief that the head and backbone are both the seat of *mana* "vital essence," which is somehow depleted by poor posture. It may be that the Hua have a similar belief that I never heard them articulate. If so, this rule protects against not only the appearance but the actual loss of *nu*.

Third, the firstborn may not touch his or her parent on the head or shoulders. The position of the head and shoulders is a symbol of status and of the power of *nu*. Only when this power has declined does the parent tolerate such contact from the firstborn.

These constraints on body contact, as well as constraints on *nu* transfer, suggest an ambivalence between a Hua parent and eldest child. Further independent evidence supports this claim. Normally parents are proud and fond of their children. Normally they also resent the curtailment of their liberty and the end of their youth. This ambivalence is allowed no culturally sanctioned expression in Western society and is forced to seek furtive outlets. In a classic article on the subject, Fortes (1974) surveyed a wide range of tribal and oriental societies in which this perfectly

natural ambivalence is sanctioned and allowed institu-
tionalized expression, particularly in "various forms of ritually enjoined and socially sanctioned avoidances" (p. 91).
Fortes did not say whether societies in which such avoidances are standard give independent expression to parent-
child hostility. Hua parents certainly do. The firstborn is
habitually described as the child on which the parents
waste their strength. His or her body is one into which
large amounts of their *nu* is drained. Like the first fruit of a
plant, the firstborn child is said to be the largest, strongest,
and most vital, having been produced at the time of the
parents' greatest strength. The male firstborn, informants
say, is feared as the child eager to usurp the father in physical and social power. A man may not carry his firstborn
baby (male or female) on his shoulders lest he be pre-
maturely "put or pressed down." Nonetheless the Hua are
warm, loving, and gentle with their children: resentment
of the firstborn is expressed verbally and symbolically,
never to my knowledge physically.

Very similar constraints operate between a man and his
agemate and between a woman and her *komipa'* "co-wife."
A man may eat food prepared by his agemate but may not
allow the shadow or the body of his agemate to pass over
his food, implements, or person. Nor may he eat foods that
his agemate has killed, cultivated, or bred, in other words,
that are consubstantial with him. Similarly, a woman may
eat food prepared by her co-wife. Apparently there is some
disagreement as to whether she may eat a pig tended by
her co-wife, but otherwise she may not eat any food that
her co-wife has cultivated. There is also disagreement as
to whether she may allow the shadow or the body of her
co-wife to pass her body, food, or implements. If the
co-wife relationship is, as informants aver, simply the sym-
metrical female counterpart of the male agemate relationship, then the greater latitude allowed women may reflect
the fact that the rules are intended more for the protection
of men than of women.

Finally, both men and women are subject to the rules

that prohibit body contact: a man may not let himself be groomed, touched on the head, or approached from behind by an agemate, nor is it advisable for a woman to permit such liberties to her co-wife.

There is also independent evidence that the relationship between agemates is characterized by considerable rivalry and hostility. Agemates are frequently played off against one another in matters of speed, growth, strength, and general level of achievement. A man's agemate is his rival throughout his lifetime. Informants say that a man's shame at lagging behind his agemates in growth, sexual prowess, gardening skill, bravery, or fortunes of the hunt can be so severe as to cause suicide. Sexual jealousy and suspicion among agemates may be so extreme that a man may enjoin on his wife a total avoidance of his agemates. She may be forbidden not only to enter their houses or gardens but to talk to them or even look at them.

The sexual rivalry between agemates is latent; that between co-wives is not. The most frequent category of physical violence is a fight between co-wives. The elder wife may make the life of her junior co-wife miserable in the hope that she will decamp. This is in fact a not infrequent conclusion to polygamous marriages.

In some ways the most remarkable of the exceptionally dangerous alters, one whose *nu* pollutes and must therefore be avoided, is the actual wife, or any woman of the class from which a wife is usually chosen, a classificatory female cross-cousin who is not actually a true cross-cousin (such a relative is reckoned too close for marriage). The prohibitions enjoined on a man in relationship to his new wife are total: he may eat no food she has prepared or produced, nor may he allow her shadow or her body over his, nor may he permit her any of the proscribed forms of body contact. Traditionally, cohabitation did not begin until all the men of one age category were married.

A new wife is alleged to be loyal still to her consanguines rather than her affines. In any dispute between her husband and her brothers, she may side with her brothers. If

need be, she can provide them with her husband's fingernail parings, hair, and spittle, to be used in sorcery against
him. She may introduce menstrual blood into his food in
an attempt to kill him. She is, literally, the enemy within
the gates, at least until she has demonstrated her allegiance
to the affinal community by investing children in it. With
the passage of time, as the wife becomes accepted into her
affinal community, her *nu* becomes less *siro na*, until at last
she achieves a status of relative purity as a mother.

It should be emphasized, if it is not self-evident, that this
is peculiarly a male ideology: the hostile intentions of the
wife are imputed to her by men alone. And there is a striking and remarkable asymmetry between men and women
in their pollution content: only women are polluting in
marriage. While men fear their wives as witches, women
are enjoined not to fear their affines. She is a threat to
them, but they are not a threat to her.

There is, however, one set of affines that a woman must
carefully avoid: potential adulterous partners (who are also
potential husbands on the death of her husband). If the
woman does not practice the prescribed avoidance rules
with such men, this lapse is taken as an indication of illicit
sexual passion. The avoidance rules are generally an index
of ambivalence, though in this instance, not of ambivalence between the woman and the party to be avoided, but
of ambivalence between the husband and that party.

Hua males maintain that *nu* from sources genealogically
too close or too far is dangerous. Ego must, in effect, eat
only from the middle distance. For example, no person,
male or female, may eat any meat or prize garden produce
that is consubstantial with the self (either in the more immediate sense that he or she produced it or the more extended sense that his or her child or grandchild did). To eat
such foods is to consume oneself, an act comparable, they
say, to that of a dog licking its genitals. Physical degeneration is a likely consequence because, informants say, "My
nu will turn around and put me down." Barth (1975:35)
and Salisbury (1965:62) report similar idioms among the
Baktaman and Siane.

To eat a food that comes from too great a genealogical distance is also dangerous for a male as it involves the ingestion of an untested and potentially hostile *nu*. Thus, a male may not eat food that has been stepped over or crossed by the shadow of his affine or that is consubstantial with the affine.

The marriage rules parallel the eating rules: the preferred wife lies within the middle genealogical distance. A marriage with a closer relation is as dangerous as eating one's own produce. Similarly, a marriage with a stranger community holds the same dangers as eating its food—contact with an alien *nu*. Presumably these eating and marriage rules reflect the social dangers of community withdrawal and introversion on the one hand and indiscriminate community expansion and extroversion on the other.

Pollution may also be determined by generational direction. The senior generation female and male can give blood let from its veins, the largest and best produce from its garden, animals it has raised or shot, and its flesh after death to members of the junior generation, but the junior may not make the same gifts to the senior. The adult's *nu* is nourishing to the child, but the child's *nu*, particularly that of the firstborn, is polluting to the parent, because the child's *nu* on entering the parent's body *bi aina to-* "puts or presses it down," perhaps "degrades it." The result is that the parent is physically weakened and in some cases sickened as well. Some informants add that as a consequence of the child's pollution of the parent, the parent ages more quickly and the child matures more quickly.

Although the child's *nu* is *siro na* to the parent, it does not appear to elicit revulsion or disgust (as does, for example, the female's *nu* to the male). But it does seem to have a connotation of moral repugnance. For a parent to eat the prize produce from the child's garden or, worse, the child's blood, or even for him or her to profit from the daughter's bride price, is described by all as "like a dog licking its genitals." To be used properly, *nu* must be shared with others, never consumed even indirectly by its originator.

A similar idea appears among the Wid-Mungkan of Australia (McKnight 1973) and the Diola-Fogny of Africa (Sapir 1970). A Wid-Mungkan child may not give food resembling sexual substances to either parent. For a parent to eat such foods would be to rob the child of his growth. The Diola-Fogny forbid parents from eating food that has touched the bodies or lips of their married children. Sapir (1970:1336) says that this rule reflects a native belief that there are proper and improper directions of blood flow. The mother and father, according to the Diola-Fogny, have sent their blood into their children. For their children to send it back through food or other means would be disastrous for the parent.

Two Hua rules reflect this generational principle, but the restriction is not directed at actual body substance. The broad underlying principle seems to be that anything that is the child's or is done in the child's honor must not be a source of profit to the adult. The first rule is that the mother, the father, the father's agemates, and the wives of his agemates may not eat any food out of an earth oven made in honor of their real or classificatory child (as, for instance, at the child's initiation or first menstruation ceremony, or the child's marriage). The second is that these persons may not receive and use, spend, or eat any of the valuables of their daughter's bride price. The wealth must be distributed beyond and outside this inner circle of real and classificatory parents. To eat from the earth ovens or most particularly to use some of the bride price of one's child would be like eating one's own child, an act that is morally contemptible.

I believe that these Hua, Wid-Mungkan, and Diola-Fogny rules, in addition to encouraging exchange and the formation of extrafamilial ties (Lévi-Strauss 1969), are also directed toward easing a conflict inherent in the parent-child relationship: the conflict about reciprocity. Parental resentment of the child may arise from an expectation of a return on goods and labor invested. The message of these rules is that there is no return, that reciprocity has no place in the nurture relationship, that *nu* transfers are from the senior to the junior generation, and that they are properly one-way gifts. To expect a return, to hope for reciprocity, is base and contemptible.

BODY SUBSTANCES AS FOODS OR CURES

The prohibitions discussed above primarily concern foods that we would simply consider foods. I wish to emphasize that they also apply (rather redundantly, it might seem) to body exuviae. This will become apparent when we consider relations of exceptional closeness in which products of decay may be ingested for their nutritive or curative properties.

The Hua are no less aware than are we that in decay and death lie regeneration and life: stagnant water is prescribed as a cure for sick pigs; possums are thought to be engendered by leaves left to rot in the marsupial pouch; and human fertility is believed to lie in the dark, unwholesome, rotting interiors of women's bodies.

Whether or not *we* consider exuviae repulsive depends to some extent on whether they are ours. A German proverb says *Eigener Dreck stinkt nicht* "One's own waste does not smell bad." This line of thinking is merely carried a step further among the Hua.

Semen and breath, as we have seen, are potentially *siro na*. Are they then to be avoided at all times? No, for a woman acquires both from a man in the act of intercourse. And in this transaction, men believe, the woman profits and the man loses, for she acquires valuable *nu*, which contributes to her general vitality and weight, and he loses a limited resource. (Herdt 1981 provides a detailed description of oral insemination of initiates for purposes of growth among the Sambia of the Eastern Highlands.)

A man smears sweat, oil, and vomit over the bodies of his real and classificatory sons to increase their growth.

Although not foods, these substances are ingested through their pores. At the ceremonial termination of a food constraint, the previously tabooed food is passed to an initiate under the armpit of a classificatory father. In this way, the young man acquires some of the *aune*, the positive aspect of *nu*, from the sweat of his father's armpit and will be better equipped to cope with the dangers posed by the once forbidden food.

A man's hair clippings were traditionally burned and then sprinkled over food intended for his real or classificatory sons (and possibly his brothers as well). A packet of a dead man's hair or a dead woman's fingernail parings is said to have the power to increase the growth and fertility of his or her children and to relieve pain if rubbed on an affected area.

A person's body after death, his or her blood, pig, largest and best of garden produce, and child after its death, all have the power to increase the growth and vitality of certain eaters. In fact, it is feared that if a person fails to eat the corpse of his or her same-sex parent, that person and his or her children, crops, and animals will become stunted and weak, having forgone their rightful inheritance of vitality. By the same token, a boy whose growth is stunted or whose health is impaired will be made to drink blood from the veins of his real or classificatory fathers.

Feces also have positive uses. One of the recommended cures for a man suffering from *kupa* is that he eat a fragment of his elder brother's wife's feces. It may also be recommended that a sickly or stunted person drink from the Tua River, which flows at the bottom of the valley and which is alleged to be full of the *aune* of the valley's residents, carried in the feces washed down by rain.

Urine has similar curative functions. The relatives of a sick man may commission a sister married into another community to place a stalk of ginger in an area where it will be urinated on or stepped over by the men of the village. The ginger is then returned to the sick man, who, on eating it, is thought to capture some of the *aune* of the members of his affinal community.

Aune capture relates to saliva and hair as well. Married-out sisters were commissioned to retrieve partially eaten bits of food and the reeds with which the men of the affinal village traditionally plucked their beards. These items were burned and sprinkled over the food of ailing men.

Menstrual blood and parturitional fluids were and are viewed as the most dangerous and polluting of all substances. They are also recognized as the most creative: *aune* transfer is effected through them more than through any other substance. Although there is no indication that either of these substances is used as a cure or a tonic—as among the Arapesh, who eat menstrual blood as an antidote to sorcery (Mead 1940:421–422)—substances that the Hua associate with menstrual blood are so used. Various plants that release a reddish juice when cooked have curative uses. They include *visge, dekma', rihima, kogiva, fitupa, kovrena',* and all the red *kito'* (leafy vegetables), including *ruvarokorarome, hgerua, bokome,* and *sagrekre.*[2] The juices of these plants are reported to have the power to dissolve a clot of blood located in the abdomen and to force its evacuation through the intestine. Both the immature fetus and menstrual blood originate as a ball of clotted blood within the woman's womb. In the Hua male view the consumption of the reddish juices triggers a process in males that is similar to menstruation and abortion in females. Men ingest these juices to cure themselves of pregnancy or to eradicate a more general state of pollution.

The Hua conceive of the emissions of the body as infused with a person's "self," as carriers of the owner's essence, as symbols or mementos of him or her. (Even today in secular North America a dead person is felt in some sense to be present in the bones at the grave, in the ashes of the body, in a lock of the hair.) If the dead person was loved, contact with or possession of some of these remainders of the body is desired; in fact, the Hua carry small bones of loved ones in packets around their necks. If the deceased was disliked, contact with his or her remains is

2. See chapter 3, note 3.

abhorred. As with the dead, so with the living. Where the relationship between persons is positive, contact with some of one another's emissions is easily accepted if not desired. In the event of illness or weakness, receipt of the *nu* substances of certain categories of others (most typically consanguines who are one generation senior) is imperative.

In Western culture substances detached from the body are labeled as waste and must be gotten rid of. We attribute a negative value to all these products, whether feces, fingernails, semen, or saliva.[3] Most, though not all of us, tolerate our own personal body substances and those of our infants and lovers. Among the Hua these substances may have positive or negative value. For blood, semen, flesh, hair, saliva, sweat, body oil, nasal mucus, and fingernails, positive and negative values are more or less equally balanced. This is not so for menstrual blood, feces, urine, and vomit, which are not used frequently and regularly for nourishment or body boosting but rather are administered in very restricted amounts as cures for people who are seriously ill or in acute need of physical stimulation (vomit, for example, for the young male initiate). They conform more to our Western model of a drug, while the other body substances are more like food.

In Western culture foods and medicines are taken into our bodies for nourishment and cure; body substances are expelled and flushed, washed, wiped, or sprayed away. Body substances in their natural form—I exclude semen, in part, and blood in medical transfusions and skin in medical transplants—have no positive uses: they carry germs and are mildly to very disgusting. Breast milk, which unlike all the other substances produced by the body is nourishing, deviates from our model of body substances as waste. But it is peripheral to our overall conception of body substances, which seems to focus on feces and therefore on pollution.

3. Semen, of course, is somewhat more complex in that it has a salient positive "use" while it is still abhorred in many contexts as waste.

The Hua by contrast allow a central role to breast milk in their conceptualization of body substances. Just as breast milk nourishes, so also can all the other body substances. These substances are important sources of power, valuable and useful products of the body, tools with which to work significant effects on others and oneself. They may be used as foods to nourish or as medicines to cure, or conversely as polluters or poisons. Whether the positive or negative use is effected depends on the situation.

The Hua attitude is profoundly different from our own. To them pollution is not inherent in body substances, as in our feces model. Instead a substance that in other situations may be nourishing may become temporarily polluting through the contexts of its production and distribution.

Chapter Seven

NU AS A
WORLD HYPOTHESIS

Anthropologists often describe a whole culture in terms of one overarching, central metaphor, whether this is called a "theme" (Opler 1945), a "pattern" (Benedict 1934), a "focus" (Herskovits 1945), or a "world hypothesis" (Pepper 1948). For the Hua, such a metaphor is the idea of vital essence, or *nu*, a theory of broad scope that attempts to explain, if not the whole world, then at least the biological and social aspects of life.

Vital essence occurs in three states: as a solid, it is *haugepa*, as a liquid, it is *nu*, and as a gas, it is *bu'* "steam." All living creatures have these three states of vital essence in varying proportions, and the processes of conception, maturation, intercourse, menstruation, and aging are understood in terms of the shifting balance of the three in a creature's total makeup.

Vital essence in the liquid or gaseous state may be transmitted from one creature to another. Depending on whether the transfer benefits the recipient, transmitted *nu/bu'* can be either good *aune* "spirit" or harmful *siro na* "pollution." Whether or not the transmission is harmful to the recipient depends entirely on the nature of the social relationship between him or her and the donor. The complexities of social life are thus phrased in terms of a more fundamental metaphor that is basically biological in nature.

Any biological liquid is *nu*: thus water, blood, urine, sap, and fat are all a kind of *nu*. In some cases the relationship is recognized at the most transparent level of lexical compounding: *nuti* "nasal mucus" and *koa nuti* "semen" are obvious compounds based on the root *nu*. In all cases, *nu* is conceived as the source of life, vitality, and fertility.[1]

1. Other highland languages with the same root are more transparent in their taxonomies. In Karam, *mok* "sap" closely approximates *nu*: *tiy-*

Haugepa represents the solid counterpart of *nu*: a clot of blood is the *haugepa* of blood; ground or earth is the *haugepa* of soft mud; and an adult is the *haugepa* of his child. *Nu* develops from *haugepa* as the consequence of a sort of explosion that opens passages in the solid *haugepa*.

The Hua *nu/haugepa* metaphor is curiously reminiscent of the cosmogony of the ancient Greek philosopher Thales, according to which water was the generating substance of all matter (Burnet 1960:21). In Hua thinking, however, *nu* is an animating principle only. There seems to be little metaphysical speculation on the origin of matter or on the nature and structure of the physical universe in general. A closer parallel to Hua thinking is provided by modern biology, which recognizes water not only as the source of life but as the major ingredient in all living things (Sherrington 1955:113).

The exemplar of the generation of *nu* from *haugepa* is undoubtedly the germination of soft shoots from a hard, dry seed. Conception and menstruation, as well as a number of other phenomena, are viewed as analogies to this proven and attested process. Conception, according to Hua thinking, occurs with the development of a soft wet fetus (to which the parent may allude as *d-nu* "my *nu*") out of a *haugepa* clot of menstrual blood. The logical and empirical basis for this theory is fairly evident: because menstrual flow and pregnancy are seen to be mutually exclusive, their identity is inferred. A fetus is just another form of menstrual blood.

The release of *nu* from *haugepa* is analogously attributed to some plants and even various kinds of mud. In Hua thinking, several trees release *nu* "sap" once a month at *a'di kuna* "women's time" (the new moon, when women are supposed to menstruate). The fruit of the *have'* (Moraceae *Ficus*) tree releases a white sap when picked. The shape of the fruit has a surprising resemblance to the fe-

---

mok "breast-sap" is milk; *wan-mok* "penis-sap" is semen; and *jn-mok* "head-sap" is brain (R. Bulmer 1967).

male breast, the sap to breast milk. The sap in fact may be rubbed on the breasts of women who have insufficient milk.[2] *Iomepa* (Moraceae *Ficus pungens*) is a tree marked by an abundance of yellowish-green fruits and a white soap-like sap found on the underside of some of the leaves. From the roots of the enormous *kemo'* (Monimiaceae *Levieria*) tree oozes a dark sap that leaves a sootlike stain. This stain makes the roots look as if they had been burned.

The *ktitosva*, *mamusva*, and *dkugea'* mushrooms are said to appear only at women's time. (Unfortunately, I never saw any of these.) These mushrooms are said to represent the *nu* of the soil in the same sense that the sap is the *nu* of the tree.

Some muds are also alleged to appear, that is, to soften up and be released as *nu* from the *haugepa* of the rock at women's time. These muds are particularly desired for use in self-decoration and love magic. They are *daruki* and *koe*, perceived by the Hua as reddish; *kumu* and *pinepogu*, perceived as black; and *kumu* and *aurua*, two muds I never saw.

The emergence of *nu* from *haugepa*, of what is soft and wet from what is hard and dry, is made possible by a kind of explosion. The *nu* is released through *ki'* "passages, orifices," which are formed during the *haugepa fku fu-* "explosion, bursting of the *haugepa*." Passages and orifices play a central role in the Hua conception of the generation of life, as the following origin myth shows.

> Roko [one of the original Hua ancestors] caught birds [the ones with the colorful feathers used as valuables in bride prices]. He collected nuts and salt [also important exchange items]. He went off and finally came to a place where he saw a round house that had no door, in fact no openings at all, but from the roof of which some smoke was rising.

2. Hutton (1928:404) claims an association of *Ficus* with fertility (because of the milklike fluid it releases when broken) in many societies, including those of the Naga Hills in Assam.

Roko went up to the house and poked a hole through the thatch, peeked in, and called out, "Are you in here?"

The creature inside replied only, "Muuuuu."

Roko then asked, "Where is your door?"

And the creature again responded only with "Muuuuu."

Roko circled the house, again looking for a door, but was unable to find one. He asked himself, "By what door does this creature come in and go out?"

Roko then went back to the hole he had poked through the thatch and called, "Hey, my cross-cousin, Kunei," to which again the creature responded only with a "Muuuuu."

At this Roko broke down the wall of the house and entered. And there he found an enormous creature. It had ears but these ears lacked openings. It had a mouth but it was sealed. It had eyes but they could not open. It had legs, and arms, and hands, but these had not been freed from the body.

Roko took a knife and cut open the mouth. And then he cut open the eyes [*fuke* "caused them to burst"]. Then he cut free Kunei's legs and straightened them out for him.

Kunei then said, "My cross-cousin, what have you done to me?"

To which Roko replied, "I have made it happen to you. And now I will give you salt, and nuts, and ginger."

Kunei cooked these and ate them and his mind awakened.

The theme of the opening of passages pervades the story. First Roko opens a passage into the house, then into his cross-cousin's mouth, and then into his eyes. Then he gives his cross-cousin ginger, to which is attributed the power to open passages, most particularly the passage through the ear into the brain. Moreover, the form this creature takes prior to Roko's activity is like that attributed to the fetus prior to the bursting that creates its head, orifices, and limbs. It also resembles the form of a seed, and the releasing and unfolding of the limbs are similar to germination.

Passages, then, are central in the Hua conception of the generation of life. In fact, the amount of vitality, endurance, sexual potency, and fertility attributed to an animate

object, whether plant, animal, or human, is directly corre-
lated with the number and size of its passages and orifices.
Thus the fast-growing, fertile *pitpit* is credited with many
passages (the minute pores in its stalk), while *kimi*, the
black palm, which is quintessentially *hakeri'a*, is seen to
have only a few. A relative absence or smallness of orifices or passages is directly related to infertility and slow
growth. Males claim that the lower body openings of
women are much larger than men's, and that the rate of
women's growth and the amount of their vitality are correspondingly greater.

Maturation, like conception, is conceived in *nu-haugepa*
terms. While conception starts with the *haugepa* from
which *nu* is alleged to emerge, maturation converts *nu* to
haugepa. The infant at birth is thought of as pure *nu*. To
survive, she or he must rapidly become more *hakeri'a*. To
this end the infant is rubbed with the leaves of two *hakeri'a*
trees, *hakru* (Symplocaceae *Symplocos*) and *zarvu* (Lau-
raceae *Cinnamomum*). In a further effort to dry out and thus
to harden the infant's body, the mother's assistant rubs the
infant's body with hands warmed in the fire.

The subsequent growth of the child is understood in
terms of expenditure of *nu*, of which each child at birth
possesses a finite amount. *Nu* is the source of growth, and
once spent, growth ceases and a state of *hakeri'a* sets in.

This conception of growth, particularly male growth, as
the expenditure of a limited reserve of *nu* lies behind a
number of the prohibitions placed on the behavior of the
male initiate. These prohibitions represent an effort to protect the male's *nu* from contamination, wastage, and theft.
The steady decline in the *nu* reserve, the movement from a
korogo to a *hakeri'a* state, is, however, inevitable. By old age
men are dried out, withered, impotent, weak. They can, in
fact, be referred to as *haugepa*, just as the newborn can be
referred to as *nu*.

The female's cycle follows a similar course from *korogo* to
hakeri'a, from *nu* to *haugepa*, but with the complication of
the reproductive cycle. Women on occasion refer to men-

struation as "my *korogo* thing." The onset of menstruation involves a welling up of a new source of *nu* in the body. Pregnancy and childbirth are similarly associated by the Hua with the release of vast quantities of *nu*, which men fear and avoid. At menopause there is, to everyone's relief, a considerable drying out of the woman's body. Ultimately she becomes as *hakeri'a* or *haugepa* as a man.

Conception, menstruation, growth, and aging are all understood in terms of gradual gains and losses of *nu*, of steady shifts between *korogo* and *hakeri'a* states. Kelly (1976) discusses a very similar kind of thinking among the Etoro. The Hua view sexual differentiation through the same lens: females are most commonly differentiated from males as *korogo* while males are *hakeri'a*. Similarly, one of the most common ways for a Hua to talk about sexual intercourse is in terms of *nu* loss.

The Hua conceptions of *korogo* and *hakeri'a* states, dependent on the varying proportions of *nu* and *haugepa*, represent a theory based on certain incontestable observations. People clearly differ in their vitality, speed, endurance, rate of growth, and resistance to inevitable aging. Some of these differences correspond grossly to sexual differences: females mature more suddenly, if not more quickly, than males, and age more slowly. Men, on the other hand, are physically stronger than females. How do these differences correlate with the female mysteries of menstruation and conception?

The theory of *nu* attempts to relate these observations: it does not follow from them logically, but it is compatible with them and thus satisfies what Guthrie (1962:70) has called "a perennial and universal . . . search for unity in the universe behind the multiplicity of phenomena." Like all scientific theories, it has an aesthetic appeal that alone may serve as its justification. As ethnographers, we risk falling into error if we too casually discount the value of such aesthetic appeal and automatically search for justification in terms of structural-functionalist or cultural ecological, "practical" explanations.

This is not to deny that the *nu* metaphor may symbolize

social relationships, but, as I have already argued, the function of such rules and constraints is not, for the Hua citizen, to perpetuate the social order. Rather, the social order is taken as a given, and the purpose of the rules is to protect the citizen from the evil influence of his or her inescapable enemies.

The fact that social relationships also are phrased in terms of *nu* and its transfer from one person to another suggests that the social order itself is interpreted as biological, and that the ultimate reality is not society but the mysteries of the body. At an even deeper level, however, stating social relationships in terms of *nu* transfer may reflect not so much on a biologically oriented world view as a passion for generalization, a wish to explain as much of the world as possible through the agency of a single principle, which only incidentally happens to be a biological one.

The power of this principle is demonstrated by the number of social relationships, both friendly and hostile, that are expressed in terms of the opposition between *aune* "spirit" and *siro na* "pollution" manifestations of *nu* (see chapter 6). The basic rule of self-preservation is to avoid the ingestion of *siro na*, which withers, stunts, and kills, and to increase the consumption of *aune*, which strengthens and preserves.

As mentioned earlier, the Hua are explicit that the growth of children is dependent on an expenditure of *nu* by parents, an expenditure that weakens and ages the adults. The *nu* that brings the child into being and sustains it has literally been drained from the parents' bodies. The process of the child's growth is conceived as the process of the parents' decline. Implicit in this conception of growth and development is the idea that human *nu* is not a renewable resource, or at least not an easily renewable one. It is not generated by the individual's effort (except in a marginal sense as, for example, in the rejuvenation ceremony). Rather, he or she receives it from other people, who have themselves received it. It is a finite quantity possessed by the community as a whole.

A careful and rational appropriation of all energy is

required. Overexpenditure on sexual activities results in an abundance of dependents (*ainu ba'de bre* "he has a diarrhea of children") and less energy with which to provide for them. Entropy is implicit in the Hua conception of energy as finite. The *nu* that exists continues to do so only because of its convertibility into transferable forms, primarily food. Leakage from such a system inevitably occurs: the Hua frequently comment that individuals today are less powerful and well built than their ancestors, and balding, which Hua males abhor, is said to occur in ever-younger men. This sense of entropy underlines the conception of human interdependence in a single closed system of *nu* transfer.

Nu is perhaps most significant in relation to food. Many North Americans think of foods as impersonal things produced by unknown farmers that nourish them in impersonal physiological ways. The Hua conception of food and nourishment is profoundly different, and it is different by virtue of *nu*.

It would not be an exaggeration to say that for the Hua food is *nu* and *nu* is food, and further, that there is nothing—apart from the homeopathic properties of foods (see chapter 1)—that nourishes other than the *nu* with which the food is associated.

The associations of foods with *nu* are multiple. Foods resemble *nu* substances and therefore participate in their power. Initiates may not eat red pandanus oil because it looks like menstrual blood, *zokoni* mushrooms because they smell like menstrual blood, and foods that are dark on the interior because they resemble female interiors, which are full of *nu* and therefore fertile. The absolute prohibitions enjoined upon young male initiates presuppose an identification of the various substances of the female body, all of which are *nu*, with the various substances of the diet. The ends of sweet potatoes are tabooed not because they are sweet potatoes or ends but because they resemble the ends of women's feces; snails are tabooed not because of their slime but because their slime resembles vaginal secretions. And so on.

Foods are also associated with *nu* through contagion. A mature male may not eat leafy green vegetables picked by his real or classificatory wife or firstborn child because these vegetables are contaminated by spots of menstrual blood, genital waste, sweat, and body oils transferred from the hand to the food in the process of picking it. In Hua thinking all foods are contaminated (in either a negative or a positive sense) by the *nu* substances of those who harvested and prepared them. Food is a carrier of *nu*.

Moreover, foods are permeated with the *nu* substances of their producers. The pigs that people raise, the animals they shoot, their prize garden produce are thought to contain their *nu*, their physical essence, lodged or invested there in the act of production. The Hua rarely come into contact with foods produced by people they do not know. All the foods they eat are produced by people they know and whom they either trust (in which case they eat the food) or distrust (in which case they do not).

Finally, in Hua culture, unlike our own, substances of the body are actually used as foods. Blood, flesh, semen, sweat, body oils, hair, fingernails, and saliva, all are *nu* substances, and all are ingestible, even edible, to the Hua.

Food is thus one more mechanism of *nu* transfer. Many New Guinea cultures use the idea and reality of body substance to talk about physiological and sociological categories and processes (Meigs 1976, Weiner 1980, Herdt 1981). Weiner points out that not just material goods but also the actual substances of the body are exchanged; through the exchange of body substances states and relations of age, gender, and so forth are established and elaborated. The Hua exchange food both as a valuable in social prestations and as an intimate, personal body substance, a means of transferring physical essence between otherwise discrete bodies. These transfers effect changes in physical status— in sexuality, aging, growth, and health.

Nu thus connects food, sex, and pollution. Food and sex both provide an avenue of exchange of physical substance between bodies. In the sexual act the male puts out semen, which the female takes in. The food producer invests a more generalized kind of *nu* in his or her product, which the eater incorporates into his or her body. Eating and sex are both acts of incorporation of the substances of another person's body. Not surprisingly, given the parallels, eating has its incest rule too: a person may not eat food that he or she or his or her offspring have themselves produced. Eating and sex are two versions of the same behavior and both are subject to pollution, which is merely the transfer of body substance under negative social conditions.

To live is literally to feed on another, on another's flesh and blood, even on another's exuviae, but most of all on the food products of another's labor. The losses in one's own *nu* system must be made up in gains from the *nu* system of others. Social interdependence and cohesion are expressed through the reality and the metaphor of cannibalism.

Chapter Eight

A RELIGION OF
THE BODY

Religion is usually defined in anthropology as a belief in spirits or in the supernatural (Tylor 1920, Spiro 1966) or a class of metaphors and symbols whose hidden referent is the society (Durkheim 1965, Douglas 1975).[1] Certainly these two definitions have governed most studies of New Guinea highland religion. The search for gods, spirits, a mind-body split, cosmological beliefs, sociological functions, and symbols dominates the standard anthology on New Guinea religion, *Gods, Ghosts and Men in Melanesia* (Lawrence and Meggitt 1965). Yet among the Hua, and apparently some other Eastern Highlands peoples as well, these religious concepts appear to be peripheral to the central body of religious thought.

The single extant Siane god, according to Salisbury (1965:55) "is rarely referred to and no ceremonies are explicitly directed to him"; further, the numerous spirit beings immanent in the physical universe are "generally indifferent to human action." Salisbury identifies the central religious concept as *oinya*, which he translates as "nonmaterial, non-discrete spiritual essence," a "supernatural aspect" of men, pigs, and certain other animals that resides in the blood, hair, sexual organs, breath, and shadow but is particularly identified with *oko* "white mucous secretion" (ibid., pp. 55–56).[2] This concept is remarkably similar

1. Spiro's (1966:94) definition is perhaps the most succinct: "To summarize, I would argue that the belief in superhuman beings and in their power to assist or to harm man approaches universal distribution, and this belief—I would insist—is the core variable which ought to be designated by any definition of religion."

2. Given that the Hua and Siane languages are related, it is quite possible that the Siane *oinya* and Hua *aune* are cognates (John Haiman, personal communication).

to the distinctly nonspiritual and nonsupernatural Hua notions of *aune* and *nu*.

Descriptions of rituals that center on bodily goals and concepts abound in ethnographies from all areas of the highlands. Berndt (1965:93), discussing the Kamano, Usurufa, Jate, and Fore of the Eastern Highlands, says, "The stress on strength and physical well-being, especially for men, appears in almost every aspect of ritual action." R. Bulmer (1965:151) says of the Kyaka of the Western Highlands, "The objectives of the [Sandalu initiation] cult were to foster the health, strength and prosperity of the individual participants, to strengthen the clan in war and ceremonial exchange, and to weaken its enemies." And of the Kuma of the Western Highlands, Reay (1959:155) states, "Unobtrusive as the women's part is in the most spectacular of all the men's ceremonies [the pig festival], it expresses the central purpose of the whole sequence of events comprising the Pig Ceremonial—the fertility of the clan and its pigs and gardens."

Scholars of the late nineteenth and early twentieth centuries, in particular Robertson Smith, James Frazer, and Emile Durkheim, separated the notions of purity and pollution from the "sacred" ideas of deities and souls, which to them constituted the proper stuff of religious thought. Concepts relating to the purity of inner body states were regarded as secular or "profane." Douglas (1966) proposed that notions of primitive hygiene and body magic no longer be discounted as eccentric ideas of "profane" culture but be reintroduced as important symbolic forms in the mainstream of religious life. The new status Douglas advanced for the twin concepts of purity and pollution may also be claimed for life-cycle rituals and taboos, customs often discussed separately from the dogmas, deities, and rituals of traditionally defined religion.

This broader conception of the scope of religion invites a new perspective on religious themes in the highlands. I suggest that four themes are central to Hua religion, at least as it is practiced by males. The first is a focus on internal body states, on the conservation and accumulation of *nu*. At menarche the inside of the Hua girl's body is represented as a caldron of potent and dangerous substances that not only must be conserved to guarantee the undiminished strength of the girl's reproductive power but also must be isolated from the community to safeguard the health of males. The Gururumba view of menarche appears similar. The Gururumba girl "must not drink water since it might 'cool' the 'hot' sexuality developing within her and rob her of her procreative abilities" (Newman 1964:263).

Hua males conceive the inside of the adolescent male body in terms opposite to those reserved for females. The male is relatively devoid of fluids, odors, and textures; the inside of his body is white, hard, clean, odorless, and, in comparison to the female body, strikingly impotent. Efforts to enrich this environment through the accumulation and conservation of *nu* substances are a central theme of initiation rites throughout New Guinea. In secret ceremonies, Hua initiates are fed blood let from the veins of older men for this express purpose. Marind Anim (Van Baal 1966), Etoro (Kelly 1976:45), Keraki (Williams 1969), and Sambia (Herdt 1981) initiates serve as passive parties in ritualized homosexual acts in which they consume their elders' semen to strengthen their marginally sufficient powers. Hua males consume soups made of jungle leaves that they believe are rich in the growth-producing powers in which they themselves are deficient. While girls at menarche must observe taboos to protect those around them from the dangerous powers emanating from inside them, boys at initiation endure taboos to protect their already insufficient internal powers from any further diminution. The taboos on speech, an active role in sex, and motion protect the initiate from unnecessary expenditures of *nu*, and the taboo on the use of water avoids the dilution of *nu*.

Through the symbolic medium of food rules Hua males paint in broad strokes and loud colors their conceptions of the inner landscapes of the female body. Foods that are

dark on the inside or appear rotten, that release a repugnant smell, that are swamped in a profusion of fluids, that
exhibit mysterious and disturbingly rapid growth or ease
and speed of reproduction, or that are simply shaped like
some aspect of the female reproductive apparatus—these
foods are singled out for special condemnation as replete
with the deadly powers of the repugnant female substances and states they stand for.

The inside of the body is the temple, the place where the
awesome powers reside; internal body states are imagined
in intense detail. It is odd, though, that former cannibals,
who had numerous opportunities for observing internal
body states, hold so fanciful a conceptualization of these
states. I was at first baffled by how little the Hua knew
about their bodies, by their absence of interest in or observation of them, by their cult of ignorance in regard to reproductive anatomy.

An explanation of this Hua ignorance lies at least in part
in realizing that the body, when not taken for granted, is
for the Hua very largely a religious object, which may be
understood through dogma and respect. It is a place where
powers defined as unknowable operate. To attempt to understand its operation through observation and experi-
mentation would be analogous to a Christian's attempt to
know and understand the deity through the medium and
tools of science.

A second religious theme among Hua males is that of
purification, the notion of a physical space that must be
cleared of material impurities to insure the proper functioning of its resident properties. This space is usually conceived as male and as threatened by the contaminating and
hostile influences emanating from affines, particularly
from nonconsanguineal females, and from resented or
hostile consanguines. When the defenses provided by
food and avoidance rules break down and the internal state
is contaminated, rites of purification are performed. Nose
bleeding and vomiting among the Hua (Meigs 1976), Gururumba (Newman 1964), and Bena Bena (Langness 1967);

tongue piercing among the Bena Bena; tongue scraping among the Kamano, Usurufa, Jate, and Fore (Berndt 1965); penis bleeding among the Bena Bena, Arapesh (Mead 1940), and Wogeo Islanders (Hogbin 1970); sweating among the Hua and Gururumba; and eye washing among the Huli (Glasse 1965), Mae Enga (Goodenough 1953), and Kyaka (R. Bulmer 1965)—all are aimed at stimulating health and vitality by removing foreign substances, female or otherwise.

The third theme is vital essence or the animating principle, the Hua *aune* as a positive manifestation of *nu*, Siane *oinya* (Salisbury 1965), Gadsup *aumi* (Du Toit 1975), Gururumba *GwondEfoJE* (Newman 1964), Etoro *hame* (Kelly 1976), Daribi *noma'* (Wagner 1967), Dani *edai-egen* (Heider 1979), and Huli *dinini* (Glasse 1965).

Among the Hua an enormous structure of ritual and taboo exists for the precise purpose of managing the community's *nu* from the birth of its individual members through their deaths. Whether in a female attempt to reduce her inner *nu* or a male effort to increase his, an infant being "hardened" with *hakeri'a* substances or an old man being "softened" with *korogo* ones, *nu* is always at the center of life-cycle events. It is similarly the central theme of both absolute and relative food rules: in absolute rules tabooed items are symbols of *nu* substances, in relative rules they carry or contain the *nu* of distrusted others.

In the absence of a belief in a god or gods or any developed body of beliefs in the spirits of the dead, the Hua conceptualize *nu* as the source and sustainer of life. It is a distinctly nonspiritual substance, yet it provides the focus of most of the rituals and taboos of which I am aware; in ritual the individual seeks to maximize his or her advantage in relation to *nu*. More significantly, *nu* is conceived as the means of saving oneself. Spiritual concepts and concerns, states of grace and sin, simply do not exist. The Hua monitor their bodies, not their souls, and it is with their physical state of being, itself determined by *nu*, that their religion is concerned.

Although I cannot argue that the male components of other highland societies similarly have religions of the body, many are concerned with a concept of vital essence. Among the Etoro of the Southern Highlands a central equation is that augmentation of the *hame* leads to life, growth, and vitality, while its depletion leads to weakness, respiratory illness, senescence, and death (Kelly 1976:48). Kelly focuses on sexual modes of transmission, concluding that male homosexuality is culturally approved as a means of passing life force on to boys, while heterosexuality is viewed as "fundamentally anti-social behavior" that depletes the vital communal reservoir of male force (ibid., p. 45). Hua male anxiety about *nu* loss is manifested in the injunction to heterosexual abstinence for initiates and continence for adults, both of which are found throughout New Guinea. Hua males, in fact, pride themselves on the infrequency of their heterosexual acts.

The goal of accumulating life force or essence is central to the sweat house rituals in which men, sealing themselves off from the world and its erosion of essence, deliberately promote the production and accumulation of the inner and outer fluids identified as the substances of vitality. Participants in the Hua body oil house attempt to increase their *nu* content through consumption of *korogo* substances, to stimulate heavy production of sweat and body oils through exposure to heat, and to avoid any expenditure of inner *nu* or erasure of outer *nu* through reduction of motion and speech. The sweat house ritual completed, the rejuvenated and revitalized male, confident of his *nu* adequacy and sexual potency, proudly displays his gleaming body in a parade before women.

The Fore sweat house ceremony is remarkably similar. Males seclude themselves in a special communal house for several days, baking at a blazing fire and eating special substances for the express purpose of producing sweat. The more obvious and extensive the pattern, the greater the strength, prowess, and sexuality attributed to the males (Berndt 1965).

The male spirit cult among the Melpa suggests a similar focus on the efficacy of enclosed and accumulated moisture. A garden is planted and subsequently torn apart, and the pieces of plants are dropped into a spring. Tree oil is poured into the spring, which is then covered and left to rot, cool, and "thus promote fertility" (A. Strathern 1970:582).

The image of a pool of fluid identified as the source of life, growth, and fertility is, I believe, central to much Hua thinking. This pool must not be excessively depleted or overly contaminated if growth and health are to be maintained. Bodily needs are set in opposition to social needs: to have a wife and children, both prerequisites for social maturity, a man must allow both the dreaded contamination and the abhorred expenditure of his *nu*; he must be prepared to "waste" his body altruistically on others. Temporary and partial recoveries of both the quality and the quantity of his *nu* may be achieved through rites of purification or rejuvenation and through the consumption of substances containing the *nu* of others. Nevertheless, the course of a male life leads inexorably to contamination and to loss.

Ironically, however, the most dramatic way in which Hua males can replenish their waning supplies of *nu* and thus stimulate their vitality is through rituals of imitation, adulation, and control of female reproductive power. This is a powerful fourth theme of the religion of Hua males.

What is religious about the male imitation and adulation of female powers? Any *nu* is powerful, but female *nu* is most powerful. Any body is awesome, but the female body, possessor of the mystery of fertility and nurture, is the most awesome. In this religion of the body the female body plays the star role.

Thus, although males denigrate females as ignorant and treacherous in the social sphere, they admire and laud their magnificent biological powers within the arcane enclave of the men's house. Through the imitation of menstruation and the consumption of foods homeopathically related to the fertile and fast-growing qualities of women,

men attempt to stimulate their lagging growth and recover their waning vitality. Through their secret claim to a fertility comparable to that of females, males assert physiological equality with the envied and powerful opposite sex. And finally, through the secret prescription of possum, the abhorred symbol of female reproductive power, males gain the strength to cure themselves of the damaging consequences of mundane contact with females or with other alien or suspected persons.

The Siane male feeling of dependence on female reproductive powers is explicit in the male attitude toward female blood as the embodiment of clan spirit:

> Women, although themselves purely material, capricious and unpredictable, continually produce spirit in the form of blood and may at any time become purely spirit without men being able to see any difference. . . . They are the ultimate ideal of society. Thus, in a concrete example, the 'oldest sister' is the *atarafo* (literally 'house post person') of the lineage; she *is* the lineage and her first menses are a threat to the clan of losing a lineage. (Salisbury 1965:75)

Being a prime source of power and vitality, female blood is a resource the Siane community cannot afford to lose. The rite of departure at marriage involves a ceremony in which the departing woman's spirit, identified with her blood, is exorcised and transferred to the body of a younger female still residing in the community (ibid., p. 74).

The Huli bachelor's cult centers on this notion of male dependence on female blood (Glasse 1965). Each bachelor cultivates a bog iris, a cultigen said to have originated in ground saturated with female blood, a belief analogous to the Hua myth of the origin of the red pandanus and the Daribi myth of the red yam (Wagner 1967:65). The Huli bachelor group as a whole owns a small bamboo tube that contains a sacred portion of an ancestral female's blood. This blood together with the bog irises guarantees male health and vitality and, paradoxically, protects males from the evil emanations of living women (Glasse 1965:43).

Numerous ethnographers have reported ritual attempts by males to assert their access to and control over not only the allegedly female powers of growth, vitality, and fertility, but also the same powers of the soil. Control of the soil is viewed throughout the highlands as a female prerogative (Reay 1959, A. Strathern 1970, Barth 1975, Buchbinder and Rappaport 1976, Lindenbaum 1976). New Guinea men have an uncomfortable sense of being dependent for food on a labor source over which they have insufficient control (Lindenbaum 1976:59–60). It is this sense of the wildness of women which, Lindenbaum says, motivates their association with the wild red pandanus among the Fore. Hua males circumvent this unpleasant feeling of dependency and inferiority to females through a metaphor that represents sex as a feeding act in which males are the prestigious providers, and feeding as a sexual act in which innocent and passive males are impregnated by corrupt and rapacious females.

Buchbinder and Rappaport (1976) analyze a Maring ritual in similar terms. They report a three-way association of the earth oven, from which females produce foods; the vagina, from which females produce human progeny; and the fertile earth, which produces its own progeny. (The American slang for pregnancy "to have a bun in the oven" uses two of these associations.) The ritual in which males plant cultigens in and around the earth oven represents, they say, the male effort to achieve a semblance of control over the fertility both of the vagina and of the soil (ibid., pp. 29–30).

The Melpa female spirit cult, which focuses on the ritual manipulation of smooth, unbroken stones, identified with the closed female genitals, suggests similar themes. These stones are alternately buried in a sacred grove and exhumed for ceremony in the cult house. They represent a virgin spirit who is controlled by males and not only protects men from the menace of their wives' sexuality but also allows them access to some of the fertility and growth-producing powers attributed to females (A. Strathern 1970:575).

It is consistent with these male feelings of inferiority to female powers that initiation among the Hua as well as other New Guinea highland people is perceived as a compensation to males for their natural physical disadvantages. The flutes revealed to initiates represent, Hua men say, the male counterpart to menstruation. Rites of initiation, they add, represent the Hua male answer to the challenge posed by the more rapid female growth and more dramatic female manifestations of maturity. Baktaman informants maintain that if women were also to have initiations, they would so exceed men in growth and strength that they "would want to be on top when copulating" (Barth 1975:48), an image also used by the Hua to describe the female lust for power. Gururumba informants declare, "In initiation, males assume ritual control over the same vital power that is actually conferred upon females when they menstruate" (Newman 1964:267).

The widely distributed sacred flutes also suggest, in the Hua case at least, male perceptions of the vulnerability of their own sex. Although serving as prime symbols of male hegemony and forbidden to the sight of women on pain of death, these flutes are alleged by males to have been originally produced and possessed by women, who are believed to have been the aboriginal rulers of Hua society. The flutes are said to have been stolen by men. Not only are male physical powers inferior to female powers, but male political dominance is revealed as illegitimate. Many Hua comments attest to a male fear of a return to subservience. If women were to see the flutes, the identity of which they supposedly no longer suspect, they would ridicule men for the stupid ruse by which they maintain their power. If women were to see men eating possum or blood, they would realize the extent of male inferiority and seize power.

It is common male knowledge among the Hua that women of reproductive age are dirty and powerful, repugnant and dangerous—to be discussed with contempt and approached with caution. Through initiation males, and ultimately females as well, enter an abrupt new world of ideas in which females and their powers are considered in a dramatically opposite light. This reversal of knowledge and the constant playing of both sides of the common-arcane border provide an intellectual challenge and thrill.

This book began in the field with a flood of bewildering and exotic food rules; their investigation ultimately led to the discovery of indigenous conceptions of nutrition, growth, sexual differentiation, reproduction, and aging. Further, an intimate connection between the alimentary and sexual processes was uncovered and their religious significance was explored. These processes are perceived as paired and parallel systems by means of which the fluid contents of individual bodies are shared, a notion of social interdependence as physiological reality.

These fluid contents are the various forms of the single life essence, or *nu*, which may manifest itself in positive life-enhancing forms or negative polluting atrocities. To gain access to and preserve *aune* and to avoid and expel *siro na* is the central goal of the taboos and rituals of the religion of Hua males.

It is a religion of physiological fitness and survival. Religious goals of heightened vitality and sexual potency are achieved without recourse to sacrifice, obeisance, meditation, worship, or prayer. Spirits, deities, and the supernatural in general play no role. Instead, the body, sacred temple of all power, is approached directly, its contents assessed and monitored, its intake and output carefully regulated. Sexual and eating behaviors have religious significance in that they occasion transfers of *nu* between otherwise discrete and separate body interiors. To avoid the depletion of one's own limited inner reserves and simultaneously to gain access to and accumulate the growth- and health-stimulating *nu* of trusted others, all the while not only avoiding but also expelling the polluted *nu* of distrusted others, constitute the daily practice of this male religion.

A more esoteric and private level of religious practice may be described as a male search for the female principle, conceived as the ultimate source of fertility, growth, and vitality, as life itself. This embarrassing and thus secret quest by politically dominant males for access to and control of the physiological powers belonging to their political subordinates is the constant theme of ritual and taboo.

Growth and aging, sexuality and fertility, health and illness—these processes and conditions are determined by unseen organs and hidden fluids. Physical life itself, uncontrollable and frightening, is the central mystery of the religious thought of Hua males. It is a religion that presupposes an extensive opposition between the sexes. It is a religion of segregation and exclusion. The extent to which it is a religion exclusively of males is, at this moment, unknown. It is exciting and hopeful to speculate that Hua women have developed a system of religious ideas to counterpoise the weight of the male ideology I have described. I was not able in the course of my research to discover one but I did not have time to probe extensively. This is the task that remains to be done.

Appendix A

ABSOLUTE FOOD RULES FOR INITIATES

Appendices A, B, and C comprise almost exclusively statements made by Hua informants themselves.

The food rule system appears in its fullest, and most elaborated form in reference to the young male initiate. The hundreds of food rules he must observe have varying durations. The foods are listed below in their order of importance in the Hua diet.

SWEET POTATO

Some informants claim that there are no absolute rules prohibiting the consumption of sweet potatoes, while others claim that the ends of sweet potatoes are prohibited because they resemble the ends of women's feces or that the *komanegoza* species of sweet potato is prohibited because it is wild.

All informants agree that undercooked sweet potato, and for that matter any insufficiently cooked food, must not be eaten for two reasons: the fact that it is underdone suggests that women have contaminated some of the substances used in preparing the earth oven, and the whiteness of an underdone sweet potato resembles the whiteness of a possum's eyes.

It is generally agreed that initiates are forbidden to eat any food, including sweet potato, that is cooked in ashes, unless the ashes have been completely removed from it. The fear is that the initiate's skin will become ashy, dry, and unhealthy looking.

YAM

All of the many species of yam are eaten with the following exceptions:

dagasgu: because it is wild.

kakaiva: because, according to one male informant, it is used by women to masturbate.

fanu hgu: because it smells *be' ftu*, that is, like menstrual blood.

ame': because it smells *be' ftu*.

minava: because it grows and ripens slowly, that is, it is *hakeri'a*.

vai: because it grows and ripens slowly, that is, it is *hakeri'a*.

There is not good agreement about the last two on the list. The ambivalence about *be' ftu* (on the one hand, a dangerous and repugnant smell and on the other, desirable) appears in relation to *fanu hgu* and *ame'*.

TARO

The following are prohibited:

ekremu': because it is *hnitriri atve* "taro with a dark interior" (and is, according to one informant, like a woman's vagina). If the initiate eats it, his breath will smell or his liver will darken and he will become repugnant to girls.

kinarikogu: because it is dark on the inside, because girls are named after it. (According to one informant *kinarikogu* is just another name for *ekremu'*.)

koraiziziya: because it is dark on the inside, because it is like blood on the inside. (The first two syllables of its name are *kora* "blood.")

runera: because it is wild. If its leaves touch a pregnant woman, she might bear a child twisted like the leaf of the *fera'atve* "wild taro."

zore'a: because its leaves are very small.
mura: because it is small.
kai atve: because it is red and white on the inside and the red is like blood.

The following are permitted:

ritina: eaten freely because it is *hakeri'a*.
amamo'a: ?
vareto'a: ?
zagaura: ?
toto'a: ?
kome'a: ?
so'dara: ?
fofozavea: ?
soapu atve: ?

HEVIA' (PIDGIN ENGLISH *KUMU*) "LEAFY GREEN VEGETABLES"

Most of the rules regarding the leafy green vegetables are relative ones and are listed in appendix B. Nevertheless, there are some absolute rules. *Kisrepa*, *hnikutoza*, and *kobritara* species of *hevia'* are tabooed to initiates because they are wild and because they are *hakeri'a*.

Any *hevia'* onto which a bird has defecated is tabooed because it would produce a sore on the mouth. Raw *hevia'* may not be eaten because it is supposed to cause bad breath. In particular, any *hevia'* plant from which a *ruza* "lizard" has run must not be eaten raw. According to one informant, the lizard's presence indicates that a woman has recently stepped over the *hevia'* plant because lizards are attracted to vaginal odors. According to another informant, lizards copulate in *hevia'* plants.

KITO' (PIDGIN ENGLISH KUMU)
"LEAFY VEGETABLES"

Although the most important rule in regard to this category of leafy vegetables is a relative one, there are a number of absolute ones. An initiate may not eat *hmavi* and *higopa* because they are wild. One informant said, "If you eat things planted with human hands, you will grow well, but if you eat wild things, you will be stunted." Another informant suggested that these *kito'* were prohibited because they are black. Eating them would make one's *kota* "face, nose" turn black. A third informant volunteered that if a boy ate them, girls would not be attracted to him.

All the red *kito'* (*ruarokorarome'*, *are maita*, *azovuzea*, *zafare'*, *hgovia*, *hgerua*, *bokome*, *sagrekre*) are prohibited because they are like blood or women; because women wear them as decoration on their buttocks; and because they are "*kito'* that shines in the eyes."

PIG

Meat on the bone is prohibited because of the resemblance between pig and possum bones. Fat is prohibited because the fat may locate itself in ego's joints, which then would become loose, making him unable to work. Eating fat is also thought to lead to weight problems—in particular a fat and swollen belly. The consumption of fat may extinguish the internal fire. Blood, although normally eaten by the Hua, is firmly prohibited for an initiate. Groin, stomach, and intestines are tabooed because they may be contaminated by menstrual blood or feces. Males are afraid to eat the intestines and stomachs of the scavenging animals for fear that they may ingest some filth.

Heart is prohibited because of its identification with *kora haugepa* "blood clot." Liver is prohibited because it contains large quantities of *kora haugepa*. Kidneys and lungs are prohibited for reasons I never learned. Womb is tabooed because it contains menstrual blood, and genitals are tabooed because of their association with sex, although elderly men are said to eat them.

Pork that has been smoke dried is tabooed because it might stunt growth by reducing the *nu* content of the initiates' bodies.

WATER

Water, the only substance traditionally drunk by the Hua, was totally prohibited during certain phases of initiation. Initiates were cautioned against drinking excessively at any time lest their internal fires go out. This fire, identified with vitality, is located at the base of the chest. If it ceases to burn, the sparkle goes from a man's eye and he loses his power to attract women and to compete successfully with his agemates.

In addition, initiates must observe for several years a prohibition on water from the forest (the wooded slopes of the mountains above the Hua villages). Possums are said to have polluted this water with their feces and urine.

In the past it was forbidden for a bamboo water tube to be passed over a male's head because such an action could extinguish the internal fire. A person who thoughtlessly passed a bamboo tube over another's head would have to pay compensation.

Even today the Hua do not permit water of any kind, including rain, to fall on butchered or cooked pork. Water, they say, will cause the meat to rot more rapidly.

Lures for game birds were traditionally set by the side of puddles where these birds were known to bathe. Birds killed during or immediately after bathing were taboo to men. Entering the water, according to informants, is like intercourse. Furthermore, water, like a woman, is a *vravra na* "damp, wet thing."

SALT

The Hua traditionally made salt by a complicated process that included burning leaves down to ash, pouring water through the ash, then boiling the liquid until it became salt. Two types of salt were made: one from leaves from the grasslands and the other from leaves from the forest.

Salt made from leaves from the grasslands is freely eaten with the exception of the last liquid to be drawn from the ash, which is tabooed because it is the *ai'a* "feces" of the salt. Salt made from leaves from the forest is tabooed because these salt cakes have a curve that is like the curve of a possum tail, and because possums may have urinated and defecated on the forest leaves from which they are made. Salt in its liquid form is tabooed because it resembles women's urine.

MUSHROOMS

The following reasons are given for not eating mushrooms:

1. They resemble the vagina.
2. They smell *be' ftu*.
3. They grow only during *a'di kuna* "women's time" (the new moon).
4. They grow on the ground, which is identified with women and filth.
5. They are associated with possums.
6. Their ashy, dry surface can be transferred to the eater.
7. They are red.

Because there was much disagreement among informants, I have presented all the data in table A-1 rather than attempt a summary. Busa (B), Fova (F), Kiafuri (K), and Momoti (M) are the four informants.

Table A-1
PROHIBITIONS ON MUSHROOMS

Mushroom	Busa	Fova	Kiafuri	Momoti
zokoni	−	−		−
ktrgu′	−			−
tane	−	+		+
knegu	−	+		−
ktitosva	−	+		−
dguripa	−	+		−
harru	−	+		+
himoria	−	+		−
mamusva	−	−		
dkugea′	−	−		
hemahera	−	+		
kegikoma	−	+	−	
zagihva	−	+	−	
arerua	−	−		
degesva	−			
futu hva	−			
kuhara		+		
fuaurga′da		+	−	
niniknuva hva			−	
hevia hva			−	
remu hva			−	
kvrgi hva			−	
hove			−	
indova			−	

Note: A minus (−) indicates the informant thought the mushroom was tabooed; a plus (+) that it was not.

Below are the reasons they gave for the taboo or absence of taboo on the various kinds of mushrooms. In some cases informants gave no reason.

zokoni:
    (−) (B) because in one folktale it is pasted to women's vaginas; because it smells *be′ ftu*.
    (−) (F) for fear of its smell.
    (−) (M) because it smells like a woman's body; if you eat the *zokoni* the smell of your mouth will disgust girls.

ktrgu':

(−) (B) because it is soft and flabby like the vaginal labia.

(−) (M) because it is *korogo* and because it grows on the ground.

tane:

(−) (B) because it grows on the ground, where humans and animals may have defecated and urinated on it.

(+) (M) because it is *hakeri'a* and when eaten makes a crackling noise.

knegu:

(−) (B) because it makes the oil come out of the blackheads on one's nose.

(−) (B) because possums defecate and urinate on it; because it is a ground-growing mushroom; because it grows in the forest.

ktitosva:

(−) (B) because it grows only during women's time or new moon.

(+) (F) because it is good, it is white, it grows on dried out, dead trees.

dguripa:

(−) (B) because its shape resembles a young woman's breasts before she has children.

(−) (M) because it is like women's vaginas.

harru:

(−) (B) because it grows only during women's time.

(+) (M) because it is slippery; when you try to touch it, it slips away. Slippery foods are favored for their suggestion that after a person eats them he will be able to slip away from those who are trying to ensorcell him.

himoria:

(−) (B) "because it is a possum," that is, it grows at the base of trees in which possums live; because possums defecate and urinate all over it;

because it grows very fast, goes *hakeri'a* fast, and therefore stunts growth.

(−) (M) because it is like a woman's vagina.

mamusva:

(−) (B) because it grows only at women's time; because it grows and dies fast and then releases a horrible black *nu*.

(−) (F) because it grows at women's time.

dkugea':

(−) (B) because it grows only at women's time.

(−) (F) because it grows in the holes of trees and therefore is like women's vaginas.

hemahera:

(−) (B) because it has that dusty ashy look, which the eater will also get.

kegikoma:

(−) (B) because it grows on the ground, and ground-growing mushrooms have a bad *nu*.

(−) (K) because it grows on the ground.

zagihva:

(−) (B) same as for *kegikoma*.

arerua:

(−) (B) because it is red.

(−) (F) because it is red; because it grows at women's time.

degesva:

(−) (B) "because it is a possum," that is, it grows at the base of trees in which possums live and they defecate and urinate on it.

ftu hva:

(−) (B) because it grows on the ground.

kuhara:

(−) (F) because it is red and grows on the ground.

fuaurga'da:

(−) (F) because it grows on the ground.

niniknuva hva:

(−) (K) because it grows on the ground.

hevia hva:

(−) (K) because it grows on the ground.

remu hva:

(−) (K) because it grows on the ground.

kvrgi hva:

(−) (K) because it grows on the ground.

hove:

(−) (K) because it grows on the ground.

indova:

(−) (K) because it grows on the ground.

BANANAS

There was such disagreement among informants about the different species of bananas that I felt it better not to summarize the data but rather to present it all in table A-2. There was reasonably good agreement between Busa and Fova, though Busa himself made two different statements about the *hara* banana. Where Rohakivi disagreed with them (about *opne* and *kta*), the other three informants agreed. Momoti, who is much younger than the other three men, had the most aberrant list. His generalization was that the *korogo* bananas cannot be eaten because of the way their trunks bend over toward the ground, while the *hakeri'a* ones are safe to eat because their trunks are erect. *Hzapa, vugeta, airvia,* and *mnimniva* bananas, being *hakeri'a*, are considered edible by Momoti.

The generalization made by the three other informants was just the reverse of Momoti's. They called the *hakeri'a* bananas *keva egemo* "stunted, dried out bananas." They said that if initiates were to eat them, they would become stunted. The *korogo* bananas, being soft and fast-growing, are safe to eat.

The second reason for which a banana may be tabooed is that its skin is used by women to wash their bodies.

hzapa:

(−) (B) because it is *rapuru ege* "a banana whose skin

Table A-2
PROHIBITIONS ON BANANAS

Banana	Busa	Rohakivi	Fova	Momoti
hzapa	−	−	−	+
vugeta	−	−	−	+
airvia	−	−	−	+
mnimniva	−	−	−	+
opne	−	+	−	−
borua	+	+	+	+
figa	−	−	+	−
zofa	+	+	+	+
kta	−	+	−	−
bupa	−	−	−	−
hirofira	+		+	+
oma	+	−	+	−
hara	+/−	−	+	−
oganua			+	−
havosege			+	−
rauri	−		−	
emipa	−		−	
rafuria		−		

is dry and flakey," which has no *nu* inside it;
because it is *hakeri'a* and therefore grows very
slowly and ripens slowly.

(−) (R) because it grows slowly, its growth is stunted,
and it is *hakeri'a*.

(−) (F) because it is slow-growing, stunted in growth,
hakeri'a.

vugeta (a kind of *hzapa*):

(−) (F) because it is slow-growing, stunted in growth,
hakeri'a.

airvia (a kind of *hzapa*):

(−) (F) because it is slow-growing, stunted in growth,
hakeri'a.

mnimniva (a kind of *hzapa*):

(−) (F) because it is slow-growing, stunted in growth,
hakeri'a.

opne:

(−) (B) because it does not ripen quickly, is stunted,
and grows slowly.

(−) (F) because it is red on the inside and *hakeri'a*.

(−) (M) because it becomes soft and ripe very quickly and its branches do not become *hakeri'a*. Momoti characterizes this species of banana as soft and fast-growing—just the opposite of the characterization given by the other informants. But Momoti's characterization conforms with his system, namely, that soft things cannot be eaten. Perhaps he remembered that this banana is tabooed and then made its characteristics fit his system.

borua:

(+) (B) because it is yellow inside, ripens fast, and grows fast.

(+) (R) because it is *korogo*.

(+) (F) because it grows extremely rapidly.

(+) (M) (given Momoti's generalization, he should have listed this banana as taboo because it is soft.)

figa:

(−) (B) because it is stunted, slow-growing, *hakeri'a*.

(−) (R) because it is stunted, slow-growing, *hakeri'a*. Initiates are not forbidden to eat those bananas which grow fast and are *korogo*.

(+) (F) because it grows extremely rapidly. Fova perhaps has characterized this banana wrongly, though his characterization conforms with his theory that it is not taboo.

(−) (M) because it is stunted, slow-growing, *hakeri'a*. Momoti here slips into the theory of the others, namely, that *hakeri'a* items must not be eaten.

zofa:

(+) (B) because it grows very fast and ripens fast. It has much *nu*, and women do not wash themselves with it.

(+) (R) because it is soft, fast-growing.

(+) (F) because it grows rapidly.

(+) (M) because it is *hakeri'a*, slow-growing. Here is another example of how Momoti seems to have remembered the rule correctly but the reason for the prohibition wrongly. According to Momoti, a banana is prohibited because it is *korogo*. If it is not prohibited, it must be *hakeri'a*. This rule is, of course, just the reverse of what the other informants say.

kta:

(−) (B) because it is *hakeri'a*. Women wash with its skins after their sojourn in the menarcheal hut.

(+) (R) because it is the initiate's banana, it is *korogo*, it ripens easily.

(−) (F) because it is "bad pollution"; it grows very fast and bends over, which makes it pollution.

(−) (M) because women wash with it after their sojourn in the menarcheal hut.

bupa:

(−) (B) because it is *korogo*.

(−) (R) because women use its skins for washing their bodies.

(−) (F) because women use its skins for washing their bodies.

(−) (M) because women use its skins for washing their bodies.

hirofira:

(+) (B) because it is a good banana, not *hakeri'a*.

(+) (M) because it is *hakeri'a*.

oma:

(+) (B) because it grows fast.

(−) (R) because its trunk bends over toward the ground. This happens because it is *korogo*, is soft, and grows fast.

hara:

(+/−) (B) on one occasion Busa said it is permitted because it ripens fast and is soft; on another occasion he said it is prohibited to new initi-

ates because although it is a good banana
and has sufficient *nu*, it wanders at night!

(−) (R) because it grows fast and very tall although it
is *hakeri'a*.

(+) (F) because it is very tall.

(−) (M) because it wanders at night! (I could not find
out how or why.)

oganua:

(+) (F) because it is very *korogo*.

(−) (M) because it is stunted, slow-growing.

havosege:

(−) (M) because it is stunted, slow-growing.

rauri:

(−) (B) because it is wild, stunted, slow-growing, and
does not ripen fast.

(−) (F) because it is wild but is *korogo*.

emipa:

(−) (F) because it is wild. Women do not eat it prior to
old age, according to Fova, for fear of making very yellow urine. Women prefer to have
urine like water.

rafuria:

(−) (R) because it is stunted, slow-growing.

RED PANDANUS

There was total agreement that all species of red pandanus are prohibited to initiates. This prohibition is based
on the resemblance drawn by informants between the red
juice of the pandanus and menstrual blood, an association
also made in the origin myth of pandanus. The original
pandanus plant grew at the site of an abandoned menstrual hut in the Gimi area. According to my informant, it
grew out of the menstrual blood and was nourished by the
polluted material that continued to be dumped there.

Although all the species of red pandanus are prohibited
for the new initiate, the taboos vary in duration. Unfor-

tunately, I discussed this variation with only one informant, Fova. He attributed it to the following:

mena': ?

trua': a relatively long taboo because it is *hakeri'a*, slow-growing, stunted.

rinokoa: a relatively long taboo because it is a short, ground-hugging pandanus.

riketiva': ?

haravo: a relatively short taboo because it is very large; initiates can eat it once they have married.

agumaguarea: ?

zuaiva: a relatively long taboo because its yellow juice is said to resemble a young infant's feces.

WHITE PANDANUS

There is general agreement that no species of white pandanus is eaten until the initiate has grown up and married. Various reasons for the prohibition were suggested by Momoti, Aza, and Fova:

1. It is wild and therefore must not be eaten.
2. It is a *kaso na* "sharp, scratchy thing."
3. It is *hakeri'a*.
4. It is cooked in ashes and becomes dusty. Most foods cooked in ashes are prohibited for fear that the new initiate's skin will take on the ashy quality of the food. The Hua prize oily skin as an indicator of abundant *nu*.
5. In a story a possum says, "Don't eat the white pandanus because it is something that I, who am polluted, eat. If you eat it, you will get the big belly of pregnancy."

MISCELLANEOUS VEGETABLES

The following are prohibited:

fga (winged bean): because it is a stunted, slow-growing plant; because it smells (one informant said the smell was *be' ftu*); because it grows on the ground.

kembi (a tall edible grass with a marked swelling in the lower part of its stalk): because of the swelling in its stalk, which is like the pregnant womb (*pmurua aima'namo ne* "it is something that is pregnant"). One informant said that if an initiate ate *kembi*, he would get *kupa*, though several other informants denied this. However, when a Hua girl first menstruates and is secluded in a menarcheal house, her real and classificatory parents eat lots of *kembi*.
  A second reason for the prohibition on *kembi* is that it is sharp and scratchy. If the initiate were to eat it, his skin might lose its oil.

auge' (a small, edible purple, white, and yellow flower from, I believe, the winged bean): because it is "the vagina of women," "a woman's clitoris," like a woman's *rutu* (some part of female genitals), "something that comes and peeks out of a woman's vagina."

okza (unidentified): because it is *hakeri'a*. It would make the initiate's skin dry and flaky.

heva' (broad bean): because it is like possum kidney or liver.

corn: because its leaves are sharp.

fera okani (unidentified): because of its bad *zorgeva* "hair"; because it is like women's necklaces.

Informants disagree about the cucumber. All comment that its interior is full of water. Those who say that cucumber is permitted cite its juiciness. Eating it makes the initiate grow faster, they say. Those who claim that cucumber is prohibited cite the crunching sound made when eating it. This sound is said to resemble the Hua words *dgau'di dgau'di* "my vagina, my vagina."
  The following are permitted:

ki'zava (unidentified)
okani (unidentified)
rike (unidentified)

SUGARCANE

Although informants disagree about which sugarcanes are prohibited and which are not, as shown in table A-3, there is complete agreement on the reasons for prohibition: a short sugarcane must not be eaten—it is short like a woman and it can be called "woman's sugarcane"—and the *heva eve* "stunted, slow-growing sugarcanes" must not be eaten because they might retard the initiate's growth. These two rules do not account for the prohibition on *kzo* and *arava*. *Kzo* is tabooed because knives to cut possums are made from it. *Arava* is tabooed because contact with it causes itching.

When asked why a nonprohibited sugarcane was freely eaten, informants replied either that the sugarcane was tall or that it grew fast.

Table A-3
PROHIBITIONS ON SUGARCANE

Sugarcane	Fova	Rohakivi	Momoti
sekave	+	+	+
zavavaria	+	+	+
zape'bo	+	+	−
fuvua	+	−	−
arava	−	−	−
kmoria	−	−	−
auruamo	−	−	−
hriga	+		−
hagarama	+		+
kengo	+	+	→
roruava	+	+	−
seva	+		−
anani	+		
vaimua	+		
kzo	−		

One final rule: sugarcane may not be eaten outside the men's house because the pulp might be left exposed on the ground, where a woman might defecate or urinate on it or a person who had recently had intercourse might step on it. If any of these things were to happen, then the initiate would *bi aina to-* "be put down"—his growth and strength would be damaged.

POSSUM

Possum is the most heavily tabooed of all the Hua foods. Informants say that a male who eats possum will become pregnant and that, unless countermeasures are taken, he will burst and die when the growing fetus has cut its two bottom teeth. Initially I could elicit no reasons for the possum taboo. Ultimately, however, one informant volunteered (and others confirmed) that possum "is the counterpart of women." Incidentally, initiates are forbidden for a short while after initiation even from entering the forest because it is the home of possums.

The Hua class eighteen animals as *zga* "possum." Of them perhaps five would be classified as a rat by Westerners because they have no pouch. The Hua group these five with the possums because they bear litters of only one or two. The Hua say that possums, like humans, bear only very small numbers of young, while rats bear large litters.

Of the eighteen animals classified as *zga* (*kai'*, *keni'*, *hmia'*, *viva*, *bo'zga*, *izomu*, *kehova*, *hazubre'*, *krirope*, *zanepa*, *mainu*, *muigi*, *hazo'ai*, *kepu*, *kimi'*, *vare'*, *zaviasu'*) five (*kai'*, *keni'*, *hmia'*, *kehova*, and *kimi'*) are classified as having the *be' ftu* smell. This smell, which informants usually maintain is both dangerous and repugnant, is in some contexts reckoned to be attractive. Once a man is permitted to eat possums, he prefers the ones with the *be' ftu* smell. There is also a preference for the very dark or black possums.

Vare', probably bandicoot, became publicly edible in the

past to men in early old age, but today it is eaten by some younger men freely. The reason for the relatively relaxed nature of this taboo is that *vare'*, although now a wild animal, was originally tame like a pig. According to myth, the original Hua ancestors led not only pigs but also *vare'* on leashes. The pig stayed leashed but the *vare'* slipped his leash and ran down into the grasslands and became a wild animal.

Although the Hua recognize at least eighteen species of possum, I elicited only these few species-specific in taboos. For purposes of taboo the separate *zga* species seem to be treated as a single class.

Finally, the taboo on possum is a public pose. Males secretly eat possum in ceremonies in special houses, called *zga zu'* "possum house," to increase their health and strength. The fact of their eating possum is secret from women. In the past if a woman found out, she was killed, males say. Even today, no woman admits knowing that males secretly eat possum.

MOUSE/RAT

Though there are many different species of mouse (*avru'*, *do'to mumo*, *ai'*, *totopoa*, *hokro'*, *evamu'a*, *zagiokara*, *haga-memo*, *hagameza*, *murva'*, *aupa*, *hakreva*, *kairoganoruane*, and *keve'da mua*), I was not able to elicit different rules for the different species. The class *mumo* "mouse, rat" seems to be prohibited because it is *siro na* in that it eats feces from the ground, because it crawls and smells like a possum, and because its hair is like a possum's. Incidentally, the original possum is said to have been born of a mouse.

The result of eating mouse is general physical degeneration or pregnancy. The belief that an initiate can become pregnant from eating mouse emerged only after many months of fieldwork, whereas the belief that pregnancy can result from eating possum emerged immediately.

DOG

Initiates are not allowed to eat dogs until old age for three reasons. First, because dogs are *kopa na* "dirty, polluted." They eat we know not what, we know not where. They eat raw mice and possums. They eat in the area allotted for defecation. They eat women's feces. One can look in their mouths and see black filth. Second, because "they are things with hair." And third, because their backs curve when they sleep. A straight back and erect posture are carefully preserved signs of virility and strength.

FROGS

All informants agree that frog is prohibited if not until death, then until just prior to it. The reasons are that frogs are like women's vaginas; that frogs have no fat (they have skinny buttocks); that frogs are *mnipina na* "water things," and will cause males to get water in their joints, preventing them from running fast in battle and so forth.

The Hua make a very close identification between frogs and women. A man who dreams about frogs can be expected to have female children. When a child is born, it is traditional for the father to call to the mother, "Did you catch a frog or shoot a bird?" If the woman answers, "Frog," the man knows he has a baby daughter; if she says, "Bird," he has a son.

Frogs have an ambivalent status. If asked what males cannot eat, informants always list frogs. However, frogs are also listed as a food that males eat to avoid being ensorcelled. Frogs both pollute and provide powerful protection.

FISH

There is some disagreement about the taboos on fish. Of the eleven informants with whom I discussed fish, six said that all fish with the exception of *dgopo'* "catfish?" were edible to new initiates, while four said no fish were permitted. One informant (one of my best) on one occasion said fish are permitted and on another said they are prohibited.

Fish are no longer caught and eaten by the Hua, having been replaced, I presume, by the canned fish available at local trade stores. The fish traditionally available were *sosoga'*, *raiva*, *feni* (an eel), and *dgopo'*. Informants agree that the *dgopo'*, being "like a possum," is prohibited for males until very old age. When asked how this fish resembles a possum, informants reply that it lives in holes in rocks or that it has whiskers.

Those informants who maintain that fish were traditionally prohibited cite the following reasons: fish are *mnipina na* "water things" like women and fish are *rnitni na* "cold things" like women, who are classified as *rnitni na* in opposition to men, who are *buko* "hot." Women are reckoned as cooler than men because women have more interior liquid and because their larger lower-body openings enable them to take more air into their bodies.

Those informants who maintain that fish except for *dgopo'* are permitted cite one of the following reasons: fish are *korogo* because they live in the water, or fish are *hrufre'na* "things that slip away easily." Foods that slip away easily are usually considered efficacious in helping to avoid sorcery.

Fish may be one of that large class of animals and plants that are considered dangerous for eating in some contexts but powerful cures in others.

SNAKES

About ten snakes are recognized as edible by the Hua. All are taboo to the new initiate. The Hua no longer eat snakes, which perhaps explains the vagueness in snake prohibitions. When asked why a particular snake was prohibited, informants replied that it is a *hepa kvuvina brema'na* "bad thing of the bush," that is, wild; that it has no arms and legs; or that an initiate who ate it would get the flaky, scaly skin of the snake.

There is one allegedly fierce snake, the *kuzu'*, that is eaten several years after initiation in order to make the boys fierce in battle.

SNAILS

These are prohibited because the slime they secrete is said to be like female vaginal secretions. Also, its *korogo* quality is said to resemble the vagina.

BIRDS

Although I worked quite hard on birds with some ten informants, I never felt I really got reliable information, perhaps because birds are now only a peripheral part of the Hua diet. In any case, the following information represents simply the point of view that most informants seemed to agree upon. But much more work on birds is needed.

The following birds are prohibited:

aurme': may be eaten once a man has married and had a child.

baho: may be eaten once a man has married and had a child.

beguvara: may be eaten once a man has married and had a child.

bipi': may be eaten once a man has married and had a child.

bume: because it has a hideous face, is nocturnal, eats possum and other dirty foods, and sleeps in a hole, as a possum does. Males never eat it after initiation. Older women do eat it, but young women do not for fear of bearing children with hideous faces.

bumo: ?

butupa (bird of paradise): because it is a *rema' nma* "one of the birds with feathers that are bright and beautiful." No man ever ate these birds.

doto nma: may be eaten once a man has married.

feta': because it is a *vaima'nma* "one of the birds whose feathers are used in decoration," or a *sivanma* "one of the birds into whose feathers people put spells."

fio': because it bathes in puddles (and water is associated with females), it is not eaten until late middle age; also some prejudice against eating it because it is white.

fopotenara: because it goes into the water and because it *ivi ivi fu-* "nods its head sleepily," a behavior identified as typical of old age. It is eaten only in late middle age.

hago': because it is a *sivanma*. It is eaten only in late middle age.

hakreva': because it is an *aigopa nma* "ground bird." It may be eaten once a male's beard has started to grow.

hane': because it is a *rema'nma*, *vaima'nma*. It is the age-mate of newly married women. It may be eaten only in old age.

hagive: because it is a *sivanma*. If a man gets a bit of a woman's hair and mixes it with the feathers of this bird, then the woman will leave her husband, never settle down happily with another man again, and become a wandering, promiscuous woman. This bird is prohibited also because it sleeps in holes in trees.

hazuifi'a: because it is nocturnal; because of the loathsome abundance of feathers located around its mouth; because it has a face like the female pudenda; because it lives in a hole; because it kills and eats mice and possums. It is eaten only in old age. There is a song about this bird:

> *Bipevenvene zaipaneveneve.*
> *Hugamageo dendvaru baisimato'.*

This song says that a man must eat carefully, as the bird *rio'* does. If he eats indiscriminately, as the *ha-*

zuifi'a does, then his face will become ugly and he will lose his wife to his agemates.

heseva: because it is a vaima'nma. Only men in old age eat it.

hge': because it is rema'nma and sivanma. It is eaten in old age.

hgiro': may be eaten once a man has married.

hgive: because it sleeps in a hole.

hisi': because it is nocturnal, is a thief, and sleeps in a hole.

ho'ene': because it is a vaima'nma; because it lives on the ground. It is eaten only in late middle age.

ta'ai': because it is a vaima'nma; because its tail wiggles the way a woman's skirt swings.

kaitgina: because it is a rema'nma.

kiage': because it is a sivanma.

kikipa': because it is big and thieves. It is eaten only in middle age.

kirigitaia: because it is a sivanma.

kitrora: because it is a sivanma.

kokofua: because it has a hot, unpleasant taste (so no one eats it).

ktrupe: because it is nocturnal, sleeps in a hole, is a thief, has a feathery face, which is likened to female pudenda, and nods its head sleepily as an old man does. It is eaten only in late middle age.

kurikuripa: because it is extremely large and if eaten causes very rapid aging. It is eaten only in old age.

kvzgo': ?

muti: because it is sivanma.

nmavza: because it is rema'nma, because it is the agemate of women.

opoi: because it lives in holes.

repi: because it is big, lives on the ground, and eats feces. It is eaten only in late middle age.

rio': because it is big, nocturnal, kills and eats possum, and has an ugly face. It is eaten only in old age.

rokamura: because it is big, lives on the ground, lays a

huge egg, and when the egg is in its belly, it is like a pregnant woman. It is eaten only in old age.

ruhipa': because it is big and is known to steal food. It is eaten only in late middle age.

rurumane: because it is *vaima'nma*.

sindre: although it is a ground bird (most of which are tabooed), it is also a small bird and therefore males may eat it when they first marry. One informant mentioned as a reason for its taboo the way in which it wiggles its tail, which is like the way in which the genital apron of a woman swings when she walks.

taverenara: no one eats it because it has a sharp bad taste.

tetero: because it eats feces; also because it wiggles its tail the way a woman's genital apron swings. It is eaten in old age.

uvvu': because it is big. It is eaten in late middle age.

vihotu: because it is a ground-living bird, has a yellow face, and is *vaima'nma*. It is eaten in late middle age.

viva': because it lives on the ground and eats feces and worms. It is eaten in old age.

vivio'a: because it makes a sound like the flutes. It is eaten in late middle age.

The following birds are permitted:

hvi: because it is very small and flies high. It is identified with the high air and mountains.

ifu'ai'a: because it is very small.

kevove'dero: because it is small and flies high and light.

ktroma': because it is small, *tunoga nma* "up in the air bird."

kugofa': because it is small, *tunoga nma*.

kuimo: because it is small, *tunoga nma*.

pri': because it is small, *tunoga nma*.

rinokoa: because it is small, *tunoga nma*.

ruvi: because it is small, *tunoga nma*.

visge: because it is small, *tunoga nma*.

vzo': because it is small.

zanupa: ?

Informants disagreed about some birds. Most informants agreed that the cassowary, although freely eaten today, was traditionally prohibited to initiates for two reasons. First, it is considered exceptionally wild. Informants maintain that the meat of the dead bird spontaneously increases in bulk! Second, it is *hakeri'a*—it does not have much fat. Those informants who claimed that cassowary was permitted said that it is like pig, although they did not say in what way.

The *knava'* bird was generally prohibited because it is a ground bird. When moving on the ground, however, it makes a strange trail, which suggests escape from a sorcerer. This is the reason, according to one informant, that it is freely eaten by new initiates.

FLYING FOX

Most informants agreed that the flying fox was prohibited because it resembles possum and has its *be' ftu* smell, because it is nocturnal, or because it is a ghost of *vemo* "dead people." Siane initiates, incidentally, are fed a meal of flying fox, which they are told is their ancestral spirits (Salisbury 1965:60–61). Those Hua informants who maintained that the flying fox was always edible said that it chases away from food the *rga'*, a form of pollution released from the bodies of humans (for example, from the vagina of a woman at childbirth). The reference here is to the way the flying fox flaps its wings when it approaches bananas and other foods, thereby chasing away insects. There is a ceremony after childbirth in which men, likening their action to that of the flying fox, brush leaves over food to remove the *rga'* with which it has become covered.

Another reason that the flying fox was said to be edible is that the animal is thought by the Hua not to defecate. They vomit out all the food they eat. Hua males admire this practice as particularly clean (traditionally males induce vomiting to keep their interiors clean and white).

INSECTS

The Hua traditionally ate insects, though they rarely do so today. Many of the rules apply, as indicated below, for varying lengths of time during the male initiation.

Informants disagreed about whether termite larvae were permitted. A few informants said the larvae were not prohibited to new initiates because they are *korogo* and would therefore help to increase the initiate's growth rate. Two informants, however, said these larvae were prohibited—because the holes in which they work inside trees do not have exits (very like the despairing comment made in reference to a pregnant male, "But there's no exit"), according to the first informant, or because the action of the larvae inside the tree is like that of the sexual members in the act of copulation, according to the second.

The following insects were prohibited:

vesnu': may be eaten after one week of abstention.

fravakopieva: because it is red. It may be eaten after one week of abstention.

futupara eva: because it is an indiscriminate eater, eating anything and everything from off the ground. It is eaten once the beard begins to grow.

ririma: eaten after one week of abstention.

ririma sirigine: eaten after two weeks.

aigava sagva: eaten after two weeks.

ekremu': because it is black; eaten after one month.

fikutare: because it eats feces; eaten after one month.

ktuktu: eaten after one week.

roposia: because it is black and therefore associated with internal uncleanliness; freely eaten after two weeks.

zorakuru eva: eaten after one week.

rukva: because of its indiscriminate eating habits; eaten after one week.

fomipara: because it has six legs; eaten freely after about three weeks.

buge': because it comes out of a hole in the ground. It may be eaten again only in middle age.

krikoma: same as for *buge'*.

kakva: because it crawls around on the ground; eaten after four weeks.

fumo airoga bugera "the insect that is on pig feces": because it eats feces. No male eats it until late middle age.

koripa kva "peanut bug": eaten again after only three nights because it has a good smell.

igari: eaten after two nights.

karinde: eaten after two nights.

The following insects were permitted:

ufgura: ?

kotakurueva: is eaten to make people not stare at a person when he is eating pig.

sese eva: freely eaten because it is a *tunoga gnu* "up high creature" and therefore has associations with cleanliness.

erieri kva: ?

kokva: ?

HUMANS

By the time I was at Lufa cannibalism had not been practiced for twenty years, according to informants. Because of this long lapse and because there was considerable Hua embarrassment about the custom, I felt I would probably not get reliable data. Consequently I made no effort to elicit information on this topic, though I wrote down what data came my way.

I am aware of only one absolute rule in regard to cannibalism (the rest are relative): an initiate could not eat any human blood other than that of old, sexually inactive males because of the identification of all blood with menstrual blood. Men in general are allowed to eat other men's blood but not during the new moon, when women are supposed to menstruate.

Appendix B

RELATIVE FOOD RULES

Table B-1 presents the pattern for three relative rules of prescriptions and proscriptions for an adult male in the various social relationships of which he is likely to be part. The rules are those for a mature male, one who no longer needs to observe the severe restrictions of the new initiate or newlywed but who has not yet achieved the relative invulnerability and relaxation typical of late middle age. It must be emphasized that the rules apply to both real and classificatory kin.

The following abbreviations are used:

B	Brother
Cc	Cross-cousin
Ch	Children
D	Daughter
F	Father
Hu	Husband
M	Mother
S	Son
Wi	Wife
Z	Sister

MB means mother's brother, FF means father's father, and so on.

Complete sets of data were collected from eleven male informants. In most cases informants agreed; where they disagreed, I selected the majority viewpoint.

Each rule has a separate and autonomous status to the Hua, although the groupings do reflect Hua thinking. Rules 1a, 1b, and 1c all protect ego from the danger of *nu* (in the form of sweat, body oil, spots of menstrual blood, and traces of urine or feces) spread by means of alter's sometimes contaminated and almost invariably unwashed hand. Rule 2 is concerned with emanations that may drop

Table B-1

AVOIDANCE RULES FOR A MATURE MALE IN HIS RELATIONSHIPS WITH ALTERS

	Self	F FF MF	M FM MM	B	Male Cc of FZ or MB lineages	Female Cc of FZ, MB lineages	Z	MB	FZ
1. Can ego eat:									
a. leafy green vegetables picked by	+	+[a]	+[b]	+[a]	+[a]	+	+	+[a]	+[b]
b. food cut or peeled by	+	+[a]	+[b]	+[a]	+[a]	+[b]	+	+[a]	+[b]
c. food otherwise prepared by hand of	+	+[a]	+[b]	+[a]	+[a]	+[b]	+	+[a]	+[b]
2. Can ego allow his body, food, or any implements to be crossed by body or shadow of	?	+[a]	−[c]	+[a]	+[a]	+[b]	−	+[a]	−
3. Can ego eat:									
a. deceased body of	0	+	−	+/−[d]	+	−	?	+	−
b. blood of	−	+[a]	−	+/−[d]	+[a]	−	?	+[a]	−
c. deceased child of	−	+/−[e]	+/−[e]	−	−	−	0	?	?
d. pig of	−	+	+	+	+	+	0	+	+
e. largest and best garden produce of	−	+	+	+	+	+	0	+	+
f. wild animals shot by	−	+[a]	0	+	+	0	0	+	0

Note: A minus (−) means proscribed; a plus (+) means permitted; a zero (0) means not relevant. A question mark (?) means unknown.

[a] Unless alter has recently had intercourse.

[b] Unless alter is menstruating or has recently had a child.

[c] The body or shadow of a woman who has been initiated into the male society is permitted to cross ego's body, food, and implements.

[d] A distinction is made within the category of brother. Ego may not eat the body or blood of a brother with whom there is extensive sharing of *nu*, that is, with a real brother. Classificatory brothers' bodies and blood may be eaten. There is one additional complexity: a real brother who is very different in age from ego is thought not to share much *nu* with ego. Thus his body and blood are edible.

					Affines							
Later-born Ch	Later-born ChCh	Agemate	First-born Ch	Ch of First-born Ch	Wi	Wi F	Wi M	B Wi	Wi B	Z Hu	Later-born SWi	Later-born DHu
+[a,b]	+[a,b]	+[a]	−	−	−	+[a]	−	−	+[a]	+[a]	+[b]	+[a]
+[a,b]	+[a,b]	+[a]	−	−	−	+[a]	−	+[b]	+[a]	+[a]	+[b]	+[a]
+[a,b]	+[a,b]	+[a]	−	−	−	+[a]	−	+[b]	+[a]	+[a]	+[b]	+[a]
+[a,b]	+[a,b]	−	−	−	−	−	−	−	−	−	−	+
−	−	−	−	−	−	−	−	−	−	−	−	−
−	−	−	−	−	−	−	−	−	−	−	−	−
−	−	−	−	−	−	−	−	?	?	?	−	−
+	+	−	−	−	−	−	−	+/−[f]	−	+	+	+
+	+	−	−	−	−	−	−	+/−[f]	−	+	+	+
+	+	−	−	−	0	−	0	0	−	−	0	−

[e]The rule depends on the sex, generation, and genealogical closeness of alter. A female alter would not be eaten. A male alter one generation senior to ego (FFS or MFS) would be. A male alter of the same generation as ego (FS) would be eaten if there is not too much sharing of *nu* (see note d).

[f]If BWi is either much older than ego (and thus approximates the category of mother) or much younger (approximating the category of daughter), ego may eat her pig or the largest and best produce from her garden. If she is about the same age as ego, she approximates the category of wife, and in fact may become his wife if her husband should die. As such, she is a person whose *nu*, in any of its manifestations, must be avoided.

from alter's body when he or she crosses over ego's food, tools, and so forth, because loincloths are the traditional dress. This rule is also directed at the shadow, which, as an immaterial manifestation of alter, transmits *nu*.

Rules 1 and 2 are both concerned with the contagious social value of food: the preparer's essence, like a germ, is carried on the surface of a food. Rules 3a through 3f are concerned with the consubstantial social value of food: the essence of an individual is suffused into the products of his or her body or its labor. A person may not eat any substance that is endowed with a significant amount of his or her own *nu* and by extension cannot eat substances identified with the body of his or her children. A rule not listed on the table has a similar theme:

> The mother, father, and any of the father's agemates and their wives may not eat any food out of an earth oven made in honor of their real or classificatory child. Nor may they receive, use, spend, or eat any of their real or classificatory daughter's bride price.

To "eat" any of the above would be comparable, they say, to eating one's child.

Several other relative rules do not appear on the table. Unless otherwise specified, these rules follow the general pattern of the first three: the food or behavior usually is prohibited to ego if alter is an affine but not if he is a consanguine unless he falls into the category of firstborn child, agemate, or real or classificatory wife.

> Ego may not wear the clothes or carry the string bags of certain alters.

This rule provides protection against the sweat and body oil of a contaminating alter.

> Ego may not eat any tuber partially eaten by, share a knife with, or drink from the same bamboo tube [or cup] as certain alters.

These rules, according to informants, provide protection from socially prohibited saliva.

> Ego may not pass close behind the back of certain alters.

Through such a movement ego *bi aina to-* "presses him [alter] down," a phrase that refers to dominance and submission.

> Ego may not touch alter on the head or shoulders.

Again the issue is one of *bi aina to-*.

Several rules are relevant exclusively to *kakora* "initiated persons":

> *Kakora* must vigorously expel air from their nostrils after inhaling in the vicinity of a menstruating woman.

If her *rga'* "polluting odor" enters the bodies, it will cause sickness.

> *Kakora* may not eat any food cooked over a fire into which a menstruating woman has blown [in order to liven up the flames].

Informants maintain that her pollution could be spread through the medium of the fire to the food she is cooking.

> *Kakora* are forbidden to eat any food on which women have spat seasoning.

Traditionally salt, ginger, and various other "spices" were masticated and then spat onto food as a seasoning. Female saliva is polluting to a male.

> *Kakora* are forbidden to eat red pandanus prepared by a woman.

If a female were to prepare it, males say that it would become polluted with the genital filth with which her hands are alleged to be contaminated. This is one of the few foods prepared exclusively by males.

> *Kakora* may not eat any food that has been picked or peeled by a new wife.

Once again the fear focuses on the menstrual and genital filth alleged to contaminate their hands.

> *Kakora* may not eat from an earth oven into which a new wife has placed some leafy vegetables.

The menstrual and genital filth, collected under the fingernails of the new wife, would be on the *kito'* "leafy vegetables" she had picked and would spread from there to contaminate the whole earth oven.

Another group of rules applies exclusively to males in the process of being initiated. The intention of these rules appears to be to isolate initiates from the *nu* substances of reproductively active women and of outsiders—in effect, to restrict eating contact to full members of the men's house.

> Initiates, for a period of approximately four months, are forbidden to eat any food not prepared by men or not harvested from gardens belonging to women in late middle age.
>
> Initiates are forbidden to eat pork from villages other than those with which the initiates have a close association.
>
> Initiates are prohibited from eating pork cooked in the large common drum or earth oven.

They must eat pork that has been cooked separately in a small drum lest they eat some pork contaminated by a food contributed by a woman or stranger.

> Initiates may not drink water from the same bamboo tube or cup as any woman or as a middle-aged man.

The men's mouths may be polluted from sleeping with women.

Finally, a few other relative rules follow the same principles but apply to different categories of people.

> Infants may not be held by either a man or a woman who has had sexual intercourse within the last day.

Otherwise the *hepa ftu* "bad smell" from the skin and mouth of the sexually active person will penetrate the infant's body and cause him or her to cease nursing.

A man may not eat pork given to his wife. To eat such pork would be like eating the wife's vagina. When the woman's name is called at the time of the pork distribution, it is *pgau kiope figasi'bo* "as if they are calling her vagina." Further, at the moment when the pork is lifted up into the air and the woman's name announced, her vagina in response answers, *Ve* "Yes, me?" or, as other informants delicately put it, *kaumu'bo bu'bo bre* "her vagina expresses its appreciation."

> A man may not share sugarcane with a woman until he is married.

Sugarcane and semen are directly associated in many contexts.

> A man may not share sugarcane with other men until old age.

Consultants suggested indirectly and with embarrassment that if a man gives another man some sugarcane, it is like giving him semen.

Table B-2 shows the avoidance rules that apply to adult females.

Table B-2
AVOIDANCE RULES FOR A MATURE FEMALE IN HER
RELATIONSHIPS WITH ALTERS

					Consanguines				
	Self	F FF MF	M FM MM	B	Male Cc of FZ or MB lineages	Z	Female Cc of FZ or MB lineages	MB	FZ
1. Can ego eat:									
a. leafy green vegetables picked by	+[a]	+	+	+	+	+	+	+	+
b. food cut or peeled by	+[a]	+	+	+	+	+	+	+	+
c. food otherwise prepared by hand of	+[a]	+	+	+	+	+	+	+	+
2. Can ego allow her body, food, or any implements to be crossed by body or shadow of	+[a]	+	+	+	+	+	+	+	+
3. Can ego eat:									
a. deceased body of	0	+	+	+	+	+	+	+	+
b. blood of	−	+	+	+	+	+	+	+	+
c. deceased child of	−	+	+	−	−	−	−	+	+
d. pig of	−	+	+	+	+	+	+	+	+
e. largest and best garden produce of	−	+	+	+	+	+	+	+	+
f. wild animals shot by	0	+	0	+	+	0	0	+	+

Note: A minus (−) means proscribed; a plus (+) means permitted; a zero (0) means not relevant. A question mark (?) means unknown.
[a] Unless alter is menstruating or has recently had a child.
[b] Informants disagree.

First-born Ch	Later-born Ch	Later-born ChCh	Affines							
			Hu	HuM HuF HuZ	HuB (much older)	HuB (much younger)	Spouse of first-born Ch	Hu Age-mates	HuB of same age as ego	Co-Wife
−	+	+	+	+	+	+	−	−	−	+
−	+	+	+	+	+	+	−	−	−	+
−	+	+	+	+	+	+	−	−	−	+
−	+	+	+	+	+	+	−	−	−	+/−[b]
−	−	−	+	+	+	−	−	−	−	−
−	−	−	+	+	+	−	−	−	−	−
−	−	−	−	+	?	−	−	−	−	−
−	−	−	−	+	+	−	−	−	−	+/−[b]
−	−	−	−	+	+	−	−	−	−	−
−	+	+	+	+	+	+	−	−	−	0

Appendix C

TABOOS IN RELATION TO A FIRSTBORN CHILD

FOOD TABOOS

Informants occasionally commented that the firstborn must avoid the same things as the young male initiate. Firstborn children, male and female, are from infancy identified with initiated males, while later-born children, at least in childhood, are exclusively identified with women and other children.

These prohibitions are not automatically laid on the firstborn. As one informant said, "Only men who had pigs put a fast on their firstborn." It is my impression that only men who are ambitious for themselves and their children invoke these restrictions.

The following is a partial list of the foods prohibited to the firstborn son or daughter: possum; dog; mouse; birds that new initiates do not eat (see appendix A); red pandanus; anything wild; frog; leafy green vegetables picked by young, sexually active women; flying fox; snail; fish; taro that has a dark interior; bananas; and pig intestines, blood, liver, and fat (meat is permitted).

If the firstborn eats any of the above (assuming the father has laid on the taboos), it is said that the child will lose strength and be stunted in growth. The taboo period lasts from birth until shortly before initiation for males and until menarche for females. The restrictions are terminated in a feast in which the firstborn is ceremonially fed these foods. In the case of the male firstborn, initiation reestablishes the same set of taboos.

Informants describe the firstborn as the one who made the mother's "passage open up." He or she represents "the two parents' first *nu*" and is expected to be larger than all subsequent children, just as the first fruit of a plant is larger, produced at its parents' period of maximum strength. The firstborn is, according to some informants, or may be, according to others, made from a mixture of the semen of several men—the husband plus the men with whom the mother is assumed to have had intercourse prior to her marriage. The child may be called "the child of all men." As a result one can be sure that a firstborn child will never be a sorcerer. The firstborn may be called *hairga ba'de* "the child of the outside," and a later child *ainga ba'de* "the child of the inside." Inside and outside refer to the community and the source of the semen from which the child was made.

A firstborn female child is like a male. If the firstborn child is male, he is expected to assume the position of family leadership.

TABOOS LAID ON FIRSTBORN COMMUNITY LEADERS

These taboos represent the community's effort to protect their leaders from sorcery. The leader must not spit sugar-cane pulp out on the ground, must urinate and defecate only in water (which will carry his *nu* away, making it inaccessible to would-be sorcerers), and must not have intercourse outside his house (lest he leave some semen on the ground, which could then be ensorcelled).

TABOOS LAID ON ALTER IN RELATION TO A FIRSTBORN CHILD

These taboos apply only to an alter who is one generation senior to the firstborn child, that is, who is in the relationship of real or classificatory parent to the firstborn. Such a person may not:

1. eat leafy green vegetables that a firstborn child has picked
2. eat any food that a firstborn child has peeled, cut, or prepared, or an animal that he has shot
3. eat any food that has been stepped over by a firstborn child
4. eat any food orally contaminated by a firstborn
5. eat any pork cut by a firstborn
6. eat any food out of an earth oven from which a firstborn has eaten some banana or red pandanus
7. let the firstborn touch his or her hair
8. let the firstborn's shadow cross his or her body
9. let the firstborn's hand touch his or her head or shoulders
10. let the firstborn enter his or her garden
11. touch the firstborn when it is an infant (this rule applies only to the male parent, who may only poke at it playfully with a stick)
12. carry the firstborn on his shoulders (this rule also applies only to the male parent).

If alter does not observe these restrictions, then he or she will lose both health and strength. Alter will suffer a decline and the firstborn child a corresponding ascent.

Paradoxically, the Hua associate the firstborn child with both the vulnerable male initiate and the dangerous new wife. The firstborn is thus as vulnerable as the purest category of person and as dangerous as the most polluted. This special polluted status of the firstborn is formally terminated when he or she has married and had one or two children.

Garden produce may also be treated as a firstborn. A man, his real and classificatory brothers of approximately the same age, and his agemates cannot eat out of the *baru bai'a* "first garden" planted by his wife. Informants say that the harvest of this garden is contaminated by the wife's sexual substances.

GLOSSARY

abade girl

a'di kuna women's time, the new moon, when for purposes of ritual simplification, all women were assumed to menstruate

aita lineage

aune positive or nourishing aspect of *nu*; shadow or spirit

baru' firstborn child

be' ftu the smell of a menstruating woman and of certain rotting substances

bu' steam, the gaseous form of *nu*

fgagetava womb

figapa uninitiated person

haga sweet, good tasting

hakeri'a dry, hard, slow-growing, infertile, hot

haugepa the solid counterpart of *nu*

hauva a' newly married woman

kakora initiated person

kau vagina/urethra

kembige a kind of sorcery

keva ro- to become stunted, dried out, withered, debilitated

kimi black palm

kito' leafy vegetables (Pidgin English *kumu*)

komipa' co-wife

korogo wet, soft, fast-growing, fertile, cool

kosi- to grow, increase in weight, strength, vitality

kumurimo faie black coating of pig fat and soot, indication of male strength and virility

kupa the condition of being pregnant but unable to give birth

nogu' sister's son

nono' mother's brother

nu vital essence, which includes all the substances of the body but especially its fluids (Pidgin English *gris*)

pauge zu' body oil house; rejuvenation ceremonies

pitpit a vegetable

rafuri men's house

ropa a' mature or venerable woman

ropa de mature or venerable man

sa'   sibling of opposite sex

siro na   dirty thing; pollution

sivanma   species of birds into whose feathers people put spells

ta   bitter, spicy hot

tunoga nma   species of birds that live in the arboreal heights

vaima'nma   species of birds whose feathers are used in body
   decoration

vare'   grasslands wallaby classified as possum

vede   people

vi-a'   male-female

vza bu'   breath

BIBLIOGRAPHY

Ackerknecht, E. H. 1971. "Autopsies and Anatomical Knowledge." In *Medicine and Ethnology: Selected Essays*, ed. E. H. Ackerknecht. Baltimore: Johns Hopkins University Press.

Allen, M. B. 1967. *Male Cults and Secret Initiations in Melanesia*. Melbourne: Melbourne University Press.

Bailey, K. V. 1966. "Protein Malnutrition and Peanut Foods in the Chimbu." In *An Integrated Approach to Nutrition and Society: The Case of the Chimbu*, ed. E. H. Hipsley. New Guinea Research Unit Bulletin 9. Canberra: Australia National University Press.

Barnes, J. A. 1962. "African Models in the New Guinea Highlands." *Man* 62:5–9.

Barth, F. 1975. *Ritual and Knowledge among the Baktaman of New Guinea*. New Haven: Yale University Press.

Beauvoir, S. de. 1964 (1953). *The Second Sex*. New York: Knopf.

Beck, B. 1969. "Colour and Heat in South Indian Ritual." *Man* n.s. 4:553–572.

Bell, F. L. S. 1936. "The Avoidance Situation in Tanga." *Oceania* 6:175–198, 306–322.

———. 1948–1949. "The Place of Food in the Social Life of the Tanga." *Oceania* 19:51–74.

Benedict, R. 1934. *Patterns of Culture*. Boston: Houghton Mifflin.

Berndt, R. M. 1965. "The Kamano, Usurufa, Jate, and Fore of the Eastern Highlands." In *Gods, Ghosts and Men in Melanesia*, ed. P. Lawrence and M. J. Meggitt. New York: Oxford University Press.

Bettelheim, B. 1962 (1954). *Symbolic Wounds, Puberty Rites and the Envious Male*. New York: Collier.

Boehm, F. 1930. "The Femininity Complex in Men." *International Journal of Psycho-Analysis* 11:444–469.

It was only as this book was substantially completed that Gilbert Herdt's *Guardians of the Flutes* (New York: McGraw-Hill, 1981) appeared. Consequently it is only mentioned briefly in the text. But I heartily recommend it to all readers curious about the issues raised in this book.

Brookfield, H. C. 1964. "The Ecology of Highland Settlement: Some Suggestions." *American Anthropologist* 66:20–38.

Buchbinder, G., and Rappaport, R. A. 1976. "Fertility and Death among the Maring." In *Man and Woman in the New Guinea Highlands*, ed. P. Brown and G. Buchbinder. A.A.A. Special Publication 8. Washington, D.C.: American Anthropological Association.

Bulmer, R. N. H. 1965. "The Kyaka of the Western Highlands." In *Gods, Ghosts and Men in Melanesia*, ed. P. Lawrence and M. J. Meggitt. New York: Oxford University Press.

———. 1967. "Why Is the Cassowary Not a Bird?" *Man* n.s. 2: 5–25.

Bulmer, S. 1964. "Radiocarbon Dates from New Guinea." *Journal of the Polynesian Society* 73:327–328.

Burnet, J. 1960. *Greek Philosophy, Thales to Plato*. New York: Macmillan.

Conklin, H. C. 1963. "The Oceanian-African Hypothesis and the Sweet Potato." In *Plants and the Migration of Pacific Peoples*, ed. J. Barrau. Symposium, 10th Pacific Science Congress. Honolulu: Bishop Museum Press.

Crawley, A. E. 1960 (1927). *The Mystic Rose*. Vol. 1. New York: Meridian.

Currier, R. L. 1966. "The Hot-Cold Syndrome and Symbolic Balance in Mexican and Spanish Folk Medicine." *Ethnology* 5: 251–263.

Douglas, M. 1966. *Purity and Danger*. London: Routledge and Kegan Paul.

———. 1975. *Implicit Meanings*. London: Routledge and Kegan Paul.

Dundes, A. 1976. "A Psychoanalytic Study of the Bullroarer." *Man* n.s. 11:220–238.

Durkheim, E. 1965 (1915). *The Elementary Forms of the Religious Life*. Translated by J. W. Swain. New York: Free Press.

Du Toit, B. 1975. *Akuna: A New Guinea Village Community*. Rotterdam: A. A. Balkema.

Eisler, M. J. 1921. "A Man's Unconscious Phantasy of Pregnancy in the Guise of Traumatic Hysteria: A Clinical Contribution to Anal Eroticism." *International Journal of Psycho-Analysis* 2: 255–286.

Evans, W. N. 1951. "Simulated Pregnancy in a Male." *Psychoanalytic Quarterly* 20:165–178.

Faithorn, E. 1976. "Women as Persons: Aspects of Female Life and Male-Female Relations among the Kafe." In *Man and Woman in the New Guinea Highlands,* ed. P. Brown and G. Buchbinder. A.A.A. Special Publication 8. Washington, D.C.: American Anthropological Association.

Fortes, M. 1974. "The First Born." *Journal of Child Psychology and Psychiatry* 15:81–104.

Freud, S. 1909. "Analysis of a Phobia in a Five-Year-Old Boy." In *The Complete Psychological Works of Sigmund Freud,* ed. J. Strachey, vol. 10. Toronto: Clarke, Irwin, and Co.

———. 1925. "Some Psychical Consequences of the Anatomical Distinction between the Sexes." In *The Complete Psychological Works of Sigmund Freud,* ed. J. Strachey, vol. 19. Toronto: Clarke, Irwin, and Co.

Gell, A. 1977. "Magic, Perfume, Dream. . . ." In *Symbols and Sentiments,* ed. Ioan Lewis. New York: Academic Press.

Glasse, R. M. 1965. "The Huli of the Southern Highlands." In *Gods, Ghosts and Men in Melanesia,* ed. P. Lawrence and M. J. Meggitt. New York: Oxford University Press.

Glick, L. 1963. "Foundations of a Primitive Medical System: The Gimi of the New Guinea Highlands." Ph.D. dissertation, University of Pennsylvania.

Goodenough, W. H. 1953. "Ethnographic Notes on the Mae People of New Guinea's Western Highlands." *Southwestern Journal of Anthropology* 9:29–44.

Guthrie, W. K. C. 1962. *A History of Greek Philosophy.* Cambridge: Cambridge University Press.

Haiman, J. 1979. "Hua: A Papuan Language of New Guinea." In *Languages and their Status,* ed. T. Shopen. Cambridge: Winthrop Publishing Co.

———. 1980a. *Hua: A Papuan Language of the Eastern Highlands of New Guinea.* Amsterdam: John Benjamins.

———. 1980b. "Dictionaries and Encyclopedias." *Lingua* 50:329–357.

———. n.d. "Hua Folk Tales." Unpublished manuscript.

Harper, E. B. 1964. "Ritual Pollution as an Integrator of Caste and Religion." *Journal of Asian Studies* 23:151–197.

Hayano, D. M. 1974. "Misfortune and Traditional Political Leadership among the Tuana Awa of New Guinea." *Oceania* 45:18–26.

Heider, K. 1979. *The Grand Valley Dani*. New York: Holt, Rinehart and Winston.

Herdt, G. H. 1981. *Guardians of the Flutes: Idioms of Masculinity*. New York: McGraw-Hill.

Hershman, P. 1977. "Virgin and Mother." In *Symbols and Sentiments*, ed. Ioan Lewis. New York: Academic Press.

Herskovits, M. J. 1945. "The Process of Cultural Change." In *The Science of Man in World Crisis*, ed. R. Linton. New York: Columbia University Press.

Hogbin, I. 1970. *The Island of Menstruating Men*. Scranton: Chandler Publishing Co.

Hornabrook, R. W.; Crane, G.; and Stanhope, J. 1974. "Kar Kar and Lufa: An Epidemiological and Health Background to the Human Adaptability Studies of the International Biological Programme." *Philosophical Transactions of the Royal Society of London*, series B, 268:293–308.

———. 1977. "Human Ecology and Biomedical Research: A Critical Review of the International Biological Programme in New Guinea." In *Subsistence and Survival: Rural Ecology in the Pacific*, ed. T. Bayliss-Smith and R. G. Feachem. New York: Academic Press.

Hutton, J. H. 1928. "The Significance of Headhunting in Assam." *Journal of the Royal Anthropological Institute* 58:399–408.

Jacobson, E. 1950. "The Development of the Wish for a Child in Boys." *Psychoanalytic Study of the Child* 5:139–152.

Kelly, R. C. 1976. "Witchcraft and Sexual Relations." In *Man and Woman in the New Guinea Highlands*, ed. P. Brown and G. Buchbinder. A. A. A. Special Publication 8. Washington, D.C.: American Anthropological Association.

Labby, D. 1976. *The Demystification of Yap*. Chicago: University of Chicago Press.

Langness, L. L. 1967. "Sexual Antagonism in the New Guinea Highlands: A Bena Bena Example." *Oceania* 37:161–177.

Lawrence, P., and Meggitt, M. J., eds.. 1965. *Gods, Ghosts and Men in Melanesia*. New York: Oxford University Press.

Leach, E. 1964. "Anthropological Aspects of Language: Animal Categories and Verbal Abuse." In *New Directions in the Study of Language*, ed. E. H. Lenneberg. Cambridge: MIT Press.

———. 1966. "Virgin Birth." *Proceedings of the Royal Anthropological Institute* (1966):39–49.

Lévi-Strauss, C. 1963. *Totemism*. Boston: Beacon Press.
———. 1966. *The Savage Mind*. London: Weidenfeld and Nicolson.
———. 1967. *Structural Anthropology*. New York: Anchor Books.
———. 1969. *The Elementary Structures of Kinship*. Boston: Beacon Press.
Lewis, G. 1975. *Knowledge of Illness in a Sepik Society*. Atlantic Highlands, N.J.: Humanities Press.
Lindenbaum, S. 1972. "Sorcerers, Ghosts, and Polluting Women: An Analysis of Religious Belief and Population Control." *Ethnology* 11:241–253.
———. 1976. "A Wife Is the Hand of Man." In *Man and Woman in the New Guinea Highlands*, ed. P. Brown and G. Buchbinder. A.A.A. Special Publication 8. Washington, D.C.: American Anthropological Association.
Lloyd, G. F. 1964. "The Hot and the Cold, the Dry and the Wet in Greek Philosophy." *Journal of Hellenistic Studies* 84:92–106.
McKnight, D. 1973. "Sexual Symbolism of Food among the Wid-Mungkan." *Man* n.s. 8:194–209.
Mead, M. 1940. *The Mountain Arapesh*. Vol. 2. New York: Natural History Press.
Meggitt, M. J. 1962. *Desert People*. Sydney: Angus and Robertson.
———. 1964. "Male-Female Relationships in the Highlands of Australian New Guinea." *American Anthropologist* 66:204–224.
Meigs, A. S. 1976. "Male Pregnancy and the Reduction of Sexual Opposition in the New Guinea Highlands." *Ethnology* 9:393–407.
Newman, P. 1964. "Religious Belief and Ritual in a New Guinea Society." *American Anthropologist* 66:257–271.
———. 1965. *Knowing the Gururumba*. New York: Holt, Rinehart and Winston.
Norgan, N. G.; Ferro-Luzzi, A.; and Durnin, J. V. G. A. 1974. "The Energy and Nutrient Intake and the Energy Expenditure of 204 New Guinea Adults." *Philosophical Transactions of the Royal Society of London*, series B, 268:309–348.
Opler, M. E. 1945. "Themes as Dynamic Forces in Culture." *American Journal of Sociology* 51:198–206.
Panoff, F. 1970a. "Maenge Remedies and the Conception of Disease." *Ethnology* 9:68–84.
———. 1970b. "Food and Faeces: A Melanesian Rite." *Man* n.s. 5:237–252.

Paul, L. 1974. "The Mastery of Work and the Mystery of Sex in a Guatemalan Village." In *Woman, Culture, and Society*, ed. M. Z. Rosaldo and L. Lamphere. Stanford: Stanford University Press.

Pepper, S. 1948. *World Hypotheses*. Berkeley: University of California Press.

Radcliffe-Brown, A. R. 1964 (1922). *The Andaman Islanders*. Glencoe, Ill.: Free Press.

Rappaport, R. 1968. *Pigs for the Ancestors*. New Haven: Yale University Press.

Read, K. 1952. "Nama Cult of the Central Highlands of New Guinea." *Oceania* 23:1–25.

———. 1954. "Cultures of the Central Highlands of New Guinea." *Southwestern Journal of Anthropology* 10:1–43.

Reay, M. 1959. *The Kuma*. Melbourne: Melbourne University Press.

Reichel-Dolmatoff, G. 1971. *Amazonian Cosmos: The Sexual Symbolism of the Tukano Indians*. Chicago: University of Chicago Press.

Richards, A. I. 1948. *Hunger and Work in a Savage Tribe*. Glencoe, Ill.: Free Press.

Rigby, P. 1968. "Some Gogo Rituals of Purification: An Essay on Social and Moral Categories." In *Dialectic in Practical Religion*, ed. E. R. Leach. Cambridge: Cambridge University Press.

Salisbury, R. F. 1965. "The Siane of the Eastern Highlands." In *Gods, Ghosts and Men in Melanesia*, ed. P. Lawrence and M. J. Meggitt. New York: Oxford University Press.

Sapir, J. D. 1970. "*Kujaama*: Symbolic Separation among the Diola-Fogny." *American Anthropologist* 72:1330–1348.

Schieffelin, E. L. 1976. *The Sorrow of the Lonely and the Burning of the Dancers*. New York: St. Martin's Press.

Sherrington, C. 1955. *Man on His Nature*. Harmondsworth: Penguin.

Silberer, H. 1925. "A Pregnancy Phantasy in a Man." *Psychoanalytic Review* 12:377–396.

Sinnett, P. F. 1977. "Nutritional Adaptation among the Enga." In *Subsistence and Rural Ecology in the Pacific*, ed. T. Bayliss-Smith and R. G. Feachem. New York: Academic Press.

Skultans, V. 1970. "The Symbolic Significance of Menstruation and Menopause." *Man* n.s. 5:639–665.

———. 1977. "Bodily Madness and the Spread of the Blush." In *The Anthropology of the Body*, ed. J. Blacking. New York: Academic Press.

Spiro, M. E. 1966. "Religion: Problems of Definition and Explanation." In *Anthropological Approaches to the Study of Religion,* ed. M. Banton. London: Tavistock Publications.

Steiner, F. 1956. *Taboo.* New York: Philosophical Library.

Strathern, A. 1970. "The Female and Male Spirit Cults in Mt. Hagen." *Man* n.s. 5:571–585.

————. 1972. *One Father, One Blood.* Canberra: Australian National University Press.

Strathern, A., and Strathern, M. 1968. "Marsupials and Magic: A Study of Spell Symbolism among the Mbowamb." In *Dialectic in Practical Religion,* ed. E. R. Leach. Cambridge: Cambridge University Press.

Strathern, M. 1972. *Women in Between.* London: Seminar Press.

Tambiah, S. J. 1969. "Animals Are Good to Think and Good to Prohibit." *Ethnology* 8:423–459.

Tuzin, D. 1972. "Yam Symbolism in the Sepik: An Interpretive Account." *Southwestern Journal of Anthropology* 28:230–254.

————. 1980. *The Voice of the Tambaran: Truth and Illusion in Ilahita Arapesh Religion.* Berkeley: University of California Press.

Tylor, E. 1920. *Primitive Culture.* New York: G. P. Putnam's Sons.

Van Baal, J. 1966. *Dema.* The Hague: Martinus Nijoff.

Van Leeuwen, K. 1966. "Pregnancy Envy in the Male." *International Journal of Psychoanalysis* 47:319–324.

Wagner, R. 1967. *The Curse of Souw.* Chicago: University of Chicago Press.

————. 1972. *Habu: The Innovation of Meaning in Daribi Religion.* Chicago: University of Chicago Press.

Weiner, A. 1980. "Reproduction: A Replacement for Reciprocity." *American Ethnologist* 7:71–85.

Whiting, J. W. M. 1941. *Becoming a Kwoma.* New Haven: Yale University Press.

Wikan, U. 1977. "Man Becomes Woman: Trans-Sexualism in Oman as a Key to Gender Roles." *Man* n.s. 12:304–319.

Williams, F. E. 1969 (1936). *Papuans of the Trans-Fly.* London: Oxford University Press.

Young, M. W. 1971. *Fighting with Food.* Cambridge: Cambridge University Press.

INDEX

(Page numbers in italics indicate tabular material)

"You look good

Sitting at his desk, Mitch reached out one hand and rubbed the silk of her nightgown between his fingers and thumb.

If this were any other man, Kira suspected she'd have a flip comment at the ready. Because he had a way of stealing her words, the best she could offer was a reedy-voiced thanks.

He opened his legs and she stepped into the gap, settling her hands on his shoulders. His hands closed over her hips, pulling her even closer.

"Want to know why I can't concentrate?" Mitch asked.

"Probably not." It was a lie. She did want to know, especially if it involved any part of his body against hers.

"You've always made me crazy. Did you know that? You'd think after all these years I'd have gotten over it," he said. "That I could be near you without wanting to—"

In business, timing was everything, and Kira meant serious business. She leaned forward and kissed him deeply, using her tongue to tell him what she needed.

2/19

Dear Reader,

Here's one final visit to the resort town of Sandy Bend, Michigan, which we saw in *The Girl Most Likely To...* (Harlequin Temptation #922) and *The Girl Least Likely To...* (Harlequin Duets #94).

This time around, former spoiled heiress Kira Whitman is in a world of trouble. And for once, it's not her fault! Advised for her own safety to briefly leave her booming real estate career in Florida, Kira returns to Sandy Bend—where no one would ever think to look for her. She soon finds that as much as she's changed, one thing in her life hasn't: sexy cop Mitch Brewer still makes her pulse race. Despite his better judgment, Mitch is hot for Kira, too! When issues of trust collide with matters of the heart, life can get pretty tricky....

On a personal note, I want to thank you, my Harlequin Temptation readers, for the wonderful letters and notes I've received! Keep a lookout for where I'll pop up next by visiting my Web site at www.dorienkelly.com. You have been the very, *very* best!

Dorien Kelly

Books by Dorien Kelly

HARLEQUIN TEMPTATION
922—THE GIRL MOST LIKELY TO...

HARLEQUIN FLIPSIDE
 3—DO-OVER
27—IN LIKE FLYNN

HARLEQUIN DUETS
86—DESIGNS ON JAKE
94—THE GIRL LEAST LIKELY TO...

DORIEN KELLY

TEMPTING TROUBLE

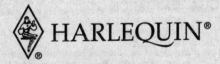

HARLEQUIN®

TORONTO • NEW YORK • LONDON
AMSTERDAM • PARIS • SYDNEY • HAMBURG
STOCKHOLM • ATHENS • TOKYO • MILAN • MADRID
PRAGUE • WARSAW • BUDAPEST • AUCKLAND

My thanks to Patti Denison of the Village Grounds
and Chris Shiparski of the Nickerson Inn for permission
to draw two of my favorite "real world" places
into the fictional realm of Sandy Bend.

This book is dedicated with much affection to Jennifer Green—
a goddess among editors. Thanks for your insight,
enthusiasm and boundless patience!

ISBN 0-373-69224-2

TEMPTING TROUBLE

This edition published by arrangement with Harlequin Books S.A.

® and TM are trademarks of the publisher. Trademarks indicated with
® are registered in the United States Patent and Trademark Office, the
Canadian Trade Marks Office and in other countries.

www.eHarlequin.com

Printed in U.S.A.

1

KIRA WHITMAN WAS SURE that if the concept of karma had any teeth to it, she'd now be a cockroach instead of one of South Florida's top-selling real estate agents. And as for those cynics who considered real estate agents on a par with cockroaches, Kira had no time for their negativity. She was too busy making hot bundles of cash.

Today was yet another perfect day in paradise. Kira and Roxanne, her partner in Whitman-Pierce Realty, had taken a long, top-down, music-cranking drive in Roxanne's beloved red Porsche. The nearly three-hour trip to Big Pine Key to check out a potential listing had been worth it. Casa Pura Vida was five bedrooms and six bathrooms of waterfront perfection.

The heels of Kira's sandals clicked against the flagstone terrace surrounding the swimming pool and guesthouse. She drew in a deep breath and smiled at the salty note in the tropical air. A humid breeze—nearly cool compared to Florida's customary June weather—eddied around her, flirting with the sheer silk of her skirt. Yes, she was one lucky girl. Far luckier than she deserved.

Kira turned back toward the house.

"Let's do one more walk-through," she said to her partner.

Roxanne's cell phone rang. She slipped it from the small designer bag slung over her shoulder. Kira watched as Roxanne checked the caller's number, muttered something blunt, then tucked the phone away without answering it. Hopefully the caller hadn't been a client, but Kira knew if she asked, she'd only be setting herself up for another of the in-your-face exchanges that she and Roxanne had been having recently.

By the time they reached the house, Roxanne's phone had stopped its hot Latin salsa ring tones, then started once again. She ignored it—something Kira was finding impossible to do.

"Don't you think you should get that?" she finally blurted.

"It'll keep," Roxanne said with a shrug that came off more like a nervous twitch. "So, what do you think we should ask for this place—five and a half?"

"No, six-four at least," Kira replied as she swung open the French doors leading into the great room.

She glanced over her shoulder. Roxanne had stopped in her tracks and was scrolling through the missed calls on her cell phone. Whoever was listed made her partner wince.

Focusing on something more positive than Roxanne, Kira moved on to scope out the gourmet kitchen, with its one-way glass wall facing the lush landscaping around the circular drive in front of the house. She had just enough imagination to know why the homeowners wanted to make sure they could see out while no one could see in. The secluded waterfall nook off the dining area brought to mind activities with more sensual sizzle than cooking a hot meal.

Kira returned to the middle of the kitchen and rested her hip against the central island where she and Roxanne had left their briefcases when they'd come in. She stood straighter as her partner finally made her way into the room.

"Six-four? Are you sure?" Roxanne asked, picking up the conversation as though it had never been interrupted.

"Positive."

Kira's ability to sniff out the last cent of value was a family gift. Her father, who she hadn't spoken to in three years, was a major real estate mogul in Chicago. He collected office buildings the same way some men his age did classic cars.

All those teenage years Kira spent half listening to dinnertime business talk had paid off. She was a natural at real estate and loved being paid to snoop around other people's houses. Even if she'd had to drastically downscale her lifestyle, earning her own income was proving to be far easier than dealing with the killer strings attached to her father's money.

Roxanne scrounged through her disaster zone of a briefcase and pulled out her PDA—her one concession to organization, and that only because she thought it made her look important. She distractedly tapped some numbers into it, then shook her head. "I say we list lower. We're talking less than a million dollars' difference, anyway. We're better off turning the place quickly."

Roxanne had been Kira's "in" to the moneyed set when she'd moved south and settled in Coconut Grove three years ago. Their partnership had made good sense when they'd first joined forces. Roxanne had kept the books and the office operating smoothly, while Kira had concentrated on sales. Both of them had loved the wild escape of the South Beach nightlife.

Then Roxanne had changed. And, to be fair, maybe Kira had, too. Still, Kira managed to have her share of fun. She enjoyed fast boats and good champagne as much as the next ex-heiress. But for the past several months Roxanne had been partying as though it was an extreme sport. She'd dropped the set of friends that she and Kira had in common, saying they'd begun to bore her. She was showing up at the office later, working less and still expecting more cash to magically come her way. Kira's tolerance was wearing thin.

"This isn't about us," Kira said. "I ran the comps, and for this area six-four is right in the market." For emphasis, she nudged the file jutting out of her own better organized portfolio. "The client deserves to get the full value. You told me that this is a second home, so there's no rush to sell, right?"

"He, uh—" Roxanne broke off from whatever she'd been about to say.

Kira followed her line of vision. An enormous black SUV had pulled up behind Roxanne's car.

Roxanne stilled. They watched a man get out of the passenger side of the vehicle and circle Roxanne's Porsche. Another guy got out of the SUV and joined him.

"Is one of them the homeowner?" Kira asked, though she already had her doubts. Roxanne wouldn't be acting this uptight if it were.

Roxanne shook her head. "Not exactly."

"Friends of yours?"

It had taken all of Kira's willpower not to pour on

the sarcasm when saying *friends*. Back in Kira's wild days, she might have dabbled in low places but never quite the depths that Roxanne was currently plumbing. These guys were so slick looking that they could trigger a run on the sanitizer market. Kira wrinkled her nose at the imagined scent of their cologne—one of those kinds with a hypermacho name like Spike or Thrust, and applied with an industrial sprayer, too.

"They're more acquaintances," Roxanne said quickly, pocketing her cell phone. "Hang on for a second and I'll get rid of them." She left before Kira could respond.

Kira watched though the front window as Roxanne talked to the men. Her arms were crossed and her stance had enough bulldog to it that Kira knew this was no friendly chat.

After a few moments, Kira was distracted from her efforts at long-distance lipreading by her phone's ring. She checked the number and fought the urge to ignore the call, figuring it wouldn't be fair when she'd just zapped Roxanne for the same behavior.

On the other end was Kira's most demanding client. Kira greeted Madeline and tried to answer her questions about the exact number of electrical outlets and light switches in an old Coral Gables mansion while she kept an eye on whatever the hell was happening outside.

Kira finished humoring Madeline, but the argument on the other side of the glass wall raged on. Just as Kira debated the wisdom of going out there to play peacemaker, Roxanne subtly raised a finger toward Kira and mouthed something that looked like *Be right back.*

Kira shot to the window wall and smacked her palm against the cool, thick glass. "Hey! What are you doing?"

Roxanne, of course, could neither see nor hear her. Kira watched in disbelief as her partner climbed into the back of the SUV.

"Dammit!"

She made a mad grab for her cell phone and autodialed Roxanne's number as the SUV backed down the drive then disappeared. Roxanne's message kicked in after one ring.

"Hi, you've reached the voice mail of Roxanne Pierce. Please leave your name, number and a detailed message after the tone. I'll get back to you as soon as possible."

Yeah, like *now* would be good. "Roxanne, it's Kira. Give me a call and tell me what's going on."

Kira snapped her phone shut and glared at Roxanne's car, since that was as close as she could get to its absent owner. She checked her watch—one-twenty—then called the office.

"Hey, Susan," she said once their receptionist answered. "Do me a favor and call my cell if Roxanne checks in…. Yes, she's supposed to be with me, but it looks like she got sidetracked." After fielding a few questions about new listings from a sales associate who had floor duty for the afternoon, Kira hung up and returned to waiting.

Fifteen minutes passed. Then twenty grew into forty. Two more calls to Roxanne's phone had produced only the same message. Kira supposed she should be worried, except this was Roxanne. The combined fingers, toes and sundry other appendages of the Miami Dolphins wouldn't be sufficient to count the number of times in recent memory that she'd forgotten an appointment, taken an unannounced vacation or otherwise left Kira to twist slowly in the wind. The only thing that stopped Kira from being totally fed up was the knowledge that just a few years ago she'd been as irresponsible as Roxanne.

For lack of anything else to do, Kira walked to the waterfall nook and touched her fingertips to the cool spray tumbling down the slate wall into the pool beneath. A bit of the tension eased from her muscles as she stood there. Kira smiled. This was definitely a house to be shared with a man. Someone sexy, tall and muscled, with slow, sure hands and a fast sense of humor...

Someone like Mitch Brewer...

Yow! Where had that come from?

Totally rattled, Kira backed from the water. Maybe Casa Pura Vida had a Fountain of Truth instead of a Fountain of Youth. Wouldn't that look great on the features sheet if she ended up listing the place?

She hadn't consciously thought of Mitch Brewer in years. Okay, months. And never mind the recurring dreams; she was willing to admit that her subconscious was beyond her control. It wasn't easy to forget a man who ticked her off as easily as he turned her on. But Mitch and the town of Sandy Bend, Michigan, were in her past. She'd been another girl, and not one she—or much anyone else—wanted to revisit.

A full hour inched by. To mark the event, Kira searched Roxanne's briefcase—a zero-guilt activity. She turned up the keys to both Casa Pura Vida and Roxanne's Porsche. At least she wasn't going to have to call someone from the office to come get her. So far she'd managed to hide Roxanne's increasingly erratic behavior from the staff.

Kira snooped around and found the command center for the house's built-in stereo system. Music made better company than the silence shredding her nerves. She wished she had something to sit on, but the homeowner hadn't left any furniture behind. Even a hard folding chair would have done. She'd hurt her right hip and leg as a teenager, and too much standing flat-out hurt.

The hour crept all the way to two-thirty and twenty seconds, enough time to play three games of solitaire on her PDA—the twin to Roxanne's and a Christmas gift from her partner.

Kira wasn't one hundred percent clear on what the correct amount of time to wait when given a be-right-back-message might be. Her mother and sisters would know; they could give Miss Manners a run for her money. Even her older brother Steve, who was far more laid-back, seemed to have a rule for every situation. If Kira had been on speaking terms with any of them, including Miss Manners, that tidbit might have been helpful. Since she wasn't, she decided to give Roxanne another half hour.

By three o'clock Kira was running on the pure steam of anger over being victim of yet another stupid Roxanne trick. She gathered her belongings and Roxanne's, locked up Casa Pura Vida and began the long trip back to the Coconut Grove office.

Whitman-Pierce's parking lot was empty and the sun was beginning to flirt with the cityscape by the time Kira pulled in next to her car. She felt fried, both physically and mentally. She quickly sorted through the jumble of stuff on the front seat, pulling out what was hers and leaving Roxanne the rest. She stopped in the empty office just long enough to check her voice mail for a message from Roxanne—there was none, naturally—and to toss Roxanne's car keys on her desk.

As she headed for home, Kira debated whether to pour herself a well-earned cocktail before or after she called her father at his summerhouse in Michigan.

"Definitely before," she murmured to herself.

She was already well aware that her company's short track record didn't make her a favorite with banks. It was going to take some world-class boot-licking to get her father to lend her the money to buy out Roxanne. A shot of vodka would temporarily numb her hard-earned pride.

Kira turned onto Jacaranda Drive, to the one-story same-as-all-the-others rental house where she'd been living for the past three years. Relatively cheap rent meant that she had a decent sum saved to buy a place she really wanted. Unfortunately that amount was nothing compared to what she'd have to pay for a life away from Roxanne.

As Kira neared her driveway, she saw two men standing on her front stoop. They didn't look familiar from behind, at least. She slowed her car to a near crawl. An older man dressed in a black golf shirt and pants hideously too tight for his gut walked around the side of her house to join the men at her front door.

On a day less weird, she would have considered the possibility that she was being paid a fund-raising visit by a door-to-door advocacy group—Polyester Addicts Anonymous or something. Not today, though.

Kira hauled butt past her driveway, turned the corner, and then proceeded at a less breakneck pace. A blue minivan was parked on the opposite side of the street about halfway down the block. As Kira neared, her gaze briefly locked with the occupant's. There was nothing special about the woman in the driver's seat. She looked like any brown-haired, conservative, suit-wearing, middle-management something-or-another pulled over to use her cell phone. Nothing in her bland expression that should have caused a jolt to Kira's nervous system. But jolted she was. Since she believed in trusting her instincts, Kira settled her foot harder on the accelerator and shot toward the main road.

A muttered litany—"Man, oh, man, oh, man"— didn't do much to calm her. Among the problems that came with being the currently celibate, overworked type was a lack of guys to call when the air-conditioning quit or goons lurked at her door. Kira had found a good AC man but remained fresh out of goonbusters. The only person she could think to call was Susan, the office receptionist. Susan's brother was a private investigator. Maybe Kira could just casually ask for his number for a friend of a friend or some other such semitransparent lie. It wasn't much of a plan but she was out of better ideas.

Watching the traffic, she sent her hand searching across the car's console for her cell phone. She'd retrieved it and was ready to dial when it rang, sending another blast of adrenaline through her veins.

Once she'd retrieved her heart from her throat, she answered. "H-hello?"

"We know you have them."

"Have what?" she managed to say to the unfamiliar male caller as she hit her right-turn signal and pulled into a dry cleaner's parking lot. No way could she drive and deal with a mystery caller all at once.

"Don't play stupid."

Sad to say but this was no act. "I really don't know what you're talking about. Scout's honor."

"Roxanne said you do. You know who Roxanne is, right?"

"Yes."

"Then you're not too stupid. She said she gave them to you yesterday. Now all you gotta do is deliver."

Kira briefly rested her forehead against the center of the steering wheel. Roxanne gave her *what*, besides enough stress that she'd taken up teeth grinding as a hobby? "Did it ever occur to you that Roxanne's lying?"

The caller laughed, but somehow Kira didn't feel charmed.

"Not this time, babe," he said. "Stick them in an envelope and leave 'em tonight at the front desk of the Hotel Coco for Suarez. And do it alone. Got it?"

Kira rolled her eyes. She wasn't going anywhere alone, and especially not to the Hotel Coco, which had some sort of cokehead-Miami-Vice-retro-sleaze attractant in its air. Roxanne loved the place as much as Kira hated it. "Yeah. Alone. Sure."

"Good."

The jerk clearly didn't grasp the finer nuances of sarcasm. Kira tried again. "Look, buddy, you're wasting our time. Talk to Roxanne again. I don't know what 'they' are and no way am I going to the—"

She drew to a stop as she realized from the absolute silence on the other end that her caller had hung up. Kira flipped shut her phone, then checked her caller log.

"Great."

According to her phone, Out of Area had just been harassing her. She dialed Roxanne one more time, since there was no one better to clear up this mess— a stinging indictment of her life.

"Hi, this is Roxanne Pierce," a new, cheery Roxanne voice-mail greeting announced. "I'm on vacation, and you're not. Leave a message and I'll get back to you."

On vacation? Kira gripped the phone tighter, fantasizing that it was Roxanne's throat.

"Roxanne, this is Kira. I don't know what kind of mess you've dragged me into this time, but I'm not playing, okay? Call me, and do it now."

Kira closed her phone and considered her limited options. She could take Roxanne at her perky vacation words and go with a no-worries attitude, but she figured she wasn't delusional enough to pull off that act.

The police were out. If Roxanne was missing—and that was an enormous *if*—she hadn't been gone long enough for them to even bother preparing a report. Kira knew she needed an outsider, though. Someone objective. Someone experienced. Someone who wasn't functioning on shot nerves and the paranoia born of spotting polyester goons on her doorstep.

She rearmed herself with her phone, called Susan the receptionist and prepared to do some private-investigator-type wheedling. As she waited for Susan to answer, the blue minivan Kira had earlier spotted illegally parked drove slowly by.

A chill chased across her skin.

Paradise had grown very ugly around the edges.

2

LIE LOW, THE PRIVATE investigator had told her. Go someplace out of the norm.

"You've got that one covered," Kira muttered to herself.

A day and a half after the visitation of the goons, she had reached her destination. Gritty-eyed from endless driving and one failed sleep attempt in a not-quite-chain motel outside Knoxville, Tennessee, she could safely say she'd sunk about as low in matters of personal hygiene as she ever wanted to.

Welcome to Sandy Bend read the sign on the southern edge of the approaching town.

"Welcome? Fat chance," Kira replied as she drove past.

It had been three years and oceans of bad blood since she'd last visited. Back in her bad old days, a stay in the quaint Lake Michigan resort town had seemed nearly as appealing as being dropped bikini-clad into Siberia.

Except for the Mitch Brewer factor.

No matter how boring she had found Sandy Bend's lack of designer-label amenities, the knowledge that he was around had always been worth a thrill. They were dead opposites and had clashed whenever in the same place. In fact, Kira had made sure of it, verbally pushing him until he'd pushed back. He'd been a tough adversary, unwilling to back down just because she was very female and very rich. Back then one of those two factors had been enough to turn nearly everyone else around her into doormats.

Out of habit, Kira slowed her car and noted the speeding of her heart as she passed the police station. Feeling that old tingle of excitement, she searched for Mitch's aged black Mustang—more salvage project than classic—in the lot. Nope, not a Mustang to be seen. Of course, she had no idea if Mitch still drove the same car.

She did know that he remained a Sandy Bend cop. She'd managed to pry that much loose in a nearly civil Christmas phone call she had exchanged with her brother, Steve. Steve was married to Mitch's sister, Hallie. Once upon a time, many screwups ago, Hallie had been Kira's friend. There was no clear definition of what Mitch had been to Kira—not friend, not lover, but definitely memorable.

But she wasn't here to see Mitch, Hallie or anyone else in town. She was here because nobody in their right mind would expect it. Including herself.

Also unexpected were the changes in town. As Kira drove down Main Street, she noted a day spa, several clothing boutiques, a jeweler and more new restaurants than she could take in. If the place had been this interesting when she was younger, she might not have spent so many bored hours trying to annoy the locals. Then again, maybe not. After a few years with a shrink and a lot of growing up, she knew now that she would have been hell to deal with no matter where she was.

Kira turned left off the main route and headed for the beach road to her parents' cottage, which bore no more resemblance to a small, homey retreat than she did to a saint. Theirs was the sort of place that made editors of glossy architectural magazines pant and drool. Kira also recognized that it was a spectacular investment, even if it was as stark and empty as a gallery of modern art. Matters of personal taste aside, since her parents were seldom in town, it remained the ideal spot to settle until matters in Florida could be sorted out.

Kira pulled into the mouth of the driveway, put her car in park, stepped out and punched the security code into the gate's lockbox. The number hadn't changed—062671, commemorating the day her father closed his first deal on a piece of Chicago's Miracle Mile real estate.

"Very touching, Dad," she said as the gate drew open. With a soft whirring hum, the security camera turned its cyclops eye her way. She waggled her fingers at whoever was watching on the other end.

Once up the winding drive, Kira parked, exited the car again and tried to smooth the worst of the wrinkles from her formerly gorgeous skirt. She knew she looked as if she'd crawled semievolved from the laundry pile, and her right hip ached more than usual.

By the time she'd trudged up the countless bluestone steps to the house's entrance, someone was waiting at the door. Not family, but nearly so. Rose Higgins had taken care of the Whitman family's Sandy Bend home for as far back as Kira could remember.

Rose took in Kira's less-than-perfect appearance and looked pleased at the flaws. "Well, if it isn't Miss Kira."

Despite the sting to her ego, Kira forgave the housekeeper the slight smirk lingering at the corners of her mouth. She'd done a great job of earning that expression through a childhood of snotty behavior. Though to fairly allocate blame, the British-born Rose hadn't exactly been Mary Poppins when Kira was little.

"Hi, Rose. It's nice to see you. And do you think we could drop the 'Miss' in front of my name?"

One efficient arch of Rose's silver brows was enough to convey the message that she had words other than *Miss* that she'd be willing to substitute.

Kira pressed on, since she wasn't ready for the death march back to her car. "Are my mom or dad home?"

"They're in London with your brother and sister-in-law and won't be back till late August."

Perfect!

Kira was now the recipient of seven thousand square feet of gated, luxurious solitude. She took a step closer to the door, nearly salivating at the thought of the steam shower in her bedroom suite.

"I don't think they'd mind if I stayed a few days, do you?" Kira asked, though she considered the question a mere formality.

Rose barred the door, one hand on its frame. "Perhaps not, but I suspect your bed will be a bit tight, what with the renters in residence."

"Renters? Come on, Rose. Dad never rents out this house."

"Until now. New business associates of your father's, you know." The housekeeper stepped back from the door and readied to close it. "Should your parents call, I'll mention that you dropped in for a visit."

Visions of steam showers began to fade into the mist, leaving Kira with the solid knowledge that she was tired, ripe and stuck in a town where she was only slightly more welcome than the tax assessor.

"Don't bother," Kira said.

Rose's smirk blossomed into a full evil grin.

"'Bye, then." The door closed with a convincing thud.

Kira squared her shoulders and ignored her stomach's grumbling that it was past lunchtime and no lunch had been delivered. She'd never been this exhausted. Or desperate, either. She was out of cash and unwilling to use her ATM card or credit cards for fear of being traced. Maybe she was overreacting, but she preferred being conservative to being goon-stalked.

"Okay, so next?" she asked herself as she wound down the hillside toward her car.

Either hunger or desperation had sharpened her mind, because she quickly settled on a plan. If Steve and Hallie were in London, their house might at least be vacant. And since their house just happened to be the old Whitman cottage, left to languish after the monument to glass and steel now behind Kira had been built, she knew its flaws—right down to the bedroom window with the broken latch that she'd slipped out nearly every summer night as a teenager.

Kira smiled. Sometimes being a bad girl was a very good thing.

THE WORST THING ABOUT LIFE in Sandy Bend was that everyone knew everyone else's business. That, Mitch Brewer felt compelled to add, could also sometimes be the best thing about life in Sandy Bend.

Thanks to a highly concerned citizen—one usu-

ally the source of complaints about misaligned garbage cans and unsightly gardens—whoever had broken into his sister's house hadn't been there very
long. Since Mitch was keeping an eye on the place for
Steve and Hallie while they were gone, he damn well
knew that no visitors were expected.

Mitch walked a circle around the sleek blue car
parked in front of the large, rambling log home. He'd
been a cop for nearly ten years. In all that time he
couldn't say that he'd run across many members of
the local breaking-and-entering set who drove a Mercedes. He checked the car's rear plate—Florida—
and called in the numbers.

A few moments later, a high-tech office worker
called the search results to his low-tech squad car.

"No sh—" managed to escape before Mitch got a
grip on his mouth.

"None at all," answered Barb over at the county
sheriff's office.

Mitch gave his thanks to Barb, then a silent one to
whatever power had just delivered him Kira Freakin'
Royal Princess Whitman. He knew she'd been in
Florida and he never expected her to return to Sandy
Bend. Finally he had a chance to return about one
one-thousandth of the crap she'd shoveled his way
over the years.

His smile grew as he walked to the house.

"Police," he called as he pounded on its door.
"Anyone in there?"

Of course there was. And damn, what he'd give
to see her I'm-dead-now expression.

Mitch counted to three, pounded and called again.
When no one answered, he fished a key ring from his
pants pocket and unlocked the house.

"Police," he repeated as the ancient oak door creaked open.

Mitch entered, then pocketed his keys. Somewhere upstairs a radio blared. Following the sound, he climbed the broad staircase. The station that Her Royal Highness had chosen was only partially tuned in, static competing with music. As he neared the source, he picked up two new noises: a shower running and a woman wailing. Not girlie sniffing, crying or weeping, but the full-out howl that he usually got from little kids who had misplaced their parents.

Mitch ventured a step closer. "Police?"

He scowled at the way the statement had come out as a question. Not that it mattered. Kira Whitman had begun to drown out even the radio.

Mitch settled his palm against the bathroom door, debating the wisdom of knocking. He'd barely begun to consider the pros when the door moved away from his hand, swinging inward. As it did, time slowed and he forgot how to swallow...and breathe.

Mitch kept a mental tally of never-to-be-repeated errors he called his Big Mistake List.

Not going immediately from college to law school? Big Mistake number one.

Not moving out of the family farmhouse the second that his older brother—and boss—Cal had gotten married and moved his bride in? Big Mistake number two.

Forgetting that Kira Whitman had a body that had kept him hard and aching for most of his formative youth? Big Mistake number three and rising fast. Very fast.

Her back was to him as she stood in the claw-foot

tub, head tipped back and water pouring down as she wailed. If he were a responsible citizen, he might warn her of the dangers of drowning, standing with her mouth open so close to that stream of water. Of course, if he were a responsible citizen, he might also turn away, since the clear plastic shower curtain painted with the occasional dragonfly wasn't doing much to hide her.

Mitch wasn't feeling at all responsible. He looked long enough to confirm that she was still sleek, blond and possessed of the finest butt that Sandy Bend would ever see.

Then he remembered how she'd swung between taunting him and being nearly tender for too many summers. How she'd gotten herself arrested during a Chicago bar brawl and never managed to make it to Steve and Hallie's wedding, diminishing his sister's joy that day. And how she'd coldly ditched her own fiancé at the altar less than a year later. Yeah, looking elsewhere got a whole lot easier with all of that to balance the action going on below his belt.

Mitch made his way downstairs to the living room, then settled in for a wait. He could afford to be a patient man…especially now that he'd seen Kira Whitman bare-ass naked.

A GIRL COULD CRY FOR ONLY SO long, and Kira for less than most. She lasted until the radio began to blare an old disco song about tough girls surviving. Even the most well-deserved bout of exhausted self-pity couldn't survive the feel-good power of Gloria Gaynor.

Kira ignored the sharp stinging of her skinned knees and elbows—victims of the fact that she couldn't climb trees and negotiate roofs quite as well as she had at age fifteen. She slicked back her hair and joined in for the song's last chorus. Then, after giving herself one last scrub with Hallie's marvelous lavender-scented soap, she turned off the tub's taps.

She dried her hair with a fluffy white towel after wrapping another around her body. Kira sighed at the soft comfort.

"Egyptian organic cotton…nothing better," she said.

And she should know, since she'd sent Steve and Hallie a dozen of these buggers as a wedding gift. That she'd done it on her dad's store account no longer sat very well. She shook off the guilt twinge. If something as simple as a mooched wedding gift was making her feel bad, she'd be flogging herself on Sandy Bend's village green before her little visit was over.

Now that she was clean enough that she could tolerate being in her own skin, food was the next order of business. Her stomach's grumbling had risen to an angry growl. She wasn't sure what she'd find in the kitchen, but unless Hallie's tastes had changed, Kira knew that survival was a good bet.

When they were teenagers, Hallie had scarfed down all the stuff Kira wouldn't permit herself to eat—French fries, chocolate, ice cream and soda with a full load of calories and sugar. And the girl had stayed downright skinny, which Kira had viewed as both unfair and unnatural. Today, though, she was thankful.

Mouth watering, she tightened her towel and made a beeline downstairs. She'd just crossed the hallway past the living room when a male voice said, "All cried out, huh?"

Kira screeched. The sound carried all the shrill

terror of an ingenue in her first slasher film. No face-less bad guy approached, though. That might have been preferable as she had six feet four worth of Mitch Brewer ambling her way. At the sight, her in-tellect turned tail, leaving only instinct to do battle.

"But you're not all screamed out, I guess," he added.

Fight-or-flight response had kicked in, and Kira was coming down on the side of fight. "Are you out of your mind, creeping around and scaring me to death? I should call the police on you." Which sounded very good until she realized that a man in blue already stood in front of her, and yes, he was in uniform. "Okay, forget the police, but you'd better give me a really good reason for being here."

He smiled, and as always she was a sucker for it. What female wouldn't be when looking up at tanned skin, white teeth and matching dimples?

"Funny, Your Highness," he said. "I was going to ask you for the exact same thing."

The real estate business had given Kira a certain relaxed glibness, but any talent she'd ever had at bald lies was damn rusty. Still, she gave it a try. "Not that you need to know, but Steve and Hallie said I could use the house while they're gone."

Mitch settled the knuckles of one hand against his lean hip and scratched at the back of his neck with the other hand. Kira could have recited in alphabetic order the names of her favorite designers—and there were many—in the interval before he spoke.

"Huh. Really?" he asked.

The Mitch Brewer she recalled was as sharp as they came, and Kira was in no mood for his clueless-country-cop gambit.

"Yes, they really said that."

"Interesting. How about the use of Hallie's clothes? Any offers there?"

She frowned, trying to get a sense of where he was heading, since Hallie was inches taller and probably still a clothing size smaller. "Why?"

"You're a little underdressed," he said, gesturing her way with a casual flick of his hand. "Now, don't get me wrong, Highness. I don't mind at all, but I thought you might."

Kira's hands tightened over plush terry cloth. Why was it that the most humiliating moments in life seemed to take the longest? Pleasure danced and flew, but the realization that you were wearing only a towel in front of the guy you'd least like to lose your dignity around—again!—took for-stinking-ever.

She glanced down in a last futile hope that he was jerking with her. But the nearly naked truth remained: she was wearing one lovely and expensive towel.

She looked back at Mitch. His blue-eyed gaze traveled a leisurely route from her head to the tips of her toes and then up again. She knew she should be angry, but more than anything she was *aware*.

Aware of the blood rushing just beneath skin growing more sensitive by the second.

Aware of the appreciation—and something more dangerous—in Mitch's expression.

Then that damned smile of his returned, playing slowly across his face. Something about it—as though he held a secret that he had no intention of sharing—really frosted her.

"I'm going upstairs," she said, letting a chill settle in her voice. "Unless you're not through staring."

"Oh, I've seen enough."

Kira turned heel. "Then you can let yourself out."

She had reached the lower landing when she heard him say, "Actually, I'll be right here when you're done dressing, Highness. We're going to give Hallie and Steve a call."

Kira stopped, shaken at the thought.

A call to Steve risked too much: her safety, her pride and most of all the potential deep pain of having her brother pitch her into the street. Considering all the grief she'd thrown his way, she could hardly blame him if he did.

She figured she had one shot left. She could derail Mitch Brewer. For the hardwired-to-flirt Kira of summers past that would have been a no-brainer. After drawing a steadying breath, she turned to face the guy who'd always seen the worst of her and offered up some more.

"How about if I just take off this towel, instead?"

3

MITCH WAS A REASONABLY perceptive guy. Good thing, since both his present and future careers demanded a nose for the truth. He moved closer to Kira. Not too close, because he was also a sane guy, which was a miracle considering his life recently. He'd survived four years of attending law school on and off while still working endless shifts on the force. Still, he knew his limits, and the sight of Kira Whitman wearing only a white towel was outside the bounds. But even from his circumspect three feet away, beneath the flowery scent that clung to her damp skin, he smelled fear.

Sure, she had a sexy purr down to an art, and the hot promise in her brown eyes seemed almost real. A more gullible guy—or even one with less conscience—would snap up her offer.

Kira's fingers toyed with the upper edge of her towel, venturing into the valley between her breasts. Until that moment, he'd been sure that she was bluffing. Now he had his doubts. Since Kira had always been mostly talk, she must be damn scared.

"Hang on, there, Highness," he said, regretting that back when he was a kid, he'd listened to and absorbed his father's speeches about duty and moral fiber. "Whether you're naked or not, we're calling Steve."

"But—but…" Her gaze skittered around the entry hall, then settled on the grandfather clock that was just outside an archway leading to the dining room. "It's after midnight in London."

It was tough not to grin at her triumphant expression, but Mitch was up for the job.

"Hallie's a night owl," he replied. "I'll bet they're still awake."

"There's no point in bothering them. Do you really think I'd move in here without my brother's permission?"

Mitch snorted. "Given your track record, I don't think you want me to answer that one." He walked to the kitchen, knowing that she would follow. He lifted the phone from its base and began to punch in the number that Hallie had left for him on the message pad.

Kira made a grab for him. "Wait! Don't call!"

He was less than impressed at the way he was rousing from something as simple as the touch of her hands on his arm. Mitch resettled the phone, and Kira backed off, fear still shadowing her expression. He was curious to see what would happen next. From the time she'd first noticed guys, Kira Whitman had been a class-A ballbuster, in a stealthy sort of way. She lulled males with her looks and then messed with their minds—himself included. He'd seen her blow hot and cold, but he'd never seen her this vulnerable.

"So?" he prompted.

"Really, I didn't break in," she said. "Maybe I came inside, but technically I didn't break in. I just—"

"Let's skip the semantics." He got enough of that stuff at school. "You're in here without permission, right?"

Her nod was almost imperceptible.

"Want to tell me why?"

"I decided to come for a visit."

This definitely placed in the top ten of total BS tales. "Unannounced? After three years?"

She didn't even hesitate. "Why not? Maybe I haven't been the best of Whitmans, but better late than never."

"So you're telling me that you drove all the way from Florida on the spur of the moment?"

She frowned. "How did you know that I've been in Florida?"

Luckily he had an easy answer to fall back on, since there was no way he'd confess that he'd known for a couple of years that she'd taken her party act south. Her ego was already plenty healthy without evidence of his continuing curiosity.

"Your car's plates," he said.

"Oh."

"Time to come clean, Highness." Saying the words only reminded him that she *was* clean and girlie-fragrant...and nearly naked. Mitch swallowed hard. "What's really up?"

Other than his hard-on.

She nibbled at her lower lip and then asked, "Haven't you ever acted on impulse?"

Bad question. Between the way his brother Cal drove him at work and the hours he spent studying, he had no room for impulse—a fact that ground at him.

"No," he said.

"Well, I have. It just so happened that I fell on a week or so that I could be away from work. I was thinking that I had relatives and old friends up here that I haven't seen…plus, uh, I just broke up with my boyfriend and I really, really needed to get away. You know, escape the places we'd been together and all that? So here I am, Brewer, and it shouldn't make any difference at all to you if I stay here."

Mitch started with the most obvious point. "Your family's not coming back until late August." He could have added that she was also seriously low on friends to visit in Sandy Bend, but that seemed too cruel—even when talking about Kira. "I can't let you stay here. I promised Hallie that I'd keep an eye on the place. If you'd let me call her, then maybe…"

He let the offer hang out there, half hoping she'd take it just so he could get the hell out of the house and not have to wonder why Kira Whitman was lying to him and why he was beginning to feel the need to help her.

"I can't."

"Then you're going to need to get your stuff and cruise on out of here with me."

She turned away from him, gripping her towel with both hands. "I can't do that, either."

Mitch hesitated—something he seldom did. He looked at the delicate curve of her shoulders, which appeared kissed gold against the white of the terry cloth. And he reminded himself once again that she was the laziest, most manipulative female he'd ever met. He almost had his hard-assed attitude back in place when he noticed that those perfect shoulders were shaking.

"Are you crying?" he asked.

"No. I never cry."

Which was another lie, but not one he could call her on, since that would clue her in that he'd been upstairs while she'd been showering. Mitch settled his hands on her shoulders and turned her to face him again, taking care not to let his grip linger longer than it had to.

"Go get dressed," he said. "I'll call one of the B and Bs in town and see if I can snag you a room."

"No!"

"What now?"

"I...um..." She brushed away the tear trailing down one cheek, and Mitch pretended that he didn't notice. He wasn't sure why he was trying to protect her dignity when she'd spent a youth jacking with others', but just because he didn't understand himself didn't mean he was in the mood to play tough with her, either.

She stood taller. Even then, the top of her head wasn't much above his chin. "I...just can't," she said.

Now, there was an explanation for the ages. Mitch did a gut check and knew he couldn't live with himself unless he said what had jumped into his brain. Of course, he wouldn't be able to live with himself once he had, either.

"You can stay with me, Highness, but just for the night. Got it?"

Her brown eyes widened. She was quiet for so long that he almost thought he was going to escape the payback for his insane impulse.

Yeah, *impulse.*

He guessed he had room for it in his life, after all.

"Okay," Kira said.

And now he had room for nothing else.

IF SOMEONE HAD ASKED KIRA where in Sandy Bend she'd least expect to find Mitch Brewer living, this would be the spot.

"Amazing," she said to herself as she pulled in behind Mitch, just in front of the Dollhouse Cottage.

She couldn't think of any image more incongruous than muscled, macho Mitch in this miniature white confection of a house. And she couldn't think of anything that would distract her from the sting of her battered sense of self-reliance better than finally seeing the inside of a place she'd secretly adored since childhood. It almost made up for crying in front of Mitch, who was definitely the last damn person she ever wanted to appear weak before again.

Kira felt a sense of peace come over her as she looked at the cottage. According to local lore, the house had been built back in the 1800s as a wedding gift from one of the town fathers for his youngest daughter. Just one story tall and dwarfed by the larger houses on the quiet residential street, it was far from the most elegant house in town, but Kira had always found its Victorian embellishments and two rose-hued stained-glass windows perfect.

Mitch climbed out of his car and walked to the white-spindled front porch. Kira trailed after him, appreciating the view...and not just of the house. As she did, she felt a waking of the awareness that had gripped her—and tripped her up—back at Steve and Hallie's house.

Mitch glanced back over his shoulder. "You coming?" he asked.

Since her mouth had gone dry, Kira simply nodded.

It seemed she could think of one activity that would distract her better than a tour of the Dollhouse. Too bad she wasn't an advocate of meaningless sex.

"I can't believe you live here," she said as Mitch unlocked the front door.

"What does that mean?"

He sounded irked, so she took a conciliatory tone. "Nothing, really. It's just this house is so feminine that it doesn't seem like your kind of place."

He stepped inside, then ushered her in. "I can afford it, which makes it my kind of place. Life's not cheap here, you know? The more the town changes, the more rent rises. But I guess that's not the kind of thing you Whitmans have to worry about, is it?"

She gave him her best socialite's smile. "We never discuss finances. Mother considers it crass." Which was true, as far as it went.

More nagging was the sense that Mitch was talking to a female long gone. He seemed to view her as some museum piece, frozen forever at age twenty. She wished she could shake him from that, but she'd learned ages ago that trying to change a guy was more painful than a Brazilian bikini wax.

Kira checked out her surroundings. The furnishings were most generously described as seventies curbside retro, but the bones of the house were spectacular. The ceilings were surprisingly high, which had to be a bonus to someone of Mitch's height. The living room floor was oak with an inlaid border of what appeared to be rosewood, and the old plaster walls were in amazing shape. She walked to the fireplace and rested one hand on the intricately carved mantel.

"Very nice," she said.

"I've been renting the place since Cal got married last year. Life on the farm got kind of crowded."

"Cal's married?" Mitch's older brother had always seemed too happy being the hot guy in town to ever marry.

Mitch nodded. "To Dana Devine. Remember her?"

"Sure." Dana was the same age as Kira and one of the few townies who'd awed her enough that Kira hadn't once harassed her. Dana was tough, smart and never backed down. All of which Kira supposed were essential qualities to have if one was, God forbid, married to a bullheaded Brewer.

"Don't you have a suitcase?" Mitch asked.

"I have a couple of things in the car. I can get them later." She always kept a change of clothes and a toiletry bag in her trunk, just in case. Still, one spare skirt and silk tank top weren't going to get her too far.

"A couple of things, huh? We're talking really spur of the moment. The sidewalk still rolls up at six around here, but tomorrow you should be able to pick up pretty much whatever you want at the shops."

True, except for that lack-of-cash problem…

"So," Kira said, "give me a tour."

"You're standing in the living room. Kitchen is that way. Bedrooms and the bath are on the other side," he said, pointing to his left. "You'll be sleeping there." He hitched a thumb toward a couch that looked like a fraternity-house castoff.

"There?"

A slow smile spread across his face. "Not quite the Four Seasons, is it, Highness?"

"I thought you said you have more than one bedroom?"

"Two. One's mine, and I guess you can have the other if you want to sleep on my weight bench."

"Oh." Kira walked to the orange, yellow and brown plaid couch and ran a hand across it. The thing was clean, even if it had the texture of a scouring pad. "This will be perfect."

The look he gave her was skeptical, but he didn't say anything. Instead he left the room and then reappeared half a minute later with an armful of blankets, folded sheets and pillows.

He tossed them onto the couch, saying, "You're going to want a little padding. The springs are shot."

Kira couldn't quite decide if she'd ever encountered a couch with springs but figured it had to be more comfortable than sleeping in her car.

Mitch glanced at his watch. "I have to get back to the station. I'll be coming in late tonight, so don't wait up for me, huh?"

"Trust me, it wasn't an option," she said. Then impulsively added, "And, Mitch...thanks."

"Sure."

He looked as though he planned to take a step toward her. She settled one hand on the back of the terminally ugly couch, bracing herself for whatever might come. For all that she'd tried to repress her memories of one particular summer afternoon with this guy, she still knew the way his muscles felt beneath the palms of her hands, still remembered the taste of his kisses and still wanted more. She wondered what he remembered, what he wanted.

As they gauged each other, Mitch's relaxed expression honed itself to something harder.

"Don't get too comfortable," he said, then left her alone, her heart pounding, her knees uncharacteristically weak.

Comfortable?

While suffering from the Brewer effect, there was little chance of that.

HALF AN HOUR LATER, WHEN IT was nearly nine o'clock, Kira had recovered enough to cushion her "bed" with sufficient padding that she thought she might sleep, but found she was still too wired on emotion and unfamiliarity.

Seeking distraction, she perused the music collection in the corner of the living room by Mitch's stereo and found only one artist who didn't sit squarely in the headbanger camp. She'd bet anything that the Sheryl Crow CD had been a gift from a girlfriend, but she set aside the niggling and inappropriate bit of jealousy long enough to put the music on.

Songs passed. As Sheryl began to sing about her favorite mistake, Kira again felt bold enough to raid the kitchen. She smiled as she padded across the linoleum floor. This was the real deal—decades old and with a patina to its black-and-white pattern that the new stuff just couldn't ape.

Next to the back door sat an apartment-size stacked washer and dryer with a basket of neatly folded laundry in front of it. On top of the pile was a white T-shirt with the Sandy Bend Police Department emblem. Kira picked it up and unfolded it. The shirt came to her knees.

"Looks like jammies to me," she said, then quickly changed out of her dead-by-travel skirt and top and into Mitch's shirt. She tucked her undies into his dirty-laundry basket, planning to wash a load tomorrow as some minimal compensation for the lumpy couch he'd offered her.

Figuring that if she had the nerve to wear his clothes, she might as well also eat his food, she opened the fridge and peeked inside. The bagged prewashed lettuce and a package of cooked chicken-breast strips would make for a tolerable dinner. After snagging a bottle of Italian dressing from the door, Kira removed her haul and put together a salad in a big red plastic bowl that she found in a dish drainer next to the sink.

Bowl in one hand and fork in the other, she wandered from the kitchen, through the living room and toward the uncharted territory of the bedrooms. Door number one was ajar, so she nudged it with her elbow and strolled in the three steps she could.

Mitch had clearly saved up his decor dollars for the piece of furniture he thought most mattered. Kira stuck her fork into the salad bowl, then tested Mitch's king-size mattress with her free hand. It felt like paradise. Part of her—the tired and whiny part, to be exact—wanted to curl up on that bed, safe in the belief that it was so big, he'd never know she was there. The rest of her pathetically rational soul knew that wasn't true. Even if the bed were the size of the entire cottage, they'd sense each other's presence. They'd been tuned to each other for too many years to have it otherwise.

Kira turned her back on the bed, with its rumpled dark green paisley comforter and distinctively male scent of wood smoke and outdoors. Some territory best remained uncharted.

Room number two proved less unsettling. In the glow from the hallway's small light fixture she saw Mitch's weight bench with some free weights next to it. In one corner sat what appeared to be a desk, complete with computer.

Kira ran her hand along the wall to a light switch. She flipped it on, then walked toward the desk with no particular plan in mind.

Mitch had left his computer on, its soft hum blending with the louder sound of the ceiling fan turning overhead. Kira balanced her salad bowl on the edge of the desk and then nudged aside a massive book to make more room for herself. As she did, she noticed the title on the book's spine: *Federal Jurisdiction*. She'd have figured him for a guy fond of lighter reading.

Once she'd settled in the desk chair, she picked up her salad and munched for a while. Computers weren't her thing. She knew exactly enough to get her job done and no more. Roxanne had always been the one to play with the accounting and e-mail programs and to keep the firm's Web site current.

Still, Kira was computer conversant enough to see that Mitch's Internet connection was enabled.

"DSL in the backwoods. Who'd have imagined?"

She went to Whitman-Pierce's Web site and used her password to get in the back door to her e-mail. She held a deletefest with the bigger-faster-longer spam, then picked through the real items. While she hadn't expected an e-mail from Roxanne, it still ticked her off that there was none.

Time slipped by as she answered e-mails and sent some reminders to Susan back at the office about clients she'd need to find an associate to cover. Kira wondered how long she'd be able to act as an absentee boss. For better or worse she was a self-professed control freak, and not forty-eight hours into her "vacation," she was losing it.

She wished she hadn't trusted Roxanne to the degree that she had. If she'd been smart enough to get her partner's computer password, she'd be fifty percent more in control than she was at this moment.

Kira speared her last bit of bland salad, returned to the Web site's entry screen and began guessing at Roxanne's password. She worked her way through dead pets, parents and Roxanne's favorite cocktail but came up blank. It was time to move on to a new category.

"Boyfriends, crushes and flings," she muttered to herself.

"Alex, is the answer 'What are Kira's fondest memories?'" sounded a male voice from behind her.

Kira gave herself credit for not screeching this time, though sending the empty salad bowl flying when she jumped wasn't much better. She quickly exited out of the Web site password screen, then turned the swivel office chair to face Mitch. He'd shed his uniform in favor of a pair of jeans and a Michigan State football T-shirt that fit all too well.

"You've got a great future as a sneak," she said.

He raised the beer bottle in his right hand and toasted her. "So do you."

"Do you always creep around?"

"My house," he said. "I'll move any way I want to. That's also my cereal bowl and my shirt," he added.

Kira stood and smoothed out her pilfered T-shirt, perilously aware that she was lacking any form of underwear.

"So, what had you so busy that you didn't hear me come in?"

"Just cruising my favorite sites."

"Right. I've been watching you from the doorway

and you've been typing, not cruising." He took a swig of his beer and said, "I'm going to be straight up with you. I don't have patience for subterfuge and the other garden varieties of BS that you deal in. And for reasons I don't plan to spend a whole lot of time thinking about, I want to help you with whatever you've got going on."

She'd done nothing to improve his opinion of her tonight. And for reasons that *she* didn't plan to think about, Mitch's opinion mattered—very much so. The old Kira he'd known had used everyone else to make her life work. Need money? Suck up to Dad. Need dinner out? Manipulate some poor fool into thinking you were hot for him. Need a place to crash? Impose on a friend.

That last one hit way too close to home.

She'd fought so hard to change, to learn to stand alone. Now even Mitch's grudging hospitality made her ready to pull up the emotional drawbridge and put alligators in the moat. Her current situation was a snag, nothing more. She could handle it without him and maybe even redeem herself a little in his eyes. Spoiled rotten user of a princess just didn't cut it anymore.

Though it was tough to appear innocent when going commando, Kira tried. "Mitch, I don't have anything 'going on.' I'm here on vacation."

"With either no clothes or a T-shirt fetish."

"I'll plead guilty to the fetish."

He lifted one lazy fingertip and traced the top of the police-department emblem where it rested above her left breast. "I'll bet you will."

She could feel her nipples grow achingly sensitive and her heart nearly jump from her chest, but she kept her bluffer's face intact, not letting her gaze waver from his.

Then he leaned down and murmured low into her ear, "You're a good liar, Highness, but not that good. I'm gonna go get some rest. But if you feel the need to confess, come wake me. I've got a feeling your story would be worth the missed sleep."

For the second time that night, he left her. And for the second time that night, Kira Whitman wondered exactly what it took to get a step ahead of Mitch Brewer.

4

DAWN CAME EARLY ON THE WEST side of Michigan's lower peninsula—especially in mid-June. It wasn't much past six in the morning and already the sky had lightened to a watery blue. Mitch stood in his kitchen, full coffee mug in hand. He'd just finished his first round of breakfast—a meal that was usually a multi-course event for him.

He knew he should go to his desk and get some studying in before he was due at the station, but the lure of the woman sleeping so restlessly on his living room sofa was too strong. More than once last night he'd awakened to the sound of Kira's sleep-talking. Or more accurately, sleep-panicking. He'd wanted to check on her but couldn't allow himself that weakness.

Addiction was a word Mitch didn't use casually. As a cop, he'd come across too many people who'd had their lives shot to hell by the real thing. Still, whatever he felt for Kira had messed with him in one way or another since he was seventeen years old. Now he was over thirty and still not free of this...hell, he didn't know what it was.

On some subliminal level he'd always measured the women he'd dated against Kira Whitman. What made it even more miserable was that many of those girls had come out on the favorable end of the comparison. Some had been smarter and sexier, and damn near all of them had been more honest and good natured. But not one woman had lingered in his mind the way she did. She had the whole package—brains, beauty and attitude.

A few summers ago, when his sister had fallen in love with Kira's brother, Mitch had learned exactly how hooked he was. In a miserable mood that summer, Kira had launched a small-scale sabotage campaign against the couple. It seemed as though she'd decided that if she couldn't be happy, no one else could. The morning of the town's annual Summer Fun parade, Mitch had finally seen enough. He'd hauled her away from the throng gathered at the starting point of the parade, ready to deliver some pretty unattractive truths.

Hot words had given way to an even hotter kiss. And then after that, hell, his hands had been everywhere—on top of her clothes, under her clothes, touching places he'd fantasized about forever. She hadn't been exactly pushing him away, either. She'd been slammed by an orgasm, and her cry of pleasure—which he'd swallowed with a kiss—had reminded him that there was a crowd yards away, just around the corner of the high school.

Mitch had felt like garbage for taking advantage of a situation. Before he could pull his act together to apologize, she'd shoved him and sent him reeling backward. While she had straightened her clothes, he'd tried to make some verbal sense of what had happened, but she'd told him to shut up. A little while later he'd returned to his family's parade float and acted as if he'd gotten the best of Kira Whitman. In truth, she'd always had the best of him.

Nearly three years older but not one hell of a lot wiser, Mitch stuck the strawberry jam back in the refrigerator. As he settled his tub of marshmallow fluff into its easy-access place of honor next to the sink, he heard Kira on the couch, stirring and muttering something edged with stress.

What could be going on in a trust-fund princess's life that money couldn't cure?

"Focus," he reminded himself as his curiosity began to stir.

His summer session at school ended in less than a month. Assuming he passed this last course, he'd have enough credits to graduate and begin to study for the February bar exam. Though he was near the top of what had been his class, he hadn't graduated with them two weeks ago. Last November, the night before deer season opened, one drunken hunter with a bad attitude and worse aim had taken care of that.

Mitch knew that he was lucky his injuries hadn't been any worse, but that didn't mean he still wasn't pissed off. From his hospital bed, he'd worked a deal with the law school administration and withdrawn from two classes. He'd made up one class this past semester, but it hadn't been enough.

What really killed was that Betsy, his study partner, had been offered a clerkship with a federal judge in Grand Rapids. Mitch had interned with the same judge the year before. If he'd graduated on time, the position would have been his.

A federal clerkship was the sort of short-term opportunity that made a résumé hit the top of the stack. Since Betsy had also been one of those women who couldn't compete with Mitch's memories of Kira, he'd ultimately decided he was happy for her—in a green-tinged sort of way. But he was equally hungry for his own bite at success. Now he damn well needed to keep his eyes on the books and not on her sleeping Highness's tempting curves.

Averting his gaze, Mitch cut through the living room, went to his desk and grabbed the hornbook for his Federal Jurisdiction course. Maybe if he studied out on the back deck, he could find some measure of peace, if not solitude. Just then, Kira was murmuring something that sounded strangely like *polyester*.

So fashion nightmares were what plagued her?

On his return trip to the kitchen and its back door, he hazarded a quick glimpse to be sure she was still asleep. He doubted she'd be pleased to know that he'd seen her with her hair looking like Medusa's and her face bearing crease marks from the rumpled sheets she slept on. He also doubted she'd believe that he liked this look on her—but he did.

Her usual practiced perfection—and he did mean *practiced,* because each summer he'd watched her facade evolve—kept him on edge. He wanted her accessible. He wanted to get her messy and real to see if she'd taste of salty sweat when she lay beneath him. He wanted to hear her cry his name as she had that one incomplete encounter three summers ago.

Bottom line: he wanted her.

Mitch shook off the image of what she'd look like and uttered a brief but heartfelt profanity as he shot out the back door to the peace beyond.

There was a boundless difference between wanting and getting. He could want all day long, but he'd never allow himself to get.

WHEN SHE WAS FIFTEEN, KIRA had starred in her school's production of *The Princess and the Pea*. That earlier affair with the stage hadn't prepared her for the reality of sleeping on Mitch's spring-shot sofa.

Unable to swing her aching legs around and gracefully sit up, she settled for wriggling her way from the couch to the floor, taking her blanket cocoon with her.

It totally stank to move like a sixty-year-old ex-pro hockey player, when the most strenuous sport she indulged in was avoiding her Pilates class. Kira squinted. A rosy pink glow bathed her from the room's east-facing stained-glass window. If she were her usual optimistic self, she'd consider this a cheery omen. Since, however, she'd had bloodstained nightmares involving Roxanne and oily henchmen, she just viewed the morning sunshine as a sign that she had no further hope of calm sleep. A check of her watch confirmed that it was nearly eight o'clock.

Kira untangled her blanket, sat up and rearranged it for walking, then strolled into the kitchen. Mitch was sitting at an antique enamel-topped table she'd vaguely noted in last night's wanderings. He seemed to be taking notes from the book she'd definitely seen. Next to the book was a plate of toast remnants smeared with gooey white and red stuff.

"Good morning," she said.

"Morning," he answered without looking up from the notebook he wrote in.

Kira wasn't fond of being ignored. "What's that?" she asked, nudging the plate.

"Toast with marshmallow fluff and strawberry jam."

"Eww. Sugar overdose."

He looked up from the notebook. "I take it I shouldn't offer that as a meal for the road?"

In yet another case of attitude overcoming better judgment, she said the first smart thing that popped into her mind. "Why? Are you going someplace?"

"No, you are," he said.

Dressed in his dark blue uniform, he was pretty sexy-looking for a cranky guy. His hand nearly engulfed the coffee mug he held. Some sex-deprived imp residing in Kira's brain whispered, *Big hands... big—*

—deal, she mentally finished for the imp, then tried to concentrate on Mitch.

He scowled at her. "Hey, are you listening to me? Remember, I told you yesterday—one night only."

"I heard the deal. Come sundown, I won't darken your doorway." She lifted her right hand. "Cross my heart," she said, action following words.

Of course, even with a blanket over the spot, her touch brought to mind Mitch's finger right there last night. It seemed that the sight spurred the same memory in him, because he now looked even crankier.

He pushed away from the table. "Have a good life, Highness. I'm going someplace with fewer distractions."

A distraction?

She'd been called worse.

Kira stepped aside and let him go.

While he banged around in his bedroom, then closed the front door so loudly that it bordered on a slam, Kira stuck a load of laundry in the washer. Despite her promise to Mitch, she didn't consider it a foregone conclusion that she'd leave his house today.

It depended on her options, and she wasn't accustomed to having them so narrow. But no matter where she went, it wouldn't be in unwashed panties.

While she waited for the laundry, Kira checked her cell phone messages. It was early, but there was nothing from the private investigator she'd hired. Don, the P.I., had told her to expect little for the next forty-eight hours unless Roxanne decided to reappear on her own. A not-necessarily-missing adult wasn't the easiest of people to track. Kira could only hope that the same held true for her, here in her Sandy Bend hideout.

It was just before ten when she slipped into clean underwear and the backup work outfit she kept in her trunk. While she stood in front of the bathroom mirror, Kira dug through the meager selection of cosmetics in her purse seeking something to cover the raccoon rings under her eyes.

Sure, she admitted to a certain measure of female vanity, but more than that, she knew how important illusion could be. By the time she left this house, it was imperative that she look like a Whitman heiress—the queen of all she surveyed. Desperation and empty pockets wouldn't get her a new wardrobe and some food other than bagged salad and marshmallow fluff.

Makeup as good as it was getting, Kira left the Dollhouse Cottage. Since Mitch's house was only five town-size blocks from Sandy Bend's limited shopping district, she decided to walk. With luck the exercise would loosen her tight muscles and clear her mind of last night's ugly dreams.

It was a perfect Michigan summer morning, with

a cornflower-blue sky and the scent of lilacs on the breeze. Kira inhaled deeply. Sandy Bend might not be as lush and exotic as her current home, but it had its compensations.

Leaving the quiet street of clapboard-sided houses with their well-tended cottage gardens, she turned onto Main Street and stopped dead. Tourists already thronged the sidewalks.

"One foot in front of the other," she told herself, then winced at her choice of words.

The last time she'd used that exact phrase was when she had fled from the almost husband her father had picked for her. Her feet—and a cab—had taken her from Chicago's Fourth Presbyterian Church straight to O'Hare Airport. It had been the right choice, even if her timing had been socially and personally disastrous. And today the right choice would be to show some of the same backbone she'd found when she'd rebuilt her life. Crowds shouldn't rattle her. They never had before.

Sandy Bend was far from the town it had been three years ago. Even then a childhood of summers had meant that most of the faces were known to her. Not so today. Other than the local market owner, old Mrs. Hawkins, no one looked familiar. And while it usually didn't bother Kira when men gave her a second glance, today she wanted them to keep their eyes to themselves. She wasn't up for the attention.

As she wove through the clusters of window-shoppers, it occurred to her that she'd fooled herself into believing that she was over the events of the past few days. Being with Mitch in the close confines of the Dollhouse Cottage had seemed somehow safe and normal. Out in the open, though, she felt like a target. Just to look busy, she dug in her purse for money. When she'd managed to mine about three dollars in change, she spotted a coffee-house called, fittingly enough, the Village Grounds. Kira headed inside.

The woman behind the counter smiled a greeting.

Kira ordered on autopilot. "A small iced mocha skim latte with a shot of hazelnut, please."

The worker's smile faded just a little. "Kira, you don't recognize me, do you?"

Brown hair…brown eyes…her age or maybe a little younger… Kira could find nothing that sparked recognition, though she did feel a twinge of envy at the woman's expression. It was one of total content-ment with life.

"I, uh…" Kira hedged.

"I'm Lisa Cantrell. We took sailing lessons to-gether for about four summers?"

"Lisa?" Kira blinked. They hadn't exactly trav-eled in the same pack of friends. She couldn't recall ever actually speaking to Lisa and suspected that if she had, the words had been some of her old snob-bery. "You look wonderful."

"Thanks. I lost a few pounds," Lisa replied as she packed freshly ground espresso into the small metal mesh funnels of the machine behind the counter. "I haven't seen you around town in a while."

Kira relaxed a little, figuring that if Lisa were out to seek revenge for whatever petty, teenage Kira might have done, the moment would have already come. "I moved south and haven't had much of a chance to make it up this way."

Lisa nodded. "This is the kind of town that you ei-

ther stay in forever or forget entirely. I guess I've
fallen into the stay-in-forever camp. Jim, my fiancé,
and I lived outside of Detroit for a few years while
he finished his orthopedics residency. It was just too
big for both of us. We moved back here and I opened
this place last summer."

"Congratulations," Kira replied. "It looks like
Sandy Bend is booming."

"Summers are great," Lisa said. "Winters are a little quieter. Not like now."

Kira surveyed the seating area in the small space.
Every table was taken, as was nearly every stool at
the counter overlooking Main Street. Young moms
laughed and chatted. Men sat at the window paging
through newspapers.

"Are you in town long?" Lisa asked over the hiss
of the espresso machine.

"I'm kind of loose on my plans," Kira replied.

"Jim and I are getting married Saturday on the
town green. Why don't you come?"

The generous gesture warmed Kira and embarrassed her a little, too. "Thanks, but I couldn't. It's
such short notice for you."

"Really, it's nothing fancy. We're having the reception right on the green, too. It's just a big, early afternoon picnic—no seating charts to worry about, or
anything like that. Come join us."

The joy of a wedding between two people who really wanted to get married sounded appealing—and
in Kira's recent experience, rare. She nodded. "If I'm
still here, definitely."

"Great!" Lisa paused and settled two miniature
silver pitchers of brewed espresso into a small tub of

ice, then filled a plastic cup with the same. "So where south did you move?"

"I'm in the Miami area. I've got a real estate business in Coconut Grove."

"Wow, that's big time."

Kira smiled. "In a small sort of way. I—"

She broke off. One of the men seated at the window had suddenly caught her attention. He wore what was left of his dark hair in a comb-over that defied both good taste and whatever he'd sprayed it into place with. His nose was crooked, as though it had been well-broken a couple of times. Kira wouldn't have noticed these details if he hadn't lowered the newspaper he was reading to stare at her. It wasn't a friendly look, either.

Kira made herself turn away.

Lisa set Kira's drink on the counter and gave her a quizzical smile. "You okay?"

"Fine," Kira said, then repeated it with more conviction. "Just fine." She put her handful of change on the counter and took the drink. "I'll see you later, okay?"

"Sure," Lisa called as Kira bolted.

She was a stronger person than this, Kira told herself as she exited the coffeehouse. She could leave the nervous imaginings of henchmen behind and have a wonderful day.

Or at least one she could survive.

5

JUST WHEN MITCH WAS BEGINNING to get a grip on his attitude, his boss and brother, Cal, walked into the police station. Since Mitch wasn't in the mood to talk—or even work up a fake smile—he tried to act interested in the paperless paperwork occupying his computer screen.

Apparently Cal didn't buy into the busy act, because he sat in the chair opposite Mitch instead of going to his own. "So, why is Kira Whitman staying at your house?"

Mitch attempted to deflect. "Aren't you supposed to be at the town council meeting? I thought the department budget was on the agenda."

Cal glanced at his watch. "The meeting doesn't start for another half hour. Now, what's the word on your guest?"

"What makes you think I have one?"

"Early this morning—and I mean very early—the ladies who walk saw a car with Florida plates parked out front of your house. Of course they shared this with me while I was buying my morning coffee."

Mitch rolled his eyes. These were the same ladies who also lunched daily. And gossiped daily. Once they knew something, soon so did most of Sandy Bend. "And what—you ran the plates' numbers?"

"No, I just saw Kira walking down the street and did the mental math. One hot Mercedes plus one blonde equals…"

Trouble. Mitch wished that Kira had quietly disappeared instead of swinging her little butt through town. Life was complicated enough.

"It's no big deal. She should be gone soon, anyway." He'd meant to sound matter-of-fact but knew that he must have come off as depressed, because Cal was giving him a speculative look that really fried his ass.

"Don't start," he ordered even though he knew Cal wouldn't listen.

"So, she just showed up on your doorstep for a night?"

Mitch shrugged. "Something like that."

"Huh. Interesting."

"Look, I've got paperwork to get through before lunch, okay?"

Cal grinned. "Far be it from me to stop you from doing your job." He stood. "And with such enthusiasm, too." When he was seated behind his desk he added, "If you wanna talk, you know I'm here."

And Mitch wished that he was far, far away.

Cal loved being a cop. Mitch had no doubt that his older brother would be Sandy Bend's police chief right up until retirement, as their father had been before him. And unlike Dad, who'd moved to Sedona, Arizona, and remarried after decades as a widower, Mitch was also one hundred percent certain that Cal would never leave Sandy Bend.

Mitch was positive, on the other hand, that he would. Maybe it was part of the middle-kid syndrome, but he'd never felt noticed here. Never felt totally connected. Back when he was a teenager, he'd secretly vented his Sandy Bend hostility by removing the carved *n* in *Bend* from the old-fashioned welcome sign at the town's southern limits.

Each time they'd replaced it, he'd stolen another and left an adolescent tribute to "Sandy Be d" in his wake. It was a dumb stunt that had gained him nothing more than a false rebel's thrill and a bunch of *ns*, which he'd ceremonially burned when he'd gotten out of the hospital last November.

His past vandalism hardly rose to the level of a felony, but he wanted a clean break from anything that might even remotely deny him admission to the bar. And he didn't mean Truro's Tavern down the street. He didn't care what it took, how many more months he went without a life to speak of, he would land a job as a federal prosecutor. End of story.

"So, did you finally get to kiss her? You know you've always wanted to," Cal called from his side of the open office.

What big bro didn't know wouldn't hurt him. "Not as much as I want to tell you to kiss my—"

Cal's laughter cut him short. "Hit a soft spot, huh?"

"I can think of a few of my own," he calmly replied while imagining how damn fine it would feel to pop Cal one on his glass jaw.

"Don't let her get to you this time, okay?" Cal said, now using his all-knowing tone instead of his push-you-until-you-snap one.

"Too late," Mitch muttered, not intending the words to carry across the room.

"Damn," his brother said. "I really hope she's gone."

Just as much as Mitch hoped in some bizarre, masochistic way that she wasn't. Then it struck him. Crime wouldn't keep him from that prosecutor's position, craziness would.

KIRA HAD BEGUN TO ENVISION her adventures as a movie: *Down and Out in Sandy Bend*. Once she'd finished her coffee and vanquished her goon hallucinations, she'd cruised the chichi boutiques that had pushed out the town's hardware store, grain supply and general mercantile. Apparently not a single local merchant believed in antiquated house accounts when the miracles of Visa and MasterCard had become commonplace.

If she didn't find a freethinker soon, she was going to be reduced to buying a packet of safety pins and altering Mitch's wardrobe to fit. Two places remained to be cased: Devine Secrets Day Spa and Marleigh's Boutique. The day spa appeared to be carrying a line of locally designed clothes, but the place's name was a strong tip-off that she'd find Dana Devine Brewer inside. Kira simply wasn't prepared to go there.

Marleigh's seemed to cater to the golf-and-tennis set, of which Kira had never been a willing member. Too much sweat was involved, and too many women with bunny names like Muffy and Fluffy. Still, it beat the safety-pin-and-duct-tape set. Kira turned a pained eye from the fuchsia-and-green color palette in the window and stepped inside.

Good thing she did, too, because she finally hit pay dirt. Marleigh was a distant acquaintance of Kira's oldest sister, Caroline, which meant that she bought into the Whitman aura but wasn't privy to the family dirt. It was easy for Kira to persuade the shopkeeper that she'd be in town indefinitely and would like the convenience of a store account.

For once in the past twenty-four hours, complete honesty was Kira's. She fully intended to pay her bills, just not until she was free of worry about being traced through her credit card activity.

While she answered Marleigh's questions about Caroline's life—fudging a little, since she hadn't talked to Caro in ages—Kira flipped her way through the racks of resort wear. Thankfully not all of it was in the 1980s preppy-throwback style she'd seen in the window. As she shopped, she was careful to select some items expensive enough to earn her unquestionable favored-customer status.

Once she'd tried those on and put them at the register, it was time for the nitty-gritty—some undies, skirts and shirts to get her through the next however many days until she could safely return home. On a whim she also selected a golden-taupe silk nightgown that was suggestive in a subtle sort of way, plus a more obvious red bikini and hip-hugging filmy sarong that showed off her curves and yet still hid her flaws.

The purchases showed just how ambivalent she was. Much as she wanted to find Roxanne and stick bamboo slivers coated with hot-pepper oil under her fingernails, she also craved more time around Mitch.

The bell on the boutique's door chimed again. When Kira spotted who'd come in, she was tempted to crawl beneath the dress rack.

"Hi, Marleigh," Dana Devine Brewer said. "I thought I'd stop by and remind you about your massage with Stacy at seven tonight."

If nothing else, Dana was direct. She hadn't managed to keep her gaze off Kira the whole time she'd been speaking to Marleigh. Kira knew when she was being hunted. With the tawny auburn streaks in Dana's dark blond hair and the predatory glint in her eyes, Mitch's sister-in-law made a fine lioness in search of prey.

"My, a personal reminder to follow your phone call an hour ago. You do believe in service," Marleigh replied in a teasing tone of voice.

Dana feigned surprise. "I called earlier? I'm slipping. It must be all the details involved in opening my new Crystal Mountain location." She pinned Kira with another sharply questioning look.

Kira wasn't comfortable with the curious glances being sent her way by the shop's patrons. The last thing she wanted was to be the daily topic on the town's gossip hotline. Marleigh, she had to be nice to. The other watchers got her don't-mess-with-the-heiress glacial glare, though the look was just frosty instead of downright cold since she hadn't used it in so very long.

"So, Kira, what brings you to town?" Dana asked.

"Just a friendly visit."

"Funny, since you're the only Whitman here."

"I didn't say who I was visiting, now did I?"

"I can think of only one possibility outside your family, and—"

"Why don't you show me your spa?" Kira cut in. "We can talk on the way." Before Dana could object, Kira turned to Marleigh. "If you could just hold my purchases for me? I'll be right back."

The boutique owner was clearly disappointed to have the action go elsewhere, but she didn't object.

Once outside Dana started up again. "So, really, why are you here? Steve and Hallie are gone until August, which I know for a fact since I'm helping cover Hallie's shifts at her art co-op."

Kira began to walk toward Devine Secrets. "I'm not sure I understand how any of this is your business."

"You stayed in Mitch's house last night, which makes it my business."

There was no outrunning gossip, was there?

Dana led Kira around the corner and to the back of the spa.

"What—no tour?" Kira asked.

Dana held open the door and ushered her in. "We'll start with my office. First door on your left."

"Great."

Kira entered but didn't take the seat in front of Dana's cluttered desk.

Dana wasted no time in starting her questioning. "This is going to sound pushy, but I'd really appreciate it if you'd tell me what's going on between you and Mitch."

"You're right. It sounds pushy."

"Look, he's been in kind of a fragile state for the past six months."

Kira grinned. "Mitch? Fragile? Forgive me if I can't picture it."

"Trust me on this."

She was so serious that it set Kira aback. She was as guilty as Mitch had been in assuming that she hadn't changed in three years. He was no more immune to life than she.

"Mitch bailed me out of a bit of a situation and I stayed with him, but nothing's going on. Really."

"So, you're not here specifically to see him?"

Kira went with the truth, as personally embarrassing as she found it. "I didn't plan to see him at all. He found me when I had, uh, slipped into Steve and Hallie's house. He wouldn't let me stay there, and for a variety of reasons I had no one else in my family I could turn to."

Frowning, Dana scrutinized her. If there had been a clock in the room, Kira could have counted its ticks as the silence stretched out.

"So, you're being honest," Dana finally said. "Good move."

"I remember you well enough to know that there's no margin in playing you."

"True again." Dana sighed, then said, "Bad family dynamics, I understand. My mom and I could be a case study in what not to do. But now I also understand good family dynamics."

Kira was about to agree that the Brewers were indeed wonderful, since sucking up seemed advisable, but Dana held up a hand and stopped her.

"I don't stick myself in the middle of Mitch's business lightly. And I wouldn't do it if I didn't know that he already has issues where you're concerned."

"Issues?" To Kira, that sounded nearly good.

"Don't look so pleased."

Dana picked up a framed snapshot from her desk and turned it toward Kira. In it Steve, Hallie, Mitch, Dana and Cal were standing on the beach, laughing as though they shared a joke. Kira suddenly felt very alone.

"This is my family," Dana said. "I don't want to be dramatic, but you should know that if you mess with Mitch's well being, you also mess with mine. And you really don't want to do that."

Yes, Dana remained dead-on direct.

Kira took the same approach. "Even if I had the power to—which I don't—the last thing I'd ever do is try to hurt Mitch, okay?"

Dana set down the photo. "The problem is, you've always been able to injure people without trying."

Kira had anticipated some tough moments when she returned to Sandy Bend, but sometimes the truth really did hurt. She let the sting subside before saying, "People change."

"Agreed, but are you one of them?"

She'd had enough. "Consider me warned, okay? I won't be here long enough to even accidentally do damage. Now, if you don't mind…"

Totally ticked, she opened the office door and walked straight into Mitch. He closed his hands on her upper arms and moved her back a step.

"Saved by the cop," she said in a lame attempt to cut some of the tension in the air. It didn't work.

Mitch checked her expression, which she assumed was hardly sunshine and rainbows, then said, "Are you okay?"

"Perfect as always."

He looked beyond her to his sister-in-law. "I had a feeling I was going to find something like this. What do you and Cal do—communicate by telepathy?"

"Cell phone," Dana corrected. "And I'm not going to apologize for butting in."

Mitch actually smiled. "Somehow I didn't expect you to. It's not your style."

"I'm family. I'm allowed to worry."

"Hey, I'm better now, okay? I can survive a few screwups."

Kira wasn't totally following whatever was going on between these two, though she did know that she wasn't very fond of being referred to as a *screwup*. She watched as Dana shook her head and gave Mitch an unwilling smile in return.

"You've got the same look you wore right before you signed up for skydiving lessons last year. What is it with you and risk?" Dana asked.

Mitch was still holding Kira by her arms. He glanced down at her. When their eyes met, it seemed to her that what had been a matter of restraint now almost felt like an embrace.

"The challenge," he said to Dana. "The biggest risks can bring the best rewards."

Kira couldn't have agreed more. If Mitch Brewer was any part of the reward, she was definitely up for the gamble.

When Mitch came home that evening, he knew for form's sake he should hassle Kira because she was still camped out in his living room. He didn't, though. It didn't seem sporting to harass her when she'd filled the house with the scents of some sort of spicy chicken and the chocolate cake he'd just spied sitting on the kitchen counter. If she was manipulating him, she was doing a damn fine job of it.

Besides, she'd taken enough from Dana today. He knew that his sister-in-law meant well. She'd been fiercely protective of him ever since she'd seen him laid up in the ICU, fighting a secondary infection he'd picked up after he'd been dumb enough to get himself shot.

But as he'd told her, he was better now. He'd healed physically and emotionally and was tough enough to do battle with Kira…just not this minute. Not when she was wearing a movie-star halter dress that made her look as though she was channeling Marilyn Monroe.

Recalling his vow not to touch her and thus avoid becoming forever obsessed with her, he nodded a greeting and said, "So, did you kidnap a cook?"

"No," she said. "I cooked."

"Amazing." And he wasn't kidding. With her posh upbringing, he'd have bet that she couldn't run a microwave.

"It's nothing much. I spent two months at a culinary institute in France. I dropped out after my second burn. Some people aren't meant to be around open flames as a career, you know?"

She handed him a cold beer, which at least gave him something to do with his hands. Left to their own devices, they'd be untying that dress.

"Dinner's just about ready," she said, then went to the counter, where she began to toss a salad that was too colorful to be any of his bland bagged stuff.

As she worked, Mitch realized the full benefit of a halter dress. Not only did he get to fantasize about the ease of getting it off her, he also got to see a sleek stretch of her back. Her skin wasn't as deeply tanned as he'd imagined a Florida girl's being, but she definitely looked tasty.

"Where'd you get the dress?" he asked, then took a swallow of beer to see if that would wash some of the roughness out of his voice, though he doubted it.

"Marleigh's," she answered, then turned to face him, salad bowl in her hands. When she bent forward to place it on the kitchen table, he was afforded a brief view of breasts plump and perfect for his touch.

"Ready?" she asked.

For more than he would ever let her know.

6

AFTER DINNER, MITCH, WHO'D been appreciative but oddly distant, retreated to his office. Kira closed herself in the tiny bathroom and slipped into her new nightgown. A cursory glance in the silver-rimmed medicine-cabinet mirror confirmed that there was nothing freakishly wrong with her.

No green bits of cilantro clung to her front teeth.

No smear of chocolate frosting ringed her mouth.

So why the weird behavior? She knew they had a mutual attraction going. And they were both consenting adults—not that he'd asked her any questions in that regard.

As she brushed her teeth and readied for sleep, she decided that she should simply be satisfied that through cooking a decent meal she'd bought herself another night's lodging. She'd felt almost giddy with the possibilities this afternoon when Mrs. Hawkins at the market had automatically put the cost of Kira's apple-and-yogurt lunch on Kira's dad's tab. Seizing the opportunity, Kira had gone back and filled a cart with foods that might tempt a less-than-gracious host. The strategy had worked. Mitch hadn't even asked her why she was still in Sandy Bend. Any guilt over sticking her father with the tab would be alleviated by a donation to a food bank as soon as she had access to her checkbook.

Unfortunately she wasn't sure what she could summon as a follow-up act to the meal, and she needed one. Don, the P.I., had finally left a message on her cell phone, and it hadn't been good. There was no sign of activity at Roxanne's house, none of her friends had heard from her and her car still sat in the lot at work.

At this rate Kira would need a regular legion of distractions. Outside of her real estate skills she'd been pretty much a dabbler in life. A few cooking classes, a miserable month as an assistant to a party planner, a whopping week working with a decorator. All in all, not a very extensive skill set.

Kira stuck her toothbrush in the holder on the sink top and smiled at her small act of dominion. As she returned to the living room, she couldn't help but think of the legend of Scheherazade, who'd bought herself a day of life with a new tale for the sultan each night. Maybe her stakes weren't as high, but somehow they had begun to feel that way.

She had never denied her sexual attraction to Mitch, but now that she'd matured—a word that generally freaked her out—she had begun to suspect that something more than hormones was coming into play. Perhaps something as fragile as the heart she'd guarded all these years.

Putting aside that thought as both absurd and dangerous, she switched on the table lamp next to the sofa and hauled her briefcase onto her lap. She began to dig though it, craving order somewhere in her life.

She sifted through the papers she'd crammed in

the middle pocket days before and ignored ever since, finding her notes on Casa Pura Vida, a listing she now had no intention of pursuing. Too much bad had sprung from a house that had seemed so wonderful. Beneath her notes were all the comparable sales listings she'd pulled in preparation for that day. She set aside the stack of papers and dredged the front pocket in search of a binder clip. Instead she came upon her PDA in its brushed stainless-steel case.

Kira frowned. The case had a new scratch running diagonally across it.

"How did this happen?" she murmured, then flipped open the PDA's cover and pressed the on button to be sure the damage was only superficial. The opening screen no longer had the picture of a shirtless Heath Ledger that she'd loaded in there for a little daily eye candy.

"Weird," she said.

But it got even weirder when she checked her address book. The data wasn't hers. As she hit the toggle button and shot through the entries *A* to *Z*, it became clear that somehow she'd ended up with Roxanne's PDA. As she recalled the angry state she'd been in when she'd returned to the office to dump Roxanne's stuff, she supposed the mix-up should be no shock.

And now it might be a blessing.

Kira walked a circle of the room, turning the PDA over in her hands. In a pure and simple world, the ethical thing to do would be to put the PDA away and snoop no more. But Kira's world was getting poached on by a partner potentially up to no good and goons who were definitely bottom-feeders. She'd have to save the ethical purity for someone with a less hacked-up existence.

Within fifteen minutes Kira was an expert on Roxanne trivia. She knew her dry cleaner, her plastic surgeon and her gynecologist. She'd read her ratings on former boyfriends, her most recent liquor purchases and what she'd bought her father for Father's Day.

But most important of all, Kira was pretty sure that she had Roxanne's password for the Whitman-Pierce Web site. Kira had found it in a memo file, set up like an office-supply shopping list. It wasn't as though Kira felt that the universe owed her a break. Overall she'd been one lucky girl. But if she were to get a break, she hoped that it would be found with this password. She hadn't felt this sort of urgency since she'd made her first house sale. She had to get to a computer and see what more she could unearth. And she had to do it *now*.

Kira padded barefoot toward the doorway leading to both Mitch's bedroom and his office. A bluish light shone into the hallway from the office. She took another step forward, then nearly groaned with disappointment. Mitch was seated at his computer.

"You want something?" he called without turning his head from the screen.

He heard all too well, just as he did most everything else all too well.

"No, nothing. Just wandering a little."

She received a distracted "Yeah, okay" in response.

Kira had never had her fingertips literally itch before, but that was how anxious she was to get her hands on a keyboard. She was totally out of luck, too. Even the new-and-improved Sandy Bend wouldn't have anything as urban as an all-night Internet café.

She tiptoed back toward Mitch, hoping to see if he

looked as if he was there for just a few minutes or if he'd settled in for the long haul.

"If you're bored, read a book," he said, again without looking her way. "There's one in the end table's drawer."

"Thanks." She lingered in the doorway.

"I can hear you back there, you know."

How? It wasn't as though she was a mouth breather, stuffy with a cold.

"Sorry."

"If you're trolling for the computer, forget it. I've got work to finish. Besides, I'm not hot on the idea of you snooping though my files."

She was hardly in a position to claim moral indignation. "Thanks for the vote of confidence," she said.

He chuckled. "Hey, I'm a realist."

As was she. Tomorrow she'd visit the library. She was pretty sure the town had one of those, though she couldn't say that she'd visited it back in her debutante days. And if they did, odds were good she'd find a computer at which she could stomp all over Roxanne's privacy rights.

Until then all she could do was burn time. She'd like to believe that she could curl up on her lumpy sofa, close her eyes and awake refreshed in the morning, but again, she was a realist. To wind down, Kira organized and refolded her new clothes. Then, to make some room to store them, she moved aside a few dusty old trophies on the shelf unit that held Mitch's stereo. One gold-dipped football player clanked against the other, and she uttered a small "Oops."

"What are you doing out there?" Mitch called from the chair she'd still do nearly anything to get him out of.

"Just a little cleaning."

"You mean you kidnapped a maid as well as a cook?"

"Funny," she called back in a tone that added a vehement *not* to her comment. Still, she was glad to hear a little of the Mitch she knew back in his voice.

Kira realigned the statues one shelf up. She remembered when he'd played football while at Michigan State. She'd still been in high school back in Chicago and had thought about inviting him to her homecoming dance. Funny, now that she considered it, she'd spent a great many years thinking of Mitch. Funny, too, that she'd had the ego to imagine that a college guy would want to come to a high school dance. Life sure had a way of knocking teenage arrogance out of a girl.

By ten-thirty, Kira had tidied her belongings, read fifty pages of the paperback thriller Mitch had mentioned and nearly wrestled the sofa's cushions into a comfortable arrangement.

Just when she'd begun to settle, music blasted through the house. She winced at the pickax-to-guitar, death through aural torture making the stained-glass windows rattle in their frames.

"I'm a guest," she reminded herself. "A squatter. An interloper."

She was running out of synonyms for house crasher, and her brain cells were dissolving in the noise.

She shouldn't get up.

She shouldn't go goad him.

Except she suspected that he was as hungry for the diversion as she was. Why else would he do this?

She rose from the sofa and homed in on the source of the noise. Mitch was still at his desk. Instead of gaining his attention through something as bland as calling his name, she used her best hail-a-cab whistle.

Mitch turned down the volume, and the band silently wailed on from the computer screen. He swiveled his desk chair to face her.

"Something wrong?" His expression was bland enough, except for a certain you-took-the-bait glint she detected in his eyes.

"I was kind of hoping to sleep tonight," she said. Never mind that knowing he was yards away had already decimated her chances on that front.

"Sorry. I study better with music when I'm getting tired. It helps my concentration."

She noted that at present he was concentrating on her chest area. Was it possible that the fabric of the nightgown she'd picked up at Marleigh's was thinner than she thought? Kira quelled the urge to look down and find out. She'd already learned that the first rule in dealing with Mitch was to show no weakness.

"You're studying?" she asked as she strolled closer.

"I'm finishing off my last law school course," he replied without ever quite getting his eyes back to hers. "I took a year's leave from the force when I could afford it, but other than that I've been attending classes in East Lansing at night."

The drive alone—over two hundred miles, round-trip—would have killed her. "That's impressive. I didn't know."

One side of his mouth quirked upward. "Should you have?"

She somehow felt as though she should, as though she'd cheated herself by avoiding this town and this man.

"Probably not," she said anyway, then gestured at the dudes on his computer monitor. "I don't suppose classical music or even techno or something would do the job?"

"Not a chance," he said.

Kira spied a set of headphones stowed on the top right corner of Mitch's desk. It wasn't so much the thought of silence but the fact that she'd get to wriggle her body into the small gap between Mitch and those headphones that prompted the next question.

"Okay, then how about if I find a way for both of us to win?" she asked.

"What do you have to offer?"

"This."

Taking her time to savor the moment and breathe in the summer-hay-and-leather scent that would always remind her of Mitch, Kira moved around him and reached for the headphones. His gaze followed her body, feeling nearly as intimate as a caress. She didn't want to think what his touch might do to her.

He moved the office chair forward, bringing his knees within inches of where she stood. Her heart picked up a rhythm more jagged than the music he had muted. She could almost swear she heard Mitch's heart pounding, too.

He reached out one hand and rubbed the silk of her nightgown between his fingers and thumb.

"Nice," he said. "You look good in gold."

If this were any man but Mitch, Kira suspected she'd have a flip comment at the ready. Because he had a way of stealing her words, the best she could offer was a reedy-voiced thanks.

He released the fabric and ran the tip of his index finger across the thin panel of lace that banded the gown just beneath her breasts. His blue eyes grew darker, more intent. She could tell that he wanted more. And she did, too.

Big risks…big rewards.

Then he dropped his hand. His smile was as regretful as it was self-aware.

"I think I've pushed my luck as far as I should. You might want to take a step back, Highness."

Stepping back was the very last thing she wanted. Kira clutched the headphones and took stock of her options.

Strong women didn't beg.

Tough women didn't melt like sweet butter simply because a man smiled at them.

And independent women took control.

She returned the headphones to his desk, then braced a hand on each arm of his chair.

He opened his legs and she stepped into the gap, resettling her hands on his shoulders. His hands closed over her hips, pulling her even closer.

"Want to know why I can't concentrate?" he asked.

For the second time she answered, "Probably not."

Again it was a lie. She did want to know, especially if it involved any part of his body against hers. And really, she wasn't going to be choosy, though mouth against mouth would be a move in the right direction.

He slowly stroked his thumbs over the curves of her hip bones. "You've always made me crazy. Did you know that?"

Ditto to that.

"You'd think that after all these years I'd have

gotten over it," he said. "That I could be near you without wanting to—"

In business, timing was everything, and Kira meant serious business. She settled her mouth over his and took in his low murmur of surprise.

Yes, he made her crazy, but he also made her feel alive down to the soles of her feet—no small accomplishment when those feet were owned by a jaded former jet-setter. And being in this moment was what she'd think of. No worries. No tomorrow. Just now.

Kira sighed with pleasure. Ah, how she remembered this mouth. It wasn't the sort of thing a girl forgot. In one of the universe's small ironies, teasing, unromantic Mitch had a romantic's mouth. His lower lip was full, just perfect to draw between her teeth and caress with her tongue.

His hands moved up, now gripping her waist and pulling her closer. She rested one knee on the edge of the chair and leaned in, at the same time opening to him. Their tongues tangled, and her heart sped. He tasted slightly of the whiskey she'd seen him pour after dinner.

The kiss lengthened. Kira could feel her skin grow warm, then warmer yet, until she was damp and craving more.

She hadn't felt this sort of fire in…

In…

Three years—*the last time he'd last kissed her.*

If she were more athletic, or the chair bigger, she'd have found a way to wrap her legs around him, to feel the contact of her body against his where she needed it most.

He murmured her name, sliding one hand up to her breast. Startled by the new feeling, she broke off the kiss and stood on both feet, straightening a little and looking down at him.

Their gazes locked. He briefly slipped his fingers beneath the silky fabric. She shivered with excitement.

"Let me touch you," he said.

She gave her assent by taking her right hand and sliding the opposite strap of the gown off her shoulder.

Mitch's hand felt hot against her skin as he cupped her breast. He ran his thumb over her nipple, and she let her eyes fall closed and head dip back as he gently played with the peak.

Far before she would have willed it—which was, like, never—his hand was gone.

"I need to see you." He gave her no time to agree or disagree. He merely worked the silky fabric out of the way.

"Beautiful," he said.

She slid her hands into his thick, dark hair and brought his mouth to her breast. He made a wordless sound of pleasure before drawing his tongue across her nipple, then sucking her into the heat of his mouth.

Kira's knees began to buckle. He must have sensed her control slipping away, because he moved his hands to her bottom, supporting her. His fingers flexed in the same slow rhythm that his tongue drew on her sensitive flesh.

She moaned, and he rubbed the curve of her butt almost comfortingly. She pushed her hips against his hands in a nearly involuntary reflex.

He took his mouth from her breast and said, "Open your legs a little for me."

She braced her hands on his shoulders again and hesitated—not because she didn't want to cooperate but because she was too lost in a haze of feelings to immediately grasp his intent.

He blew a gentle stream of air at her wet nipple. She shivered, and he made a sound she'd describe as nearly a chuckle.

"C'mon, Highness," he urged.

Kira widened her stance just a little. Through the silky fabric he traced a path between the globes of her bottom. She began to breathe even faster, trembling.

"Closer," he murmured, and she scooted in.

His hand was broad and his fingers long. She squeezed his shoulders and gasped as he began to explore his way forward, moving the nightgown with him.

Unbelievably, after three sure strokes of his fingers, she was at the precipice of an orgasm.

She wanted to get his attention, to tell him to slow down—or maybe speed up. But all she could form was "Mitch?"

He made a soft sound of comfort but didn't slow his hand. "Shh."

One hard, slamming heartbeat echoed after another. Kira felt her body tighten, then finally totally let go. She cried his name and collapsed forward. As she shuddered, he leaned his forehead against her stomach. He was saying something—she had no idea what. Words couldn't compete with the rush of sheer pleasure still making her heart pound.

Slowly passion subsided. In its place came embarrassment. Twice—once three summers ago and again now—in mere moments he'd made her come apart at his touch. She didn't like what it said about her, the way she lost control with him.

Kira came to her feet, tugging the top to her nightgown into place at the same time. Then she made sense of the bottom half, brushing the back of it from the wet folds to which it still clung.

"I—" She stopped, realizing she had no idea what she'd been about to say.

Mitch was sprawled in the office chair, his head tipped to the ceiling. His erection rode hard against his jeans, and Kira was mesmerized by the sight of him, more at a loss for words than ever. She figured that thanking him was both insincere and dangerous right now.

Mitch looked back at her, his jaw set tight and a dark flush coloring his cheeks. "Like I said, you might have wanted to take a step back."

This time Kira listened.

7

THE SUN HAD RISEN AND MITCH was gone when Kira finally gave up any pretense of sleep. Last night, after she'd pulled on the police department T-shirt and curled up on her couch, she'd heard Mitch in the shower, then back at his desk with his tribute to headbangers playing again, though more quietly. She wouldn't have cared if he'd blasted it. She was too emotionally fried to work up more than an apathetic dislike of his tunes.

This morning, even after another shower and the pleasure of putting on fresh new clothes, she still felt numb, as though she hadn't slept at all. She knew she'd grabbed a restless hour here and there, but nothing that took the edge off her tension.

"Gotta get a grip," she muttered to herself as she made her way into the kitchen. There she found a note from Mitch with a key settled on top of it. Kira read his broad, angular scrawl:

Would you water Hallie's houseplants? Here's the key, which as a point of law you might want to use this time.

She looked at the note an instant longer, absorbing the fact that he hadn't even made reference to last night. It wasn't as though she'd expected a love note, but since he had put pen to paper, she'd have expected some mention.

She wished she were the sort of person who could just cruise on through the rough emotional ruts in life, but she wasn't. Not talking about last night meant that she'd internalize her feelings until they became a knotted mess. She'd been there before and had the checks paid to her therapist to prove it. However, talking it out with Mitch would make for another uptight event in a day that already featured finding out exactly how much business trouble she was in. Maybe for today only she'd take the talk-free route.

Kira folded the note in half and dropped it in the trash, then pocketed the key, which she'd use later. *After* she'd made use of Roxanne's PDA.

Hungry, she grabbed some strawberries from the fridge, rinsed them and ate the sweet berries one by one, leaving only their green, crownlike stems. Then she raided Mitch's office for a pad of paper and packed her briefcase. As an afterthought, she also grabbed a towel and her new beachwear. If she was going to her former cottage to water plants, she might as well take the extra steps to Lake Michigan's sleek sand dunes.

After a quick stop at the Village Grounds for a latte fix and a hello to Lisa, Kira arrived at Sandy Bend's small library. As she pulled into the lot, she saw a police cruiser parked nearby, in the adjoining school complex where a group of kids were playing summertime shirts-versus-skins basketball. Mitch was standing on the edge of the court, joking with some of the players.

She could sense the moment he noticed her. Her heart sped and a tingle she couldn't quell reached her skin. Still, she managed to park her car and get into the building without waving a hankie or otherwise making a spectacle of herself.

Once inside she checked in with the librarian, offering her driver's license in lieu of a library card. The computer room was empty, for which Kira was most grateful. She logged on to the Whitman-Pierce Web site, then pulled Roxanne's PDA from the briefcase's outside pocket.

Seconds later she was smack in the middle of Roxanne's e-mail. Like a good snoop, she was careful to follow the prompts so the mail wouldn't disappear after being read. She wanted to leave no trace of her activities as she worked her way into the layers of her partner's life.

Kira started with the old mail that Roxanne hadn't bothered to delete from the server. Most of the items had headers like Fisher Island Home? or Closing Date—exactly what one would expect to see in a real estate agent's virtual files. Kira started through them in chronological order. At first nothing seemed unusual, and she began to wonder if all the nerves and suspicion were for nothing. Maybe Roxanne was really on vacation…with some ugly, ugly playmates.

Then Kira read an e-mail that struck her wrong. The communication was simple enough, referring to a closing date. But she was almost certain that they had never done business with the client mentioned. Whitman-Pierce's niche was small and elegant. A firm that specialized in multimillion-dollar tropical hideaways didn't do a high-volume business, and Kira recognized most of their former clients' names.

She pulled out the legal pad she'd filched from Mitch and began listing names, dates and any dollar amounts referred to. Out of the thirty remaining old messages, seven others referred to deals and clients that she couldn't recall. While it was conceivable that one or two might have slipped her memory, eight couldn't have. What really made goose bumps rise on her arms was an unread message confirming a "loan document delivery appointment" set for the day before they had visited Casa Pura Vida.

Not only didn't Kira recognize the sender's name, Kira and Roxanne *never* touched mortgage loan documents, which fell into the title companies' domain. Title company representatives coordinated the loan documents with the lender and ensured that the deed to the property was valid and that the funds were good. At that point, all Kira and Roxanne did was a last bit of client hand-holding, followed by acceptance of a hefty commission check. No deliveries, ever.

This was bad, just wrong. And yet subtle enough that Kira was convinced Roxanne had implicated their business in whatever scheme she was running. Kira pushed aside the notes she'd taken, rubbed at the ache forming in the back of her neck and refocused on the computer screen. She needed to somehow double-check the mystery clients before forwarding the names on to her investigator. There was no point in sending Don off track if her business was simply outgrowing her brain.

Still, she didn't want to start talk by giving a find-the-mystery-client request to Susan. Kira was sure that the office antennae were already sensitive to weirdness, since both owners had never been gone at the same time before. That left her with her least best friend—the computer—as her only source of info.

About a year ago she'd sat through a meeting with
Roxanne and the software designer she'd hired to
put all the company's accounting information in a
database that would be retrievable on line by their
accountants. Because this stuff bored Kira comatose,
she'd paid attention to only about every tenth word.
If she were a contortionist, she'd be kicking herself
in the rear about now. Since she wasn't, being forced
to muddle through the program alone would be punishment enough.

Time crawled as Kira searched. Just when she
came up with the monthly reports she was seeking,
Sandy Bend's mothers must have made a mass decision to get some time away from their children, because about two zillion kids poured into the computer room and clustered around the open computers.

A few came to stand behind her, sending brain
waves urging her to leave. This she didn't need.
Bowing to strength in preteen numbers, Kira exited
the Web site, packed her briefcase and departed. In
a way she was relieved to be done for the day. She
needed time to absorb what was going on, time to
combat the stress sawing at her nerves. And she had
just the place to do it.

Fifteen minutes later she was back in her childhood summer home. Kira doubted that she'd ever be
able to fully distance herself from this house, to see
it as Steve and Hallie's and in no way hers. Which
went a long way toward explaining why she'd broken in without a second thought.

She had to admit that using a key to get inside was
certainly easier on a girl's elbows and knees than
climbing a tree and crawling across a roof. Kira

closed the front door and then set her briefcase and swim gear by a low cocktail table in the living room. While the room bore the stamp of an artist in residence, with walls in new, vivid hues and whimsical bits of art here and there, it still evoked a nostalgic sort of peace. Even with all the changes it smelled the same: old pinewood, lake breezes and damp forest. It was easy to forget that a hectic and sometimes dangerous world waited not too far off.

Once she'd finished watering the plants, Kira changed into her bathing suit to ready for some beach time. First, though, she reached into her briefcase and pulled the list she had compiled at the library, thinking maybe she should give the names one more look. Avoidance got the better of her. Before she even started, a wedding photo album on an end table caught her attention.

Weddings...

She had seriously bad karma when it came to weddings. Missing the one under the embossed white leather cover in front of her had gotten her the role of bride in another.

Kira picked up the album and settled on the sofa. She flipped past the shots of Steve and Hallie on the beach, then slowed when she came to the photos of the wedding party—one which had one more groomsman than it did bridesmaids. That hadn't been the original plan.

Kira knew that she'd been asked to be in the wedding only because Hallie was far nicer than Kira had ever been. In Hallie's shoes, Kira wouldn't have tolerated a female who out of spite and insecurity had tried to tank her romance. But that was forgive-and-forget Hallie.

Because at the time Kira could think of no way out that would fly in the face of her prior behavior, she'd gotten fitted for her bridesmaid's dress. She'd told herself right up until the weekend of the wedding that she could pull it off, too. She could walk down the aisle with Mitch Brewer.

When that moment came, she'd refuse to recall how she'd made a fool of herself in town all that previous summer. She'd forget how angry words with Mitch over one particularly rotten act toward Hallie had led to that hot interlude very much like last night's.

That Mitch was involved at all had made for the ultimate in humiliation. It seemed that ever since he'd been first on the scene for the car accident that had shattered her hip and leg when she was sixteen, he'd also been first on the scene for all the other awful events in her life.

The Friday of the rehearsal dinner Kira had meant to drive from her home in Chicago to Sandy Bend. Instead panic had seized her. She couldn't face Mitch…couldn't face Sandy Bend.

She'd ended up at a Rush Street bar, drinking whatever fruity mixed drink looked most interesting. Whether it was the alcohol or the sugar that did her in, details became blurry. Right up until the fight. With no way out and no one who appeared to have any interest in rescuing her, Kira had used the tools at hand, smashing glasses on the floor and screaming for help at the top of her lungs.

Who'd have ever thought that a bar manager would take the breakage of about twelve bucks' worth of glassware so seriously?

She'd been hauled to jail. By the time she'd been

allowed to call her father and get herself bailed out, it had been too late to make Steve and Hallie's wedding. Needless to say, the consequences had been massive.

Weeks later Kira's father had offered her one hope of familial redemption. She would settle down with a mature man, one who would be a stabilizing influence. The man her father proposed was Winston Evers, his second in command over the Whitman empire.

Yes, in retrospect it was an archaic suggestion. But two things had driven Kira. First, she was well accustomed to having others prop up her lifestyle, and a husband would suit as well as the next guy. Beyond that, she'd been conditioned for years to try to please her father, partially so that the money would keep flowing but most of all because she craved his approval.

Kira didn't think her father was inherently evil or anything. Still, his choice of Winston was far from stellar. Sure, Win was brilliant and had a sharp sense of humor. But he was over twenty years older than Kira. He'd been divorced once years ago, had no children and dated for no reason other than social necessity. He was quite possibly the only person Kira knew who was more personally adrift than she.

They had spent time together, avoided anything more intimate than a dry peck on the lips and set a date for their wedding. Between wedding showers, dress fittings and pamper-me days at the spa, she'd managed to distract herself from the end event: marriage to a man she respected but could never love.

Winston had rescued her, though. She'd been at the church, ready to do the deed, when he'd asked for a minute alone with her. He'd taken her to a window that overlooked the jewel of a courtyard in the middle of the complex, had tipped her face up to the light, then had shaken his head.

"When did you last sleep?" he'd asked.

"I'm not sure." She'd been dreaming a lot. Most had been sexually explicit and all had involved Mitch.

"You can leave, you know."

Panic—or maybe excitement—had seized her. She'd frantically shaken her head. "I couldn't. Never."

"You can, and you probably should. I'm not going to be much of a husband, you know." He'd given her that world-weary smile she'd come to appreciate. "If you leave, my reputation will survive it. Now, *yours*, darling…" He'd chuckled, then kissed her cheek.

What others thought had suddenly seemed unimportant. For the first time in months Kira had felt a sense of freedom, and it was dizzying, intoxicating. "This is crazy. Everyone's arriving for a wedding. How do I do this?"

"One foot in front of the other."

She'd nodded. "One foot in front of the other."

And so she had.

And now here she was, sorry for so much. As part of her growing-up process, she'd written letters to virtually everyone in the family, apologizing for the miserable way she'd behaved for years. Some she'd heard back from, some she hadn't. All she could do anymore was prove that she could stand alone, that she wasn't a perpetual user. And the person she most had to prove it to was herself.

Kira closed Steve and Hallie's wedding album, then returned it to the spot where she'd found it. She walked through the living room's French doors and onto the deck. If a swim in Lake Michigan's chilly waters didn't shock the past out of her, nothing would.

MITCH PULLED HIS CRUISER IN next to Kira's car. It struck him that less than forty-eight hours had passed since he'd last done this very same thing. That was pretty short timing for what they had cooking between them. Of course, it was easy to pack a lot in considering how much else in the way of work he'd let drop. Good thing that crime was minimal and his boss knew he'd soon be resigning.

Before heading up the steps cut into the forested hillside to the house, Mitch grabbed the sack holding a lunch he'd picked up for Kira and himself. Food wasn't the best peace offering for the way he'd let temptation get the better of him last night, but along with an apology, it was all he had to offer.

He knew he'd be way out of his league if he tried to pick her up a piece of jewelry. And there was a good chance she wouldn't be around long enough for flowers to be more than a throwaway—a thought he hated, because now he knew exactly why she'd stuck in his mind all these years and why she would long after she was gone this time, too.

Mitch walked into the house, which was still and silent. He checked the kitchen, where Hallie had lined up her plants—probably because she knew he'd lose track and kill half of them if they weren't clumped together. After setting down the sack of food he touched the first pot's soil and found it freshly watered.

"Kira?" he called. "Are you in here?"

Out of a newly minted sense of nostalgia, he even checked the shower where he'd found her last time, but it was bone-dry. Back downstairs in the living room he picked up her trail. Her black leather briefcase sat next to the couch and some papers were spread on the cocktail table.

Mitch glanced at them, then walked to the room's French doors. He tested the handles and found them unlocked. Since Kira wasn't in sight, she must be down the dunes at the lake. Even though his conscience—one SOB of a drill sergeant—snarled at him, he walked back toward the papers she'd left.

Last night's encounter might have been damn hot, but it hadn't totally scorched his memory. He knew that earlier Kira had wanted to get to his computer for something, just as well as he knew that she wasn't in town for a friendly visit. Exactly what she was doing…that, he didn't know.

Without picking up the papers, Mitch read the jottings a couple of times. The names meant nothing to him, which was no surprise. However, the dollar amounts in the millions with question marks by them and Kira's heading entitled Mystery Clients were more than enough to raise a few questions in him, too.

He regretted never asking Steve for specifics on what Kira had been doing these past few years. He'd been afraid that what he'd hear would fall under the category of more of the same, and he'd wanted to think better of her. Now that he'd spent some time with her—and despite the evidence in front of him to the contrary—he couldn't imagine that she was still flitting party to party, crisis to crisis. In fact, he'd almost call Kira mellow.

He grinned as memories of last night's heat and excitement came to him. Yeah. Almost mellow.

So what was she doing that involved "mystery clients" and the amounts of money she'd noted? No fan of subterfuge, Mitch figured the best thing to do was ask. Of course, he'd have to do it in a way that didn't begin with *I was reading papers I shouldn't have been....* And since nothing was immediately coming to mind, he figured he'd improvise once he was closer to her—a place he was really growing to like.

Mitch grabbed the lunch offering from the kitchen, then made his way down the steps to a sweep of the dunes. As sand sank into his uniform shoes and socks, it occurred to him that he'd have been better off ditching the footwear back at the house.

He crested the last dune and spotted Kira closer to the water, where the sand was hard packed. Her hair was slicked back as though she'd been swimming, and she was wearing a red bikini that was hot enough to rouse him past the semi-turned-on state he'd been in since he'd decided to track her down.

He laughed when he noticed that she lay on a towel he'd last seen in his own linen closet this morning. The woman did have a way of making herself ruler of her surroundings.

As he approached, she spotted him. She shielded her eyes from the sun with her hand, then after checking him out, quickly grabbed a red piece of fabric he supposed was some sort of skirt or something, scooted it under her bottom and tied it low on her hips. He watched her sit up and smooth the fabric over the scars they both knew she'd had for years. She carefully settled her right hand over the old injury before waving with her left.

Mitch's heart tightened at this show of vulnerability. She'd always made an effort to appear impervious to others' opinions. And he'd always been a little sad that she felt she had to be so perfect.

"Hey," she said as he grew close. "Overdressed for the beach, aren't you?"

He held out his purchases from a deli in town. "I'm on lunch break. I saw you leave the library and figured you had to be out here, so I brought us food."

She patted the towel next to her. "Have a seat."

As he pulled out a container of fruit salad he thought she'd like and the pasta salad he knew he'd like, Mitch tried to think of some way to launch the what-the-hell-is-going-on-with-you? topic.

While he hesitated, Kira grabbed the pasta salad. "Carbs! Wonderful carbs!"

He was torn between asking for them back and smiling at her excitement over pasta and a bunch of purportedly Greek vegetables.

She took the plastic fork he offered and dug in. "There's nothing like carbs for stress eating," she said over a mouthful of pasta shells in a very nonsocialitelike way.

Since he was a guy, he considered carbs good for everything, including curing the common cold. That and apparently giving him a hook into the conversation he wanted to have.

"So, you're stressed?" he asked.

She nodded. "Maxed out."

"What's up?"

She hesitated before speaking. "I didn't think I was ready to talk about this, but I guess I am. Last night scared me, Mitch."

Last night? He definitely needed more practice in

crafting leading questions. It was time to redirect the witness.

"So it's just last night that's bothering you? There's nothing else?"

She reloaded her fork and pushed on as though she hadn't heard him. "We've kissed each other twice in three years, and both times I ended up acting like some sort of...I dunno...porno queen. You have to have one of two opinions of me—that I'm easy or nuts."

Clearly she was acquainted with no porno queens. "I, uh..."

She shook her head. "Don't tell me which one applies. I'm better off not knowing."

Good thing, since he had no clear-cut answer for what he thought of her, except that it didn't involve porno queens.

"I don't react like that to all men, okay? Just you, and I don't know why. I mean, you're attractive and everything, but it's not as though we have the friendliest of pasts."

Mitch frowned. "I've always felt friendly toward you." Which was like saying that the beach they sat on had a couple of grains of sand.

She shrugged in an embarrassed way, then speared some more pasta. "Quite an ego boost having me fall all over you, huh?"

He smiled. It would do.

"So, do you think you could share that with me?" he asked, pointing the spare plastic fork toward the pasta.

"Sure," she said, centering the container between them. Actually a little closer to her than him. Mitch got in a few bites before she became too territorial.

Eventually she balanced her fork on the edge of

the pasta container's discarded lid. Mitch watched as she looked out at the endless blue of the lake and sky, then back to him.

"I'm not sure how much longer I'm going to be in town," she said. "It could be as little as a few days if things heat up for me. But for however long—if you'd let me—I'd like to stay at your place."

"I'd like that," he said. He'd also like the chance to figure out what was going on with her—a task more easily accomplished when she was under his roof. "Stay as long as you want."

She smiled. "Thanks."

"So, what sort of things might heat up?" he asked in a casual tone.

"Just work stuff," she said. He didn't bother trying to measure the degree of honesty in her statement. He knew it held enough that she'd spoken with confidence.

"So, you have a job other than kidnapping maids and cooks?" he asked.

"Of course I do. Being the black-sheep Whitman doesn't pay too well. Or at all, actually."

Mitch scratched another assumption from his list.

"After working as real estate agents for someone else, a friend and I got our brokers' licenses and struck out on our own a couple of years ago," Kira said. "We have a small business in the Miami area that specializes in higher-end properties."

He saluted her with his fork. "It suits you, Highness."

She smiled. "It does. It took me a while to find my niche, but I'm there."

"So tell me more about what you do."

She shifted restlessly, still careful to cover that

scar. "It's boring, unless you're a real estate geek like me."

"It can't be worse than some of the dry stuff I've dealt with in law school," he offered.

"I'd just really rather leave my Florida life in Florida."

A sudden awful thought struck Mitch. It was improbable, considering the line she'd spun when she'd arrived in town, but he had to ask. "You're not married or anything, are you?"

She rolled her eyes. "I'm lucky if I have a date every three months."

Selfish as it was, Mitch liked the sound of that. He wasn't quite as thrilled to have the same statistic apply to him lately.

Kira reached her free hand into the sand just past the edge of the towel and ran her fingers though it, leaving a wavelike pattern in her wake.

"Can't we just take these next few days for what they're worth? Not too many questions, just some fun?" she asked.

That was a man's evasion—one he'd used to defend himself from expectations more times than he could count. He'd never figured on being on the receiving end of the play. He didn't much like it, either.

"Sure," he said, just as those women had said to him before. He'd known then that it was a glossing over of the emotions involved, but he'd also been a willing recipient of the lie. Now he wanted to give her the truth and let her deal with it. Maybe she'd have more success at making sense of it than he was.

She'd never believe him, though. She'd never accept that the few days they had were worth more than hot and hungry sex.

That *she* was worth more.

But if this was what she wanted, he'd at least deliver that. And it wasn't as though it would pain him too much in the process.

Kira met his eyes with a direct gaze. "It's pretty clear to me that we're going to end up finishing what we started last night. And since that's the case, let's get the basic stuff out of the way while we're still able to think straight. I'm not on the pill or anything, so you're going to need to use protection. Which I'd expect you to anyway. And I'd also expect you to tell me that you and your doctor are recent acquaintances and that you're the picture of health…if you get my point."

Mitch nodded. He had to respect her pragmatic approach, even if it was rubbing his nose in the fact that she wanted this to be all about sex. "Yes to all of the above."

She relaxed a little. "Same here."

Mitch took her hand and brought it to his mouth for a brief kiss. "Now that we've got that squared away, I should tell you that I have class tonight in East Lansing. I'm going to be leaving at three and probably won't be back until after midnight." He grinned, figuring at least he could get in one last tease. "So, unless you'd like to…"

Mitch trailed off, gesturing at the towel beneath them.

Kira laughed. "Let me see…. I could make love with a police officer under the noonday sun on a beach that has its share of people trooping by or I could just finish scarfing carbs and look forward to being in a real bed with you."

She leaned forward and brushed a kiss against

his mouth. "Hate to tell you, Mr. Officer, but the carbs and a real bed win. Think you can wait?"

Yeah, but it was going to hurt like hell doing it.

Mitch glanced at his watch and then stood. "My lunch break's over, Highness. I'll leave you to your carbs. And stay out of trouble, okay?"

"Hey, my bad-girl days are behind me," she replied with admirable sincerity.

For his sake as well as hers, Mitch hoped that was true.

8

EYES GLAZED FROM READING ONE too many financial reports, Kira shut down Mitch's computer. She glanced at the nearby desk clock. It was not quite nine-thirty, leaving hours yet before he'd be home. Kira stood and stretched, easing tense muscles.

She felt mildly guilty for using his computer for her research. Still, she'd decided to live by the theory that what Mitch didn't know wouldn't hurt him. And the corollary to the theory also would prove true: what he didn't know couldn't hurt *her*, either. As joking as his stay-out-of-trouble request this afternoon had been, it wouldn't have sprung to mind if he didn't have doubts about her ability to handle life.

She was sure she could keep herself together while her private investigator did his thing. Mitch didn't need to be involved, and she didn't need him witnessing yet another Kira catastrophe. Tomorrow she'd call Don, tell him her concerns and give him the list of unfamiliar client names. She wished that she had something more concrete than suspicions, but the monthly reports she'd reviewed tonight showed nothing that matched the names or sums on her mystery client e-mails.

And now she'd finished up with business, it was

time to prepare for pleasure…. She peeked into Mitch's bedroom and shook her head at the clutter of books and magazines. It wasn't a disaster zone, yet it also wasn't the seduction setting she wanted, either.

She laughed at the thought of the word *seduction*. Definitely no seduction would be required on Mitch's part. She'd wanted him since he'd trapped her two days earlier.

Kira gathered the books and magazines into her arms. Mitch certainly was a guy with broad interests. There were sportsman's magazines, almost obligatory for men who lived near both a big lake for fishing and miles of forest for hunting. But there were also current-events magazines and quarterly law reviews from different schools. She felt a little like a voyeur learning about him this way, but she'd take what she could get.

Kira stowed the magazines and papers on top of the jumble of shoes on the floor of Mitch's closet. She barely got the door shut before the mess started to slide her way. As she walked to the living room and gathered the goodies she'd bought in preparation for tonight, she admitted to herself that the wanting hadn't started two days ago. She'd wanted him *forever*. As a teenager, her first sparks of sexual curiosity had always been centered on Mitch. As a woman, she could act on those feelings and planned to do so thoroughly.

Back in his bedroom she dug into the bag and unearthed one of the purchases on which she'd spent the rest of her cash. She unscrewed the top of the bottle of massage oil and sniffed.

"Perfect."

She set it on the nightstand, along with some little sweet-smelling candles in their glass votive holders. Her stint with a party planner might have been brief, but it had given her an appreciation for the importance of a theme in all events. Tonight's was Mitch's Favorite Foods.

Kira had put the box of condoms she'd found in the linen closet on the nightstand and was folding back the comforter and plumping the pillows when the phone on the far nightstand began to ring. Her first thought was to leave it except that the phone in the kitchen had no answering machine. Neither did this one.

What if it was Mitch calling? What if he was running late or out of gas or otherwise unacceptably delayed? She'd gladly drive to the middle of the state to haul him home.

As ring number four chimed out, she made her decision.

"Brewer residence," she answered.

After a short silence a woman's voice said, "This is the *Mitch* Brewer residence?" She sounded confused or maybe shocked.

"It is."

"Then, is, uh, Mitch home?"

Kira stepped into the role of crisp and official personal assistant, trying to distance herself from her own curiosity. "No, I'm sorry, he's not available. Would you like to leave a message?"

"Who is this?" asked the caller.

Kira didn't feel inclined to share. "A friend of Mitch's. And your name?"

"Betsy."

"Betsy," Kira confirmed. "Will he know what this is regarding?"

"I'm... Wait, this is class night, isn't it? I can't believe I forgot."

Okay, so she knew Mitch's schedule. That didn't mean they had any intimate connection. "Should I have him call you?"

"Definitely. Tell him it's something he's been wanting to hear."

"Does he have your phone number?" Kira asked.

The Betsy person laughed, and Kira felt her lip begin to curl, which she feared was step one in a territorial growl.

"Don't worry, he has my number," Betsy said.

After they'd exchanged goodbyes, Kira hung up, wondering who this Betsy was. It wasn't jealousy driving her, exactly. She knew that Mitch didn't have a serious girlfriend. He was straight-up honest and wouldn't have had her overnight in his house if he did—let alone touch her the way he had last night.

Still, Kira felt unsettled. Mitch had an entire existence that she knew little about. And she couldn't ask him—not so long as she was unwilling to share the details of hers.

She'd fully intended to greet him from his bed. Now she couldn't quite get herself to do that. Kira went to the kitchen and riffled through the laundry basket until she found the taupe nightgown. She'd washed it and a load of Mitch's laundry this afternoon—one more bit of playacting that she really was part of his life.

She shed her clothes, leaving them in a pile next to the washer, then slipped into the nightgown. She'd wait for him on the couch. That place was at least clearly hers.

At eleven forty-five Mitch pulled up in front of his house. He'd set what he'd bet was a new land-speed record from East Lansing to Sandy Bend. If he were a good cop, he'd write himself a ticket. But right now he wasn't a cop or a law student. No, he was one lucky and extremely thankful bugger about to have eleven years' worth of fantasies become real. Whatever the ultimate price in continuing this obsession, he decided he'd be willing to pay it.

He opened the front door, stepped inside and dropped his backpack full of books by the coat closet. Quietly he closed the door and walked into the living room.

She was asleep on the plaid beast. The sofa had come with the house. He'd kept it because it was so damn ugly that it deserved a home. He had to say it looked one hell of a lot better with Kira on it, especially when she was wearing the gold-colored nightgown that had brought him to the brink last night.

His foot nudged something—her briefcase maybe—and he took a quick sidestep to avoid ending up on his butt. The noise awakened Kira. In the meager wash of light from the front hall, Mitch saw her sit up.

"Who's there?" she asked, at the same time awkwardly scrambling up from the sofa.

He was quickly telling her it was okay when she clutched at her leg and stumbled to the floor.

"Dammit," she gasped. "Stupid hip."

Mitch strode over and bent down next to her. "Let me help you up."

"I can do it myself," she said, then clambered to her feet, leaving him there with his hand held out. He let it drop to his side.

She limped a slow circle around the room while he stood by the couch feeling useless.

"Maybe you should sit down?" he asked.

"No, I have to walk it off or I'll be stiff all night."

"I'm sorry. This isn't how I wanted tonight to begin." He switched on the lamp beside the couch, leaving the three-way bulb at its lowest setting.

She stopped by the rocking chair that had been his mother's and rested one hand on the back of it. "It's not your fault. I've always been an edgy sleeper and I guess you startled me."

Mitch walked to her and briefly touched his fingertips to her cheek. "Can I get you anything? Some aspirin maybe?"

She nodded. "That might be a good idea."

"I'll be right back," he said before heading to the kitchen for the aspirin and some water. He hadn't quite cleared the room when he heard her hiss of pain as she walked again. Funny how guilt was more effective than jumping into Lake Michigan in January when it came to calming a guy's libido.

He took his time in the kitchen, giving Kira a chance to get a grasp on the poise that he knew was so important to her. When he returned, she was seated on the sofa, her hands settled on her knees.

"Here," he said. She held out her palm and he dropped the aspirin into it. After she'd popped them into her mouth, he gave her the water. When she was through, he took the glass from her, set it on the end table, then leaned back on the sofa.

He draped one arm across the back of the old dinosaur of a couch. Kira moved closer to him, relaxing with her head pillowed on his chest. The emotion that shot through him had a whole lot more to do with the utter rightness of having her there than it did with lust.

"This feels good," she murmured.

"A far better way to start the night," he agreed.

He ran his fingers through her hair, oddly riveted by the way it still managed to shine in the dim lamplight.

"How was class?" she asked.

"Too long. Then again, so was the rest of the day."

She sighed and burrowed closer. "Agreed."

They sat in silence a while. Mitch let Kira set the pace. She would know best when the aspirin had kicked in. While they waited, he took the time to remember the details of this moment—how she smelled faintly of strawberries and how her skin felt soft and resilient under his touch.

He brought his arm from the back of the couch down so he could trace the line of the gown where it plunged into a vee, exposing the cleft between her breasts. Her nipples rose as he touched her. Soon she leaned her head back for a kiss.

Damn, but he needed her in a bed.

She must have felt the same way, because she untwined herself from his arms and stood. "You promised me a real bed."

And as he'd promised himself, he would deliver. They walked to the bedroom together. When they were there, matters didn't proceed as he'd expected.

"Hang on," Kira said, closing his bedroom door in his face. Mitch waited, figured he might as well give his self-control its final workout. He could hear her rustling about, then the door swung open.

"Okay, now," she said.

She'd been one busy camper. He took in the white

candles burning in votives on his dresser, the top of which she'd cleared of its usual clutter of books and papers. Both nightstands had received equal treatment. Each held candles, and on one the lamp shone, too.

"Just to keep us safe, don't open your closet door," she warned.

He smiled, imagining the avalanche, and then walked over to the nightstand on his side of the bed. She'd put out a box of condoms and a bottle of… something.

He picked it up, and excitement shot through him. Flavored massage oil. "Strawberry flavored? Do I want to know where you got this?"

"Definitely not," she said after giving him a broad grin.

"Try me."

"Devine Secrets," she said. "It's under-the-counter stuff, special request only. I went in for the scented variety. Cross my heart."

Hot thoughts of using the oil on Kira warred with the sure knowledge that his sister-in-law was going to give him a boatload of grief. "Yeah, like scented-only would have made it any better. You bought it from Dana?"

"It was our lucky day. She's up at the new Crystal Mountain spa. Otherwise I would have retreated with a bottle of nail polish."

"Wise. Very wise," he said as he unscrewed the top to the oil. He put his index finger over the opening and tipped it enough to coat the pad of his finger, then brought the oil to his mouth. "Not bad. How'd you know to choose strawberry?"

"Because I've witnessed your food tastes, and

they didn't have any marshmallow fluff," she replied, then came to take the bottle from his hand as he laughed.

Mitch wouldn't call what he was feeling *love*, but he would admit to his heart expanding to make room for the smart and altogether too sexy woman in front of him.

"Uh-uh. Hand the bottle back," he ordered.

For once she did as he asked. He coated a fingertip again, then ran it over the curve of her shoulder.

"Nice," he said after sucking on the spot just hard enough to draw a shiver from her.

He repeated the process, this time touching the top of one plump breast.

"Very nice," she said.

Mitch knew he could do even better. He went down on one knee and began sliding up the hem of her gown. Skipping the oil for now, he dusted kisses on the smooth bone of her right shin, pushing the silk fabric higher.

Kira stepped away.

"What are you doing?" he asked.

"Turning out the light."

He stood. "Don't. I want to see you."

She shifted uneasily. "Some things are better left to the imagination."

He'd been concerned that this moment would come. "This is about the scars, isn't it?"

Gaze fixed on the carpet at her feet, she nodded.

Mitch scrubbed his hand over his face, trying to decide how to handle this.

"Kira, they don't matter. They're in your past."

"A less-than-attractive part of it." She sat on the edge of the bed. "Look, I know this seems irrational to you, and that's because it probably is, but I don't want you to see them."

He'd seen worse, though. He'd seen her before the wounds had healed. Alerted by Hallie that Kira had taken off in a car filled with wasted college guys, he'd been the first person to arrive at the accident scene. Since she hadn't been wearing a seat belt, Kira had been thrown from the packed car.

He'd just turned twenty and had been pretty damn sure he was a true hard-ass. That was, until he'd seen that jagged white shard of bone sticking through the ripped flesh of her thigh. He'd held himself together, administering first aid as he'd been trained in the paramedics' courses he'd been taking that summer.

When the paramedic crew had arrived and he'd been sure that Kira was in good hands, he'd gone into the woods and had puked until his stomach was empty. Then he'd tried to go after the drunken—and injury-free—moron who'd been driving. Luckily by then Cal had been there to hold him off, because Mitch would have killed the guy. And would have been glad to do it.

Over ten years had passed and he could still feel that anger boiling in him. At sixteen, Kira had meant something to him. At twenty-seven, she meant even more.

"Come on, it's no big deal," he wheedled.

"That's easy for you to say."

He had her now. He smiled, and her brown eyes narrowed.

"Don't laugh," she said.

"I'm not laughing." He unbuckled his belt, then unbuttoned his jeans and worked down his fly.

"I'm not in the mood anymore," she said from her perch on the bed.

This time he did laugh because she sounded damn near like the sulky socialite he used to know. "I'm just playing some show-and-tell, Highness."

"You're assuming I want to see."

"You will." He toed out of his shoes, took off his socks, shucked his jeans, then moved closer. "Think you can beat this?" he asked, settling his left index finger on the knotted and angry red scar that ran a good five inches down his thigh. "I'm betting you can't."

She stood and traced the damaged flesh with one fingertip. He could tell by the line between her brows, by the way she worried at her lower lip with her teeth that her touch was light and careful. She needn't have bothered. His nerves hadn't fully regenerated yet, and he still couldn't feel much there. Now, a hand's length in and up…there, he could feel just fine. And he couldn't recall ever being this hard and aching.

"What happened?" she asked.

"Gunshot wound," he said, doing his damn best to sound casual.

"When?"

"Last fall. Some guys on their way up to deer camp stopped and drank Truro's Tavern dry. There was a fight in the back parking lot and my leg got in the way."

"I'm sorry." Her fingers glided upward, closer to where he wanted them. "All this from one bullet?"

Mitch closed his eyes, figuring he could hold on to some vestige of control if he couldn't see her. "No, the rest is from an infection that followed."

"Wow. I'm *really* sorry."

He shrugged. "I wasn't much to look at to begin with."

He nearly lost it when he felt her mouth settle, warm and wet, just below the edge of his short jersey boxers. Giving himself up for a goner, he looked down and caught her smiling at what had to be one tortured expression on his face.

"We'll leave the looks assessment with the beholder, okay?" she said. "Take off your shirt."

Mitch was happy to comply.

After he'd dropped the shirt to the ground, she hooked her fingertips into the elastic of the boxers riding below his waist. "Not much? I've got a feeling you're a whole big lot to look at."

Mitch started to laugh, but ended up gasping when she followed the contour of his erection with one sure hand. He settled his palm over hers, meaning to stop her, but he lacked the self-discipline to do it.

She squeezed him through the fabric, and he could feel sweat begin to pop out on his forehead. Or maybe it was blood. He'd been too aroused for too long.

But he also planned to follow through with the purpose of this whole show.

"No distracting me," he said. "I've shown you my scar, now you show me yours."

She let go of him, then nudged him back a step. For a moment he thought that it was going to be this simple to get her past the scar hang-up. But he'd forgotten that nothing with Kira was ever straightforward.

Instead she sat on the bed and shimmied up her

nightgown so that it still covered her legs, but was free from beneath her bottom. She held out her hand.

"We're going to go by feel."

And she was going to be the death of him.

He put his hand in hers, and she worked it under the raised hem of her gown. She directed his fingers until they were settled over a broad indentation that was about three inches long. "This is the leg."

"Doesn't feel too bad," he said.

She took his hand higher, over her right hip. "And these are from the socket and pelvis repair."

He had a man's hands, rough from years of football and work. He could maybe feel a small ridge or two, but nothing much.

"I think I'm going to have to look, Highness." His voice had come out kind of husky, but that's because he was having one hell of a time not letting his hand venture elsewhere, to be skin to skin with the places that last night he'd touched through her gown. "Just lie back, sweetheart. Let me…"

She acquiesced with a small sigh, her lower legs dangling off the bed. Mitch reached to his right, grabbed a pillow and tucked it beneath her head.

"It's going to be okay," he said.

She nodded, but he could still see the shadow of self-consciousness in her eyes. Using both hands, he began pushing her nightgown upward, exposing slender thighs, the right one showing the mark of the injury he recalled.

Mitch reached for the oil, poured a little into his palm and rubbed it slowly over the spot. Her muscle tightened beneath his hand.

"Relax," he murmured.

After a few moments he could feel the tension

ease from her. Slowly he moved the nightgown higher, exposing not only the thinner scars on her hip but the soft golden hair on her mons.

Mitch's erection pressed harder against his boxers until he couldn't stand it anymore. He reached down and rid himself of the last of his clothes.

When he returned his attention to Kira, a smile curved the corners of her mouth upward. "You're definitely a lot to look at," she said.

So was she. Mitch's hand trembled as he poured more oil. He gave the marks on her hip the same slow treatment that he had the one on her thigh. Then, unable to deprive himself any longer, he reached for the oil a final time, rubbing it between his fingertips.

"It's time to lose the nightgown," he said to Kira.

She sat up and pulled it over her head, then let it drop on the bed next to her. Mitch's heart slammed. God, she was beautiful. A wash of pink had risen from her chest to her face, and he knew that she was as turned-on as he was. Clearly knowing his intent for the oil on his fingertips, she opened her legs to him. This act of trust made him want her all the more.

He stroked her with oil, dipping his fingers into her tight wetness and using his thumb to work gasps from her. And when he thought she was ready, he bent forward and kissed the insides of her thighs, moving upward bit by bit until he parted her with both thumbs and tasted sweet, slick strawberry heaven.

If a guy had to die, this was the way to go.

KIRA COULDN'T BEAR ANY MORE pleasure. Knowing she was less than a touch away from completion, she tugged at Mitch's hair. When he looked up at her, she said, "I don't want to come without you inside me. Please…"

His hands slid down from where he'd been touching her, to her knees. "Any way you want it, sweetheart."

She scooted up on the bed and felt almost weak limbed with anticipation when he joined her, kneeling between her open legs.

He reached for the condoms she'd left on the nightstand. "I'd like to go slowly, to savor you," he said. "But that's going to have to be next time, okay?"

She nodded, but she still needed to touch him, to feel his heat in her hand.

"Let me," she said, taking the flat plastic packet from him.

Mitch rolled and lay back on the bed, and now Kira knelt above him. She was to the point where even the sound of the condom packet coming open was arousing. Hands trembling, she unrolled the condom down his thick shaft.

Mitch's eyes were half closed, and his hiss of pleasure resonated inside her. She leaned forward and kissed him once deeply, using her tongue to tell him what she needed. When she moved slightly away, he cupped the back of her head with his hand.

"I don't want to hurt you," he said. "Would it be more comfortable if you were on top?"

She ran her palm down the side of his face, tingling with pleasure over the feel of his day's growth of beard. "How about we try it both ways? Just for comparison's sake, of course."

She barely had the words out before he had flipped her onto her back. He entered her slowly,

An Important Message
from the Editors

Dear Reader,

If you'd enjoy reading romance novels with larger print that's easier on your eyes, let us send you *TWO FREE HARLEQUIN INTRIGUE® NOVELS* in our *NEW LARGER-PRINT EDITION*. These books are complete and unabridged, but the type is set about 25% bigger to make it easier to read. Look inside for an actual-size sample.

By the way, you'll also get a surprise gift with your two free books!

Pam Powers

Peel off Seal and
Place Inside...

LARGER-PRINT
FREE BOOKS
EDITION

THE RIGHT WOMAN

she'd thought she was fine. It took Daniel's words and Brooke's question to make her realize she was far from a full recovery.

She'd made a start with her sister's help and she intended to go forward now. Sarah felt as if she'd been living in a darkened room and some-one had suddenly opened a door, letting in the fresh air and sunshine. She could feel its warmth slowly seeping into the coldest part of her. The feeling was liberating. She realized it was only a small step and she had a long way to go, but she was ready to face life again with Serena and her family behind her.

All too soon, they were saying goodbye and arah experienced a moment of sadness for all e years she and Serena had missed. But they d each other now, and that's what
She held

PRINTED IN THE U.S.A.
Publisher acknowledges the copyright holder of the excerpt from this individual work as follows:
THE RIGHT WOMAN Copyright © 2004 by Linda Warren. All rights reserved.
® and TM are trademarks owned and used by the trademark owner and/or its licensee.

YOURS FREE!
You'll get a great mystery gift with your two free larger-print books!

GET TWO FREE LARGER-PRINT BOOKS!

YES! Please send me two free Harlequin Intrigue® romantic suspense novels in the larger-print edition, and my free mystery gift, too. I understand that I am under no obligation to purchase anything, as explained on the back of this insert.

PLACE FREE GIFTS SEAL HERE

199 HDL D7U7   399 HDL D7U9

FIRST NAME	LAST NAME

ADDRESS

APT.#	CITY

STATE/PROV.	ZIP/POSTAL CODE

Are you a current Harlequin Intrigue® subscriber and want to receive the larger-print edition?
Call 1-800-221-5011 today!

▼ **DETACH AND MAIL CARD TODAY!** ▼

(H-ILPP-05/05) © 2004 Harlequin Enterprises Ltd.

The Harlequin Reader Service™ — Here's How It Works:

Accepting your 2 free Harlequin Intrigue® larger-print books and gift places you under no obligation to buy anything. You may keep the books and gift and return the shipping statement marked "cancel." If you do not cancel, about a month later we'll send you 6 additional Harlequin Intrigue larger-print books and bill you just $4.49 each in the U.S., or $5.24 each in Canada, plus 25¢ shipping & handling per book and applicable taxes if any.* That's the complete price and — compared to cover prices of $5.24 each in the U.S. and $6.24 each in Canada — it's quite a bargain! You may cancel at any time, but if you choose to continue, every month we'll send you 6 more books, which you may either purchase at the discount price or return to us and cancel your subscription.

*Terms and prices subject to change without notice. Sales tax applicable in N.Y. Canadian residents will be charged applicable provincial taxes and GST.

If offer card is missing write to: Harlequin Reader Service, 3010 Walden Ave., P.O. Box 1867, Buffalo, NY 14240-1867

POSTAGE WILL BE PAID BY ADDRESSEE

BUSINESS REPLY MAIL
FIRST-CLASS MAIL   PERMIT NO. 717-003   BUFFALO, NY

HARLEQUIN READER SERVICE
3010 WALDEN AVE
PO BOX 1867
BUFFALO NY 14240-9952

NO POSTAGE
NECESSARY
IF MAILED
IN THE
UNITED STATES

which was a very good thing. It had been so long that she'd forgotten this sense of stretching, the near pain that presaged the pleasure to come. Or maybe she'd never felt everything so acutely as she was now with Mitch.

He stopped. "Are you okay?"

"Better than okay." She tipped her hips upward, urging him on. He received the message, because he pushed the rest of the way in. Holding still within her, he dipped his forehead down to briefly rest against hers.

"Finally," he said, then kissed her.

Kira collected enough scattered brain cells to crack a joke. "What—it's been a long two days?"

"More like eleven years," he said, bracing his weight on his strong arms and looking down at her.

She knew her shock must have shown on her face, but Mitch was too wrapped up in the moment to notice. His jaw muscles flexed as though he were gritting his teeth and his face shone with perspiration.

She wriggled her hips a little, then ran the sole of her left foot over the back of his tight calf. It was rough with hair, and she shivered at the feel.

"With eleven years of buildup, I guess I'd better make this good," she said.

He kissed her hard and then said, "Just hold on, Highness. I've got a feeling that this time's going to be mostly fast."

Mitch picked up a rhythm that had them both soon tumbling over a blissful edge. He'd been half-right, Kira thought, once thought was again a possibility. It had been fast, but, my, it had been good.

He was collapsed facedown on the pillows next to

her. She sent one hand over to settle on his muscled buttocks.

"Don't get too comfortable, lawman. This time I'm on top...."

9

FOR BETTER OR WORSE, MITCH was an analytical guy. He always began examining a situation—be it a case in law school or a real-life event—by standing on the bedrock of a single fact that he knew to be true. When it came to the woman sleeping so peacefully next to him, he couldn't find that starting point.

All he knew was this: it was possible to have sex without any deeper emotional commitment. Hell, he used to do it all the time. Something had happened, though. With Kira there was no switching off his brain. The stakes had changed for him, and sex alone wasn't enough. He wanted into her life, dammit.

His assumptions about Kira had been shot down one by one. She was smart and ambitious, not the spoiled princess he recalled—and had still lusted after. She was generous, thinking of more than just her own pleasure, as she'd shown him time and again throughout the night.

Yet, she was holding back both emotionally and with the details of her life. He had enough ego and powers of observation to know that it wasn't a lack of feelings for him that drove her. Before it became a habit, he needed to cut out the sex as a crutch. It was too simple for Kira—and for him—to equate that physical intimacy with communication.

Mitch realized that almost any other male would tell him that he was out of his freaking head to even think of giving up what he'd experienced last night. Really, it was that damn risk/reward thing. He was willing to risk *now* for the reward of maybe having a *later*.

Mitch rolled onto his side and looked at the alarm clock on his dresser. It was nearly seven o'clock and soon he'd have to leave for work. He rustled the covers with just enough force to be sure to wake Kira. She stretched and yawned.

"Good morning," she said, then smiled.

Mitch wouldn't be opposed to starting a whole lot of mornings with that smile. He realized that at this moment the odds on that happening were pretty skinny.

Kira pushed back her hair from her face and frowned. "Hey, I forgot to tell you that you had a call last night. Someone named Betsy?"

She'd end-loaded an info-seeking question of her own in the way she'd said Betsy's name. Mitch didn't plan on delivering the particulars. It would do Kira some good to have a taste of unsatisfied curiosity.

She pulled the covers over her breasts, then said, "She wants you to call her. She said it's about something you've been waiting to hear."

Mitch smiled at the thought of Bets. She'd started clerking for Judge Kilwin yesterday. Knowing Bets, she'd probably already reorganized the judge's files, not that they needed it. Bets couldn't help herself.

Kira prodded him in the side. "So, are you going to tell me who this Betsy is?"

Mitch laughed while rubbing at the sting from her pointy fingernails. Her Highness was no better than Bets when it came to control issues.

"I think I'm just going to let your imagination run wild," he said.

"It's a pretty vivid imagination."

"I figured that out last night."

She blushed, which he found an amazing contrast to her inherent boldness. In one evening and on to the dawn, they'd touched just about every square inch of one another's skin and made love in nearly all the ways a creative couple could. Of course, he held out hope for variations on those themes...once she was willing to give over more than her body.

"So, no scoop on Betsy, huh?" she asked.

"Nope."

"I do hope you plan to offer me some sort of compensation," she said primly.

"What did you have in mind?"

She reached over and stroked him. "Oh, I don't know...a little mutual gratification, maybe?"

He would have thought it impossible after last night's excesses, but already he was growing hard. Not that he planned to do anything about it.

"Actually I wanted to talk to you about that mutual gratification issue this morning," he said.

"What do you mean?"

"I can't believe I'm saying this, but we're going to have to go without. I thought I could shut down my brain and live for the moment like you'd asked, but I was wrong. You can't have just part of me, Highness."

She rose over him and stroked him. "Not even this part?"

Yeah, he was certifiably crazy. "Especially not that part. I'm not going to be inside you until you really let me in."

She dipped down and brushed a kiss against his mouth. "Maybe we could save the teasing for later?"

"Kira, I'm not teasing."

Her smile faded. "You're kidding."

"No, I'm serious." Painfully so.

She flopped back on the bed, arms spread wide in a posture of defeat. "What is it that you want?"

"Your words. All of them."

"I don't get it."

He moved closer to her, swept a stray lock of hair off her cheek, then kissed her forehead. "You've been generous with your body, and don't doubt for a minute that I haven't been appreciative. But we've experienced kind of a disconnect here. We know how to please each other physically, but otherwise we're striking out. I want words from you. Real communication."

"Words?" she echoed. "Clearly we're not talking *oh, baby* or *you're so good*."

He smiled in spite of himself. "I was hoping for something with more depth. You know, something that would let me into your life a little."

"Okay, how's this? When I was eleven, I stole an ice cream from Mrs. Hawkins's market. Every time she looks at me, I swear she knows."

"Ancient history."

She gave an exasperated sigh. "Fine. In college my first boyfriend looked just like you, except he was a lot nicer to me, so I gave him my virginity."

He moved over her long enough to plant a kiss on the base of her throat. "Flattering in a sick sort of way, but no," he said. "I want to know why you're in Sandy Bend."

"To be driven into insanity through sexual frustration?"

"That'll make two of us, Highness."

She rolled on top of him again and braced her hands on his chest. "Come on, Mitch. Play nice."

Nice? He'd thrown nice out the window somewhere around dawn. He flipped her beneath him. "I'm not playing nice, I'm playing to win. Until you're ready to tell me what's going on with you, I'm not ready to repeat last night. So what's it going to be?"

She planted both hands on his chest and pushed hard. Mitch could have stayed put, but he didn't want to antagonize her any more than he already had. She crawled from the bed, then dug through the covers until she found her nightgown, which had migrated between the comforter and the top sheet. After she'd pulled the wrinkled garment over her head, she fixed him with a very angry glare.

"Let me get this straight," she said. "You're going to withhold sex until I tell you whatever this big, dark secret is that you think I've been hiding? How damn manipulative is that?" She grabbed a pillow that had fallen to the floor at some point last night and flung it at him. "Jerk."

She marched out of the room and into the bathroom. Mitch followed. She swung around and said, "Can't I have some privacy?"

He settled his hand on the door. "You can have all kinds of it—once we've worked our way though this."

She stalked out of the bathroom and again he followed. In the kitchen she opened the refrigerator door. Mitch watched as she retrieved some strawberry jam, then set it down with serious force on the counter next to the marshmallow fluff. When she grabbed for the bread, he worried that she was going to smash it flat, but she didn't. Instead, she dropped two slices in the toaster.

She was making his breakfast? He didn't know why the act was slamming straight into his heart, but it was.

"Did it ever occur to you that I have no big secret? That I'm here for exactly the reasons that I gave you?"

"Not for a second," he replied. "And what were those reasons again?"

It was a dirty trick, but it worked. Kira stopped dead in her tracks. "I— I—"

"See? If you can't keep 'em straight, don't expect me to. Rule one—when trying to fool someone, keep it simple. Don't keep piling on stories."

She walked back to the refrigerator and pulled out some grapes. As she washed them, she said, "Why can't you just leave this alone?"

"Believe me, parts of me would like to. And if I didn't care a whole lot about you, I would. I don't mean this as manipulation, but here's the thing. In two, three, however many days, you're going to be gone. If this were going to be all about sex, we'd just have our fun and move on. But for me at least, it's not just about the sex—which, to remind you, was outstanding."

"Really?" The toast popped up, and she dropped it onto a plate, then retrieved a butter knife from the silverware drawer.

"Definitely worth repeating, but don't get caught up in the compliment, okay? The point is we could have more. I want it and I'm pretty sure you do, too."

"Hah. What makes you say that?" Tough words

for sure, but he was reading more than her speech, and even the way her lower lip was beginning to quiver.

He pointed to the toast she was busy spreading with fluff. "You're ticked as hell at me and you're still making my breakfast."

She looked at the hand holding the fluff-covered knife as though it didn't belong to her.

"Reflex," she said firmly before setting the knife aside.

"If the thought comforts you."

She smacked the toast plate onto the kitchen table, set the jam next to it, then picked up her grapes and began eating. Mitch frowned at the toast. He always went jam first, fluff second. He wasn't even sure he could get the jam to stick to the fluff. He was far too smart to point out the inconsistency to Kira, though. While he rose and got a spoon to glob on some jam, she pulled out a seat and sat opposite his customary spot.

"What I'm asking is pretty simple. I want to be included," he said when he'd returned, spoon in hand. "I don't want to be on the outside wondering what's going on. Once we handle that, the geography issues we're going to have to deal with will be nothing."

She set aside the grapes and laid her palms flat on the table. "Okay, here's the scoop. It's just a glitch with my business. It seemed a little overwhelming a few days ago, so I took off. Now that I have some distance and perspective, I promise it's nothing that I can't handle. It's just going to take some time to figure out."

At least she was no longer trying to pretend that nothing was happening, but he still didn't like the way she'd clammed up.

"Why don't you tell me about it?" he asked. "Sometimes another set of eyes on the facts can help."

"It's handled. Really."

"This is what I meant. It's like you're looking for two bodies colliding in the night—and the morning—but nothing more. That's not what I want."

"Mitch, that's all I can give right now. I haven't asked you for every little detail of your life. I don't know how many girlfriends you've had or who you've slept with in town. I don't want to know any of that. I want us to start from here, to enjoy our time together."

"And then what? We get together if you happen to be around? Then after that maybe send a Christmas card for a couple of years before we lose touch altogether?"

"I don't know, okay? I just don't see why you have to take away something that gives us both such pleasure."

"Because the price is too high for me. It's coming at the expense of my pride. I need you to want me as much as I want you."

"Mitch, I—"

Regret and rejection were clear on her face. He'd heard *no* too many times already in this discussion not to recognize it. Mitch pushed his chair away from the table and left his disaster zone of a breakfast.

Good idea, bad delivery.

"DAMNED IF YOU DO, DAMNED IF you don't," Kira said to herself—or maybe to the closest lilac bush—before turning the corner onto Main Street, where the liberty to talk to oneself was severely limited by the number of passersby to listen.

She needed to hang tough for a couple of days, but it was miserably hard to do when she knew that she was hurting someone who mattered so much to her. Last night Mitch had left her loose limbed, relaxed and without even the smallest measure of her usual reserve in place. She'd considered blurting all to him. How—like her stupid, scarred leg—nothing in her life was nearly as pretty as it appeared on first glance. How after all her effort to grow as a sharp, savvy soul, she'd been fooled for over two years by a woman she thought she'd known as well as any of her siblings. Of course, she wasn't all that close to her siblings, either.

Kira had kept her mouth firmly shut, though. In the light of day, she was relieved that she had. Mitch was as stubborn about control as she was, though for very different reasons. If—and this was a *huge* if— they found a way to pursue a relationship once she was back in Florida, she didn't want to fall back into her old needy, wait-on-me ways. She wanted to continue to stand on her own. As a second-generation cop, Mitch was genetically coded to run the show. Once she'd proved that she could deal with this crisis, she'd tell him whatever he wanted to know. And not a moment before.

In need of caffeine and companionship, Kira stopped at the Village Grounds. Maybe some of Lisa's calm pleasure in life would rub off. As she walked by the window, Kira was relieved to see that it was slow in the coffeehouse just then.

She pushed through the shop's door. The cheery chime of the bells was drowned out by a distressed "I can't believe it!" from behind the counter.

Kira blinked as Lisa dipped below counter height.

"Hiding out?" she asked as she approached.

Lisa popped back up, a sopping rag in one hand. "Cleaning a milk bomb. I spilled a gallon of skim milk this time. An hour ago I sent half a tray of blueberry muffins to the ground. I'm a menace." She turned and wrung the rag into a small utility sink, then bent to mop more milk.

Kira came around to Lisa's side of the counter, grabbed a wad of paper towels and pitched in. "So you've got a case of the drops. What brought it on?"

Lisa's brief laugh flirted with hysteria. She cleaned as she spoke. "My wedding's three days off and I haven't had my final dress-fitting. My mother is still trying to hijack my reception and turn it into a cooing-lovebirds and fluffy, huggy hearts disaster. *And* one of the girls I had hired to help me for the summer left me a note this morning telling me that she's decided she needs to see Alaska…now! So much for two weeks' notice."

"All of which definitely stinks," Kira commiserated. "Why don't you close for a few days, until you can get a grip?"

Lisa sighed. "It's tempting, but if I do, I'll tick off my regulars." She rinsed the rag, then washed her hands as Kira threw her sodden mass of paper towels in the trash. "People around here are creatures of habit. If you throw them off schedule, you hear about it forever—assuming they forgive you enough to come back. I fought so hard to actually have regulars that I don't want to lose them."

"Understandable. Word of mouth is everything."

This was a concept that Kira knew all too well from her business. Word of mouth was what had made her. It would also kill her income if the Roxanne mess didn't get straightened out. Because she was beginning to believe that old "What goes around, comes around" adage and because she was overdue to send some good stuff around, Kira made an offer that would have been unthinkable the last time she'd been in Sandy Bend.

"So, what do you need me to do?" she asked, figuring this was penance of sorts.

"Do?"

Kira stepped in front of the sink and washed the spilled milk from her hands. As she did, she said, "As in, how can I help bail you out? If I came in a few hours every day this week, would that be a step in the right direction?"

"You'd do that?"

"Why not?" she replied, drying her hands.

Lisa's expression was best described as shocked. "This isn't an easy job, you know," she said. "We alternate between too quiet and crazy busy. You'd be all by yourself, and…" She trailed off, then laughed again. This time at least the sound didn't have that teetering-on-the-brink edge to it. "You're offering me help and I'm busy talking you out of it. Just shoot me now."

Kira laughed. "Thanks, but my reputation's already bad enough in town."

"Forget 'em," Lisa said with a dismissive wave of her hand. "If you're serious about this, I have to ask…. Have you ever made espresso or run a cash register?"

"No, but I'm trainable. And I'd really like to help." Any positive step, even one not directly related to her problems, had to be a good thing.

"Okay, if you're game, do you have a few minutes right now?"

"Sure," Kira said. All she had in the works was another session at Mitch's computer, and she wasn't ready to return to the scene of the morning's emotional carnage just yet.

Lisa tossed a tan Village Grounds apron her way. "Put this on and I'll teach you coffee, Sandy Bend-style."

Kira bit back a sigh. If only someone could teach her persuasive seduction, Mitch Brewer-style.

AFTER A MORNING SPENT FEELING as if he'd been sucking the bottom of a manure hauler, Mitch came to a decision. If Kira wasn't going to put to rest his worries about her current situation, he'd have to do it for himself. Concerns calmed, maybe he could show a little more finesse and persuade her to open up to him, instead of trying to coerce her into it.

He pulled out the business card that Kira had left as a bookmark in the thriller she was reading. This wasn't really theft. He'd return the card as soon as he was back home.

"Whitman-Pierce Realty," he read aloud from the posh-looking script. "Figures you'd have first billing, Highness."

Mitch noted the Web site address at the bottom of the card. Couldn't hurt to have a look-see. He glanced over at Cathy, the only other officer in the station. She had her nose stuck in a file, so Mitch felt safe in indulging in a little extracurricular activity, at least until Cal got back in twenty minutes. Mitch typed the Web site address into his computer's Internet browser and waited for the information to download.

The Web site was smart and elegant, much like

Kira. Mitch suppressed a low whistle as he flipped through the gallery of homes currently for sale. If Kira had been telling the truth last night, her "little glitch" at work probably had a whole lot of zeros hanging off its cost. He couldn't find a property for under three mil.

He cruised to the About Us page and read the brief bios for Kira and Roxanne, the woman who was apparently her partner. Based on the glam shot of the two of them in half-flirty, half-business dresses at the ocean's edge, looks sold—both the looks of the property and of the women doing the selling. Kira had found the only environment where her bone-deep blond glamour would come off as understated. Kira was…Kira, and he'd never found any woman more attractive. Roxanne was a total knockout, probably surgically enhanced and far too high-mainte-nance looking for Mitch's taste. Plus, there was something uncomfortably brittle about her expres-sion. He'd take Kira any day…if only Kira would have him.

The more Mitch looked at the two of them—Rox-anne, especially—the more his curiosity grew. Kira came from money, and even though she'd said she was off the family dole, she sure knew how to still look rich. What about this Roxanne? Was she an-other heiress?

He plugged her name and *Miami* into his favorite search engine, then weeded through the results. Mostly he found blurbs from local magazines and newspapers—name-dropping in the gossip columns and chat about club hopping.

The phone rang, and Cathy fielded the call. Mitch barely looked up from his computer screen when she said she was going to walk down to one of the gift shops to deal with a potential shoplifter. Mitch's mind had traveled elsewhere—over fifteen hundred miles south, to be exact. And the heat had to be affecting his brain, considering the idea that had come to him.

Over the years he'd made some connections. It just so happened that Bart, one of his law school buddies, had moved down to Miami to go into practice with his older brother who had a flashy, high-roller kind of firm. Attorney to the local celebs and all that. Mitch had met Glenn, the big brother, a couple of times when he'd come to Sandy Bend with Bart for some rustic weekends of salmon fishing and rum drinking.

Glenn was the sort of guy who'd do a favor, no questions asked, which had certain benefits since Mitch didn't want to answer any.

Not even the *What the hell are you doing?* that was shooting through his brain as he pulled Glenn's card from the personal file he kept in his lower right-hand drawer. Mitch started dialing.

From the moment he touched the phone, Mitch floated into something he could only call an out-of-body experience. He'd swear he was somewhere around the ceiling while watching this Mitch clone on the phone, pretty much trashing his hard-earned integrity. Good Mitch watched from some far, ethically pure place as bad Mitch cleared a receptionist and a secretary, summoned some small talk, then secured his target.

"Glenn, I was wondering if you could do me a favor? Could you check out two women, Kira Whitman and Roxanne Pierce?... Yeah, Whitman-Pierce

Realty. You've heard of them? I'm looking for word of mouth—if anyone you know has had dealings with them, what kind of friends they hang with, that kind of stuff.... No, no crisis. Tomorrow would be great to hear back from you.... Yeah, next summer we'll get together for sure. Thanks, Glenn. Talk to you soon."

After he hung up, Mitch zoned out into space for a while. He knew that when his conscience rejoined his body, he'd be sucking major manure once again.

10

"ONE TALL NO-WHIP MOCHA LATTE," Kira confirmed as she placed a coffee in front of a customer, then rang up the sale. The reward for doing it right was the jingle of change into a jar with a tag reading Honeymoon Fund that Lisa kept by the register.

"Thank you," Kira called to the teenage girl as she left.

After an hour under Lisa's watchful eyes, Kira had been declared ready to fly on her own. Other than a couple of muffed orders and a twenty-seven-thousand-dollar overring on the cash register, she'd done fairly well. She'd even survived a visit from comb-over man, who'd scared her with his nasty stare days earlier. It turned out he looked at pretty much the whole world that way. Kira would take cranky over inherently evil any day of the week. Today was a short-term gig, anyway. Lisa had promised she'd be back once she'd stopped home to pick up any stray wedding RSVPs, then visited her caterer to tell her to forget her mother's suggestion of heart-shaped butter pats.

In the lull between breakfast and lunch, traffic into the shop slowed. Kira took advantage of the interval by checking her cell phone for messages. She found one from Don, who she'd been meaning to call with the information from last night's research.

Kira hit the autodial and reached him immediately. He had no news on Roxanne's whereabouts but was expecting some leads to solidify early tomorrow. Kira wiped down tables and listened as Don gave her a brief recap of what else he'd found.

"Then I checked with a contact in St. Louis," Don was saying, "and—"

Kira interrupted. "St. Louis? Why St. Louis?"

"That's where she's from."

"No, she told me that she grew up in California— St. Helena in the Napa Valley. Her father's a big landowner. He even has a hotel and spa." She headed back behind the counter, as if the smaller space could give her a measure of security.

"Not even close. Her father works in a meatpacking plant."

This was bad in so many ways that Kira couldn't begin to grasp them. And what she really wanted to grasp was Roxanne's throat between her own bare hands. She might be a kinder, more rational Kira these days, but Retribution Girl still lurked right under her skin.

Kira looked up when the shop bells chimed, alerting her to a customer. She was about to raise her finger in a just-a-second gesture when she realized that the customer was Mitch. Feeling oddly criminal, she turned her back on him and moved as far from his earshot as she could.

"So, it would be safe to say that she's not independently wealthy?" she asked Don in a low voice.

"It would be safer to say that she's up to her nose job in debt."

Kira assumed that also sent her partner's tales of life in a French boarding school into the land of fiction. Probably the closest Roxanne had ever come was reading *Madeline* books in her childhood.

"I need to cut this call short," she said to Don, "but I have something I need you to check out. I read Roxanne's e-mail and found some client names that didn't make sense. Could I give them to you later?"

"No problem. And, Kira, if you spot any unusual activity, you might think about freezing your business's cash accounts."

"I can't. Roxanne usually…" If Mitch hadn't been watching her, Kira would have smacked her forehead against the counter and chanted, "Dumb, dumb, *dumb*."

"I'll look into them this afternoon," she said to Don. "Talk to you later."

Call ended, she tucked her cell phone back in her purse and turned to face Mitch. There was an uncomfortable pause before he spoke. At least, it seemed uncomfortable to Kira—as though he was waiting for her to tell him who she'd been talking to. But it could have all been in her head, too. She didn't respond well to guilt.

"So I wasn't hallucinating when I walked by," Mitch said. "Where's Lisa?"

"She had a little staffing problem, and I volunteered to cover for her so she can get married on Saturday without losing her mind."

"That's right—Saturday," Mitch said. "Will you go with me?"

She hadn't been expecting that. In fact, when he'd come in the door, she'd anticipated hearing that he wanted her to move out.

"If you want me to," she said, hating the way she felt so tentative.

He gave her a level look. "I wouldn't have asked otherwise."

Seeking to focus his attention on something other than her, Kira gestured at the large coffee menu posted on the wall behind her. "Can I get you something?"

"How about a cup of regular, black? And one of Lisa's chocolate-chip cookies, too. I'm celebrating."

"Celebrating what?" Kira automatically asked as she poured the coffee.

"I've been told to expect a kick-ass letter of recommendation from a federal judge I interned for last summer."

"Really? That's great!" She handed him the coffee, then pulled the cookie from the glass-front case where they were kept. She put it on a plate and slid it across the counter to him.

He took a swallow of coffee, then said, "The letter's a start. There's a glut of lawyers out there. Anything you can do to stand out helps."

Kira couldn't believe he was even worried. Mitch had a law-enforcement background and the cachet of having been a college football player, which she knew gained notice in the good-old-boys' network. Most important, in a few short days she'd learned that there was endless grit and determination behind his lazy smile. Which of course made him all the sexier.

"Trust me, you're a standout," she said as she rang up his order. "What kind of law do you want to practice?"

"I want to be a federal prosecutor, but it might take a couple of years in private practice before I can latch on to a job like that."

Their hands brushed as he handed her a few dollar bills. She tried to show no outer sign of the tingle that went through her from a simple touch.

"Is it a tough job to get?" she asked in a voice a little huskier than usual.

He nodded. "It can be. There's background checks and security clearances and usually a lot of people vying for just a few open slots. But I feel like I can really make a difference in a job like that, so I'm willing to stick it out."

Two customers came in, and after greeting the women by name, Mitch moved to a table while Kira took care of them. When she was done, he returned to his spot at the counter.

"How about you? Do you see yourself selling real estate the rest of your life?" he asked.

"For a long time, at least. I feel like I've wasted so many years just trying to grow up."

Kira's pulse jumped. She couldn't believe she'd said that to Mitch. Whether out of reserve or some need to maintain the Whitman image, she'd never willingly admitted flaws to anyone. Half the trick of dealing with a therapist had been developing the trust to open up. Maybe admitting this shortcoming to Mitch was a reasonable step, but she didn't want to take it any further with a guy who'd seen so much of her bad side.

He laughed. "You're not even thirty yet. How many years can you have wasted?"

There was something freeing even in this small measure of honesty. "Some days it feels like half my life."

He took her hand. "Don't be so hard on yourself, Highness. I know people well into their seventies who haven't grown up."

She smiled. "That gives me another fifty years to work on it."

Mitch was still holding her hand. She knew she should draw it back across the counter, especially since the two customers weren't being too subtle in the way they were watching. At that moment she didn't care. She felt as though she was at least gaining back some of what Mitch and she had lost earlier in the morning.

"See, Highness?" Mitch said. "We've had a full conversation and we've both survived. Don't give up hope for us yet." He moved his grip on her hand so that he was cupping it. Then he brought it to his mouth and kissed the tender skin on the inside of her wrist. "Might as well give 'em something to talk about," he said low enough for just her to hear.

His gaze was intimate, and Kira leaned closer as warmth began to curl through her. "Then let's do it right."

It was a heartbreakingly tender kiss, tasting to Kira of all the things she wasn't yet able to have—love, commitment and a future big enough to hold more than one. When the bell to the shop chimed again, she drew away, regretful to lose the moment.

"Good morning," Mitch said to his sister-in-law, Dana, who'd just come in the door.

"An interesting one," Dana replied, taking in both of them with an arch smile. "How about a tall white-chocolate raspberry latte?" she said to Kira, who was more than happy to have something to do at that moment.

Mitch was saying something to Dana but kept it low enough that Kira couldn't eavesdrop successfully. Once the espresso machine began hissing, she gave up the battle.

When she was done making the drink, Mitch was readying to leave.

"Tonight I cook," he said to her on his way out.

Kira kept her comments to a generic "'bye." The two women who had been watching the kiss also trailed out, figuring the show was over. Kira took a quick glance at Dana and gauged her mood. At least Monday's fighting glint was gone from her eyes.

"You saved me some work, being here," Dana said.

"How's that?"

"I was going to track you down today anyway. I wanted to ask if we could have a fresh start."

"Any reason in particular?"

Dana took a sip of her coffee, then nodded with satisfaction. Kira was pleased to see she could do at least one thing right in this woman's estimation.

"You and Mitch are going to do whatever you're going to do," Dana said. "I could stand in your way, but I think I'll just end up getting steamrollered. So what do you say—can we try again?"

Kira weighed the request and then said, "I vote for a truce."

"It's that easy?"

"When you have my kind of past, you can't be stingy with fresh starts."

Dana laughed. "That's my philosophy, too." She took another sip of her drink, then said, "I owe you an explanation for my pit-bull act when I first saw you the other day."

"I'm used to that kind of response," Kira said, thinking of pit-bull Rose who'd been her *un*welcoming committee to Sandy Bend.

"Has Mitch told you about his accident last November?"

"I've seen the scar."

Dana's brows rose a fraction, but she didn't push the topic. "Did he also tell you that we almost lost him?"

Kira's heart lurched. "No. All he mentioned was a secondary infection."

"It was antibiotic resistant, and he started developing pneumonia on top of that. He really scared us, and I ended up going all maternal on him. There was no one else to take the job, you know? I think he's tired of having a mommy younger than he is, but I can't seem to stop."

"But he's okay now," Kira said, just to hear the comforting statement aloud.

"He is, but he's also changed. Mitch used to be more relaxed about life. I don't know if it was the brush with death or just because he's getting older, but he's almost driven now. He goes for what he wants," Dana said.

"I'd noticed."

"It was surprising seeing him kiss you," she said. "You're the only one I've seen him look at that way."

Kira's heart sped with something that was either excitement or alarm. She couldn't quite peg it. "What way?"

"Like he's playing for keeps," Dana said, then glanced at the clock on the wall. "Hey, I have to get back to work. Tell Mitch that I said to bring you to dinner on Saturday. You'll still be here, right?"

"I will," she replied. Then she added after Dana had left, "Right here, smack in the middle of purgatory."

THE TABLE WAS SET, DINNER was cooking and Mitch was feeling marginally less screwed. He wasn't sure whether he should be appalled or amazed at how he'd managed to cordon off the section of his brain that had spurred the phone call to Glenn in Miami. What little guilt had managed to sneak through, he was drowning in the vintage music of Guns N' Roses, full blast. At least as full as a guy could get with retirees living on both sides of him.

He'd decided to deal with the Glenn incident as a near miss, similar to stealing all the Sandy Bend *n*s when he was a kid. He'd never been caught, and in this instance Kira didn't have to know. Whatever he learned from Glenn he'd keep to himself. And he'd dig no deeper.

Mitch stepped out back to see if for the first time ever he'd managed to cook salmon on the grill without charring it or turning it to jerky. He made a better fisherman than he did chef. When he'd just come back in, Axl and his band fell silent. A moment later Kira appeared in the kitchen doorway.

He didn't like what he saw. There was something in her expression that made him feel as though she was working doubly hard to keep that mask of cool competency in place.

"Hard day at work?" he asked, figuring a little teasing might lighten matters. In the past it had worked like a charm.

She pulled out a chair and sat. "I don't suppose you have any wine?"

"Funny you should mention it." Mitch went to the fridge and pulled out the bottle of sauvignon blanc he'd picked up at the market after getting off work.

While he uncorked it and poured her a glass, Kira was silent. She took the offered drink, closed her eyes and sighed as the first swallow went down.

Mitch wanted to ask her what was wrong but knew better. "Are you okay with salmon?" he asked instead.

Even her smile looked tired. "It sounds great. Is there anything I can do to help?"

"Just kick back and relax."

The meal was quiet. Mitch talked a little about people they'd known in common and what they were up to these days. Kira tried to act interested, but Mitch could tell that she had something entirely different going on in her head.

Over her objections, he insisted on clearing the table and doing the dishes himself. When he was done, he took her by the hand and led her to his bedroom.

At the questioning look she gave him, he said, "Nope, I'm sticking to my word and keeping my clothes on. Stretch out, Highness. It's time for a back rub."

Kira slipped off her sandals and climbed onto the bed. "No way am I turning this down," she said before centering a pillow along the headboard and stretching out, her arms looped above her head.

Mitch kicked off his shoes and joined her, kneeling near her hips. He swept her hair to one side and began with a gentle pressure on the nape of her neck. As he did, he looked at the smooth sweep of her back down to the rich curves of her bottom. She looked so right to him, as though having her here was natural. Maybe even a product of fate.

"I like the way you always wear skirts instead of shorts," he said. "It's sexy."

"Hides the scar better. Most shorts I like are cut too high," she murmured, then shifted her face the other way on the pillow.

He hadn't thought of that and sure as hell hadn't meant to bring it up. Still, as Mitch worked his way up the back of her left leg, deeply kneading Kira's tense muscles, he considered what injury could do.

Some people recovered better than others. On the whole, he was lucky. A few days into his hospital stay, when fairly doped from whatever had been flowing through his IV line, he'd overheard his dad and Cal talking with the doctors about the odds of him kicking his complications. That anyone would be putting odds on his death had scared the crap out of him. He'd sworn that as soon as he left that hospital bed, he'd grab hold of life and do it right. Thus far he had.

"This feels wonderful," Kira said, sounding drowsy.

He slipped his hand under her top and unhooked her bra. She didn't complain. In fact, she gave a blissful sigh as he rubbed his palm down her back. Mitch could feel himself begin to stir. He knew he couldn't fight physical response, but he damn well wouldn't do anything about it.

He began sliding up her shirt, and she briefly raised herself to help him along. He loved the feel of her warm skin beneath his hands, loved the way she entrusted herself to him.

Right up until her accident, Kira had been one of those kids who'd reveled in life. Sure, she'd been spoiled. And sure, her sophistication had intimidated him a little. But Mitch had always been intrigued by her. She'd had an intellect that not much anyone gave her credit for. For Mitch, her looks had been hot, but her intelligence had made it a done deal.

After the accident, when she'd come home acting like another girl entirely, he'd tried once to talk to her about the change, but she'd put him off. She'd been good at those stone-cold dismissals, but he'd always known that the act was coming from fear. Now that she'd grown, the act had changed from superiority to silence. And how he wanted the woman beneath.

It took little time for Kira's muscles to go lax and her breathing take on the relaxed pattern of sleep. Mitch let his hands travel over her back a few more times, as much for his pleasure as for her continued rest. When he was certain that she wasn't going to wake, he went to the kitchen and grabbed a glass and the last of the wine they'd had at dinner. He sat on the back deck looking up at the clear sky with its blanket of stars.

Kira was distracted, distressed—all of those *dis* things that ate at him. What could she have fallen into? As Mitch imagined the possibilities, the air grew chilly with a breeze pushing its way though town from Lake Michigan.

Conjecture was pointless, and he was beat. Mitch left his wineglass by the kitchen sink and walked to his bedroom. Kira was still sound asleep. If he were at all sane, he'd go sleep on the beast of a couch in the living room. But it seemed that sanity wasn't his strong suit these days.

Mitch stripped out of his clothes and pulled on an old pair of flannel sleep pants. Taking care not to wake Kira, he crawled onto the bed next to her. He could smell the faint floral scent of whatever shampoo she used. Her warmth was too tempting. Mitch got as close to her as he could without actually touching her, because if he did that, he wouldn't be able to stop. He'd take the warmth and comfort of her presence for tonight. As he dozed off, his final thought was, *This is what I've been missing all these years.*

HE WAS ASLEEP. KIRA TIPTOED into the second bedroom and closed the door. She switched on Mitch's computer but left the speakers off, not wanting to wake him.

Kira logged on to her bank's Web site for the second time that day. After she'd finished up at the Village Grounds, she'd gone straight to the library and stayed until the five-o'clock closing time. They had not been pleasant hours. Even now, as she again pulled up Whitman-Pierce's client escrow account, the sight of what awaited her sent fury coursing through her.

On some level this was her fault. She should have watched Roxanne more carefully, asked more questions. It was no excuse for inattention that the account had always balanced.

The escrow account was specially set up to hold client funds, keeping them separate from the firm's operating account. Lately about all that should have been going through it were a few good-faith deposits and the rentals on some properties that they'd agreed to handle as an accommodation to a repeat client. But more was funneling through there.

Much more.

Kira looked at the prior month's activity. There alone, when she added up the suspect daily transactions—none over five thousand dollars—more than ninety thousand dollars had passed through the account. Kira had once taken a large cash down payment from an eccentric client who didn't trust banks. She knew from making that deposit that the government had to be notified on cash deposits above a certain amount. Looking at the escrow account's statement, she'd bet that amount was currently five thousand dollars and she'd bet these deposits had been cash.

Someone was trying to run below federal radar. And that someone was still missing. She didn't wish Roxanne physical harm, but the thought of her in an orange prison jumpsuit was highly appealing.

Kira had seen all she could stomach. She clicked on the print button, wincing when Mitch's printer began to squeal as the paper went through the machine. Short of throwing her body over the printer, there was nothing she could do.

"Hurry up," she whispered to it.

When it was finally done, she switched off the computer and tucked the pages into her briefcase in the living room. Documents hidden, Kira sat on the edge of the couch looking at the neatly folded sheet and comforter she hadn't used the night before. She wouldn't use it tonight, either. Her life was unraveling, and she was becoming frightened. She needed comfort, even if it was illusory.

If she stayed in her clothes, in the morning Mitch would assume that she'd slept through the night. She'd have no neediness to confess to, no difficult questions to face. Kira crept back into Mitch's bed and tucked her body snugly behind his. Her racing heartbeat, harried with stress, slowed to match his. In time she felt safe. In time she felt love.

MITCH WATCHED THE MINUTES pass on his digital alarm clock. He'd heard Kira at the computer and felt her crawl into bed. God, he was angry. And hurt, too. But he couldn't make her give what she chose to withhold. All he could do was protect her.

And it would be one hell of a lot easier if he knew what he was protecting her from. Mitch willed his eyes shut and sleep to come.

Love was a definite bitch.

11

IF PATIENCE WAS A VIRTUE, Kira required redemption. It was impolitic to boot a guy from his own house, but she feared that's what it was coming down to. When she'd awakened on Thursday morning, she'd found Mitch in the kitchen eating his way through toast topped with his favorite gunk. By the time she'd emerged from the shower and dressed, he'd moved on to coffee and cereal. He was in uniform, which meant that sooner or later he'd go to work. Much as she loved the sight of him, she was rooting for sooner. She needed to call Don from the quiet of the Dollhouse Cottage before she was due at the Village Grounds to cover for Lisa.

Kira hovered by the stove. "So, you're working today?"

Mitch glanced down at his uniform, then served up a yes accompanied by a dry smile.

She gestured at the coffeemaker on the counter. "Mind if I have some?" It was kind of a coals-to-Newcastle question, considering where she would be in fifteen minutes.

"Help yourself." As she pulled a mug from the cupboard, he asked, "Sleep okay?"

"Fine," she replied.

"You talk in your sleep, you know."

The coffeepot rattled against the side of the mug, splashing hot liquid onto the counter.

"So I've heard," Kira said as she set down the pot and mopped up her spill. "Usually it's just nonsense."

She hoped.

Mitch didn't comment.

Short of asking *Just what did I say?* she didn't know how to mine for more information. She sat opposite him. "I hope I didn't keep you awake."

"Not for too long."

"Good," she said, though the word came out sounding as tense as she was feeling. She took some comfort from the fact that he was reaching the bottom of his cereal bowl and would soon be gone.

"No breakfast other than coffee?" he asked.

"I'm not a breakfast person."

"Too bad. You know what they say—it's the most important meal."

She tried to hide her frustration as he reached for the cereal box and refilled. A quick spark in his blue eyes let her know she'd done a poor job of cloaking her emotions.

"You sure you don't want to get a bowl?" he asked.

"Thanks, but no."

He was definitely playing her. Kira stood and dumped her coffee into the sink, then put her mug in the dishwasher. "Time for me to get to work."

Between bites Mitch said, "I've got school tonight. Think you can keep yourself occupied?"

"I'll find something."

She was in the living room readying to leave when she could have sworn she heard a muttered, "I'll bet."

After a glance over her shoulder, Kira tucked the

escrow account information into her purse. Time was running out—for her and for them.

"WHAT'S UP WITH YOU? DID somebody spit in your marshmallow fluff?"

Mitch glared at Cal, who'd just walked into the police station, bottle of water in hand. Some things in life were sacrosanct, and marshmallow fluff was among them. Which Cal should know, since most of their childhood brawls had resulted from Cal thieving Mitch's fluff stock.

Mitch pushed aside the case he needed to read before tonight's class. "You might want to give me some space this morning, huh? I didn't sleep much."

Cal pulled up a chair and unscrewed the top to his bottle. "And it doesn't look like it's for a good reason. What's wrong?"

Mitch had never viewed his brother as much of a confessor, but he couldn't afford to be choosy.

"I've been checking up on Kira," he said.

Cal took a swallow of water and then asked with a deadpan expression, "Any reason in particular or just a desire to kill your best shot at love?"

Mitch looked down at his desk. "It's not love... exactly."

Cal gave a "yeah, right" snort in response.

All things considered, Mitch decided to leave the topic of love alone. Cal had witnessed enough of Mitch's relationship with Kira over the years that he'd be a tough sell to believe it wasn't love.

"Something's going on with her, but she doesn't want to talk about it," he said.

"She's never been much for sharing, if you'll recall. Maybe you should just give her some space."

"I've been trying to do that, but just before you came in I talked to a friend's brother down in Miami."

"You do have a death wish, don't you?"

"Could be. Here's the problem—I don't like what's come back. Kira's clean. She's hardworking. In fact, her whole life appears to be built around her business. Roxanne, her partner, is another story. She doesn't have the best of friends—unless you've got a real fondness for felons and dealers."

"Definitely ugly," Cal agreed. "But why'd you start snooping?"

"Kira's not sleeping. She's sneaking on to my computer in the middle of the night and generally feeding me a bunch of bull. She finally told me that she has a little 'glitch' in her business, whatever the hell that means."

Cal sat up straighter, his cop's radar for trouble no doubt now as attuned to the situation as Mitch's.

"Do you think she's up to something criminal?" Cal asked.

Mitch shook his head. "No way. Other than that bar brawl when she missed Hallie's wedding, she doesn't have a record of any kind. Not so much as a traffic violation."

"Checking out her record, too? You get a kick out of living dangerously, don't you?"

"Someone has to watch out for her."

Cal stood. "I'd give you some advice about minding your own business, but since you're one stubborn SOB, I know you wouldn't take it. Instead I'll scrape you from the pavement when Kira's through stomping holes in you, okay?"

That kind of brotherly love Mitch could do without.

THE VILLAGE GROUNDS WAS hopping, and Kira was developing a limp.

"Torture by latte," she muttered as she steamed yet another pitcher of milk.

When Kira was about ten years old, Rose, then her seminanny, had caught her stealing a corner off the block of Belgian chocolate that Chef kept for making desserts. Rose had made Kira finish the rest of the block. Kira had been all for the punishment until the last three bites. Those had been agony, and many months had passed before Kira had been able to face chocolate again. She still could do entirely without Rose and she was beginning to think she might have also killed off her latte habit.

Calm finally came at about eleven. She retrieved her cell phone from her purse, then put in a call to Don. His tone worried her from the word *hello*, and it sounded even worse after she gave him the bank account news.

"First, there's nothing I've found that makes me think your partner is anywhere against her will, okay?" he said.

"Why do I sense a *but* coming?"

"Here it is…. *But* I've also picked up a rumor that a real bad boy's bearer bonds have gone missing. Granted, the source isn't the most reliable guy you'll ever meet, but based on what you've told me about your account, he just went up on the credibility scale."

Kira frowned. "Bearer bonds? I've heard of them, but I'm not sure I really know what they are."

"They're the ultimate in untraceable funds. They've been illegal in the United States for about twenty years, but you can get them from any number of offshore sources."

"Offshore...like some of Roxanne's favorite vacation spots," Kira said.

"You've got it. Bearer bonds are owned by whoever holds them. No record of ownership is kept. You pick it up, you turn it in and the cash is yours. A lot of drug money gets cleaned by that route. Now, I'm not saying there's absolutely a connection—"

"But with the unaccountable deposits and matching withdrawals, it would make sense, wouldn't it?"

"It would," Don agreed.

Kira closed her eyes in an attempt to quell her simmering fear—and fury, too. "So, do I panic now?"

"No. Let me do some more checking. In the meantime, freeze that escrow account. You might want to give your attorney a heads-up, too."

She doubted that her starchy business lawyer dabbled in this sort of practice.

"I'll give you a call tonight...tomorrow at the latest," Don said.

"Thanks."

"Sorry this hasn't worked out better for you, Kira. I wish she'd just run off with a married guy or something."

"If all of this turns out to be true, when I'm through with her, she'll wish she'd been sucked into the Bermuda Triangle."

Don laughed. "Remind me not to mess with you," he said before hanging up.

Right. She was a regular amazon.

Gutsy talk was an easy emotional release. Real solutions were going to be far more painful. Kira worked her face into a sufficiently cheerful expression to greet a group of sunburned tourists who had just meandered in. As she poured raspberry iced teas, her mind reeled. She wanted to believe that Roxanne wouldn't throw everything away for an easy buck, but in her heart she suspected that's exactly the sort of person her partner had turned into.

At the next brief lull in business Kira pulled the escrow account information and phoned the bank. It turned out that she couldn't freeze the account without either a court order or Roxanne's permission, neither of which were going to happen today. Kira could, however, transfer all of the funds to her personal account, which Roxanne couldn't get to. She figured when stuff was through hitting the fan, a technical violation of client ethics in order to secure their money wouldn't be frowned on. At least, not as much as Roxanne's apparent detour from the straight and narrow. No matter what happened from this point on, though, life would never be the same.

Kira served the lunchtime coffee drinkers with perhaps a tenth of her attention, her thoughts centered squarely on Mitch. Drugs and money laundering. Those had to be the top two on the list of activities guaranteed to tank a romance with a future federal prosecutor.

MITCH GOT OFF WORK AT THREE, then stopped home to mow the lawn and shower up before the long haul to East Lansing. Weary, he stripped out of his uniform and pulled on shorts and an old T-shirt. As he sat on the edge of the bed to tie his shoes, he caught a faint whiff of Kira's fragrance on the pillow next to him. It was a lame-ass thing to pick up the pillow and sniff it. He was damn lucky he was alone with no one to witness the act.

If this was love, he was better off without it. It had

to be a Brewer genetic quirk that was inspiring him to try to protect a woman who had made it perfectly clear that she wanted to be left to suffer alone. He hoped future generations of Brewers would avoid that particular serving of DNA stew. But he was stuck with it and he was tired of fighting its pull.

He was by definition a doomed man. Very soon he'd have to talk to Kira about Roxanne. He couldn't keep quiet when Kira's future—and his—was at stake. And since he was already one piece of very dead meat...

Mitch walked at a gallows-steps pace to his computer. Once it was awake and awaiting his commands, he used his favorite search engine to find a keystroke-logging program, a type of spyware he'd first heard of when attending a forum on electronic privacy rights at school. The results were virtually instantaneous.

His conscience told him that he could stop now. But his compulsion to protect gave him a hard shove. Soon he was on a popular spyware site. The basic program was freeware, so it wouldn't cost him anything—except for some stabbing guilt pains.

Mitch stared at the screen.

It was his computer.

He could download any program he chose.

He just never thought he'd be installing KeySpy. Feeling a little sick, he began his download.

It was done in a matter of minutes, far less time than it was going to take him to cope with the potential consequences of this particular act. From this moment on he'd have a hidden log of every word Kira typed and every site she visited.

Mitch turned away from the computer. He'd protect Kira in spite of herself. Now if he just thought there was any way she'd ever love him in spite of *him*self.

KIRA WALKED BACK TO THE Dollhouse Cottage on aching feet. She was not made of stern enough stuff to stand behind a counter all day. Good thing she still had a day job, assuming that Roxanne didn't manage to drag down the whole company.

Once she turned the corner, the sight of the little white house nestled between its larger neighbors eased her stress. As she neared, she could hear the sound of a mower in the backyard. She glimpsed Mitch as he and the mower made a pass by the white-picket gate that led to the rear of the house. The scent of freshly cut grass wafted toward her. He had yet to mow the postage-stamp-sized front lawn.

She stepped onto the front porch and, instead of going straight inside, breathed in the moment and began a game of pretend. She pretended that she was here with Mitch because that was where she belonged, not because circumstances had thrown them together. She pretended that her future was charged with promise. She pretended that they had loved each other forever.

Just then, the sound of the mower cut out. She heard the creak of the back gate as it opened and the rattle of the mower against the drive as Mitch brought it around to the front yard. Most of all she heard the pounding of her heart as she realized that her love, at least, was very real.

The mower started again, a slow chug growing to a hungry growl. Mitch didn't notice her as he first came out, giving her the wonderful luxury of watching unobserved. If he'd been wearing a shirt, he'd discarded it, leaving his skin bare to the strong afternoon sun. He had the body of an athlete and sportsman, honed fit through activity. She also knew that he had an honorable heart, fiercely loyal to those he cared for. Including her.

Intuition and a growing sense of dread told Kira there would be no sidestepping the mess Roxanne had created. If she asked Mitch to, he would stand by her, no matter the cost to his career. But because she loved him and because she had to learn to stand on her own, she would never do that.

Mitch glanced her way once quickly, then again with more intensity as the mower's path came toward the house. Something incredible, exciting and terrifying jolted through her as their gazes locked. That instant—and it couldn't have been more than that—would live with Kira forever. It was the first time she'd let her love show. Then, in a real display of courage, she turned heel and bolted into the house.

Fifteen minutes later she heard Mitch come in the back door. He went from the kitchen to the bathroom without spending more than a second in the living room. If he'd noticed her curled up on the couch, he'd been kind enough to let her have some time to pull herself together.

Soon she heard the sound of running water in the bathroom. Kira went to the closed door and rested her forehead against it.

She couldn't bear it anymore, not being able to touch him. And she needed to be held as much as she needed to hold. He couldn't refuse her, but if he did, she feared she'd beg.

She slipped out of her clothes, then opened the bathroom door. Its hinges protested a little.

"Is someone out there?" Mitch asked.

Kira didn't bother answering with words. She pulled open the shower curtain and stepped over the edge of the tub, figuring that she might as well take advantage of his state of surprise.

He was potently male, not pretty in the way of those cold nude sculptures she'd seen in museums, but in a rugged way that stole her breath. She took the soap from his hands and turned it over in her own, creating a frothy white lather.

The showerhead was set high, as one would expect for a man of his height. Water pelted Kira—there was no escaping it. She shivered as it hit her oversensitive skin. Mitch just watched her.

"It's been the longest two days of my life. Let me touch you, Mitch. Please."

The house had been built a long time ago, when tubs were tubs only. A window still sat in the back wall of the tiled tub enclosure. Turning from her, Mitch braced his hands on the sill. Kira took the act as tacit permission.

Hands slick, she set the soap on the sill. She started with his shoulders. How she loved the breadth of them, the way hard bone and tensile muscle sat just beneath his skin.

She kneaded her fingers into his strength, closing her eyes and sighing at the sound of his low moan of approval. She took the soap again. As her hands skated over him, committing the feel of rough hair and smooth skin to memory, slowly this emotion—this *love*—became so great that she stilled.

Mitch turned to face her, settling his broad hands on her hips. "Don't stop. Ever."

They kissed as the water rained down on them,

until Kira pulled away laughing. "I'm going to drown."

Mitch switched off the taps and pulled back the shower curtain. When he stepped from the tub, Kira shivered—not because the air was especially cool in the air-conditioning-free house on this hot summer day but because she needed his touch. She needed to feel that everything was going to be okay.

He returned with two towels. One he slung low around his hips. The other he dried her with, letting his mouth precede the area he was next to touch. Kira let him lavish her with attention, though she burned to touch him, too. When he was done—and her knees were so weak that he had to help her from the tub—he led her to the bedroom.

"This isn't about need. This time," he said, "we make love."

Kira opened her arms to him. If she could keep her hands on him forever, she would, for that's how long she wanted him. But she'd take this afternoon.

Before he came to her, he stood and looked at her long enough that she began to feel restless and a little too exposed.

"Mitch…"

"Just remembering." He dropped his towel and joined her.

Kira didn't know that skin could be so hot. His… Hers… Theirs where it met.

He took his time with her, touching, nipping, caressing, until the need to give him the same kind of pleasure was too strong to quell. Kira pushed him back into the pillows and started with that wonderful romantic's mouth. She would have kissed him for hours if she'd had the patience, but there was so much else to love. His cheekbones—high, he told her, from a Sioux great-great-great-grandmother. The strong column of his throat, salty beneath her mouth. His chest, with his heart drumming strong and true.

She moved lower, grasping his erection at its base and then slowly drawing her hand upward. She rubbed her thumb over the head of his shaft, feeling the bit of moisture collected there. A yearning so fundamental and emotionally dangerous came over her that she shook.

Kira wanted to feel him inside her without the barrier of a condom. She wanted to be with him forever and maybe one day have his children. She'd grown up spoiled and willful, with true maturity only recently gained. And even now she wasn't very graceful about not getting what she wanted.

This time she would be. She'd settle for what she could have and what she could give him.

When she drew him into her mouth, his hips arched from the bed. Then he relaxed on a slow breath of pleasure. With his words and his fingertips caressing her face, he let her know how much what she was doing turned him on. He wasn't alone in that. She would have stayed there until he peaked, fully willing to accept that new intimacy.

Mitch had other ideas.

"No more," he said. "I'm not going to last."

Reluctantly she left him and kissed a path upward until she settled her head against his chest. He wrapped her in his arms and rolled so that she lay beneath him.

He kissed her once deeply before moving aside. Kira waited, heart pounding, as he reached into the nightstand for protection. He sheathed himself in quick, sure motions, then positioned himself above her.

"I need inside you now." Action followed words and he surged deep within. "Are you ready, sweetheart?" His expression was so tender that she felt her throat tighten with emotion.

"Forever," she said, running her hands over the strong angles of his shoulders.

He began to move. Kira met his slow, thorough strokes, wanting him to never leave and this moment to never end. Mitch must have felt the same way, too, because he drew out their pleasure. But his touch was too compelling, his taste too addictive for her to be satisfied by his easy pace for very long.

She urged him to move faster, harder, but he gave her a fierce smile and told her not yet. She wrapped her legs above his hips and drove her body up to meet his, trying to push him to the brink.

Mitch laughed. "We're savoring this, remember?"

Easy for him to say. Dizzying sensations shot through her, leaving her breathless. She was poised on a precipice of something amazing, and he wouldn't give her that last push over the edge. She nipped at his collarbone—the first ready bit of flesh she could get her teeth to.

"You're playing with fire," he warned, the harshness of his words softened by his smile.

"What are you going to do—tie me up and spank me?" she teased.

"Not this time. Maybe later, if you're very, very bad."

Kira laughed and then nibbled at him again. She couldn't recall ever being so aroused and full of laughter at the same time. Sex had always been a serious matter, something to do right, as though she was being judged. It seemed that with Mitch joy was the purpose of the act. And she found that the most wonderful turn-on of all.

"Tell me how this punishment is," Mitch said.

He changed his angle ever so slightly, adding delicious pressure where she needed it most. Kira was fairly sure that her eyes were crossing with pleasure.

"It's awful," she said. "Horrible. The worst."

Once, twice, three times more he surged into her. That final time he stayed.

"Tell me the truth," he whispered into her ear, "or you'll get more of the same."

The truth she gave him wasn't what he'd expected—or what she'd planned, for that matter. The words slipped out on a tide of pure joy.

"I love you."

He hesitated a moment, and their gazes locked. She watched the shock register in his eyes, making them seem almost a darker blue.

Finally he moved as she'd wanted him to before, quickly and with enough force that she braced one hand against the headboard as they were impelled toward it. Suddenly her orgasm rippled through her, starting small and finally taking her whole body. She held on to Mitch as her world changed around her. A second later Mitch cried her name and came fully, totally apart in her arms.

She had never felt so utterly, perfectly alive.

Later, when her heartbeat had slowed and passion had left drowsy contentment in its wake, Kira sorted through her feelings. She'd never before told a man that she loved him—a fairly scary admission for someone creeping up on thirty.

Maybe before she'd never been ready. Or maybe before her heart had known that those mad flashes of infatuation which marked her prior relationships had nothing to do with love.

She turned onto her side and watched Mitch sleep. Whatever the reason, she was glad that she'd waited until now.

And for this man.

12

KIRA WOKE AFTER THE SUN HAD set. She reached over, switched on the bedside lamp and looked at the clock. Nearly ten—she had two hours and more before Mitch returned home.

She stood and stretched, enjoying the slight ache in her muscles that lingered after their lovemaking. And Mitch had been true to his promise—the afternoon had been about love.

Tonight, though, appeared to be about fright wigs. She made a face at herself in the dresser mirror, where her reflection looked back at her, victim of the worst case of bedhead she'd ever seen. That would be the downside of passionate love with wet hair.

Kira showered again, combed out her hair and slipped into one of Mitch's T-shirts in lieu of pajamas. In the kitchen she scavenged a late dinner. Sheer curiosity made her sample Mitch's marshmallow fluff. One tiny dot to the tip of her tongue was sufficient to let her know that she'd missed nothing in these past twenty-seven years. She opted for the last of the vanilla yogurt she'd bought earlier in the week at Mrs. Hawkins's market, along with some of Mitch's cereal, which at least wasn't sugar fortified.

When she was through eating, Kira remained too restless to sleep. She considered reading a few more pages of the thriller she'd paged through earlier in the week, but when she found the business card she'd used as a bookmark was missing, she decided she didn't have enough interest to find her page.

Television was a poor distraction. The little set in Mitch's second bedroom was aimed toward the weight bench. She rolled the office chair over, sat and channel surfed but could find nothing that entertained her. Nothing that would push away the worries. Alone, she couldn't pretend that life was idyllic in the Dollhouse Cottage.

Kira was drawn to the computer. She had to let the outside world in, at least enough to take care of her responsibilities at work. After much hesitation she gave in, logged on to her Web site mail and began to weed through the crop. Tapping her delete key in an old fashioned Morse-code rhythm, she consigned the spam to cyberhell.

She was ready to tap again when her heart jolted. The sender of the next message was identified as HotRox. There were some pervy meanings for that phrase, but there was also a marginally less suspect one: Roxanne. On her desk in Coconut Grove, Roxanne had a small, wild looking, feathered and sequined character doll a friend had made her. The doll's name was Hot Rox.

Kira aimed the mouse over the message and opened it. Half hoping for yet another erectile-dysfunction cure or a link to an X-rated Web site, she found instead a real message.

Come back home. You'll be safer once I have what I need from you. They know where you are anyway.

Kira minimized the message to the bottom of the computer screen, but its impact remained the same. She felt as though someone were holding a knife to her throat.

She left Mitch's office and began walking circles through the small house, drawing deep breaths and making a mental list of things she was thankful for in order to calm herself. *I'm thankful I'm still alive* seemed to be lodged at number one.

Seeking another route, she went to the kitchen and got a glass of ice water. The way her hands were shaking, she could hardly get the cubes in the glass. Leaving the mess at the sink, she pulled out a chair from the kitchen table and sat.

No one had overtly threatened her, she reminded herself. She was reading the worst into the note, which was probably what the sender had intended her to do.

What could she possibly have that Roxanne needed—assuming the sender was really Roxanne? Kira didn't know all the technical terms, but she wasn't clueless. It was an easy thing to fake another person's identity over the Internet. And Roxanne would be the least of all the potential evils out there. Somehow Kira needed to sift through the possibilities. For now she'd assume the sender was really her partner.

She went to the living room and switched on the lamp next to the couch. Somewhere in her briefcase was the contact information that Don had given her when they'd first spoken. She was pretty sure he'd included an e-mail address. She found the slip of paper in the front pocket and knew a moment's relief that she could reach him now, when it was far too late to call. That he probably wouldn't read the message until morning didn't matter. All that did was that she'd feel better.

Kira hurried back to the computer. Once she'd forwarded the e-mail to Don, she deleted it from the system. She'd done all she could to exorcise that particular demon. She wasn't feeling one heck of a lot calmer, though.

What could Roxanne be demanding in that infuriatingly vague e-mail?

Kira returned to her briefcase, where she dug through the papers checking for anything she might have missed when she'd gone through them earlier in the week. Maybe it was something as simple as a note or number that Roxanne had written on the back of the Casa Pura Vida research. Kira found nothing.

Or maybe Roxanne had returned to the office and discovered the PDA mix-up, and that's what she wanted. If so, there should be some entry in there that would stand out. Kira pulled Roxanne's PDA and leaned back on the couch.

First Kira opened the date book. Luckily the entries only went back as far as December of the prior year. It was painstaking work reading every entry for every day, since Roxanne had been nearly obsessive about detailing the unimportant stuff in her life. It was after eleven when Kira finally finished checking out all of the PDA's files. Nothing stood out.

Frustrated, upset and out of bright ideas, she returned to the kitchen, put fresh ice into the water glass she'd earlier abandoned and rummaged through the cupboards for the whiskey she'd seen Mitch sip the night they'd first kissed.

She pulled out the bottle and read the label. She had no idea whether "single-malt scotch" was good or bad. All she cared was that it might numb her. Kira tried a tentative sip and decided it would serve its purpose. Glass in hand, she returned to the office, where she searched the Internet for articles on bearer bonds.

The ice in the glass had melted and her eyes were heavy with sleep by the time she decided she'd seen enough. At least now she understood what she faced. Exhausted, Kira pushed back from the computer and made her way to Mitch's bed, where she let sleep claim her.

MITCH CLIMBED FROM HIS CAR, then stretched cramped muscles. He was nearly at the end of his long-haul driving days, which was a good thing, since his tolerance for it was gone. As he pocketed his keys and walked toward his house, he noticed that virtually every light inside was turned on. He appreciated a warm welcome, but could do without the hit to his electric bill.

"Kira?" he called as he came in the front door. But no one answered. He switched off the living room light and the kitchen, too. When he reached his computer/exercise room, he halted in the doorway. His computer was on, and he was far too attached to his flat-panel monitor to have left it glowing all night. If that hadn't been tip-off enough that Kira had been there, the half-finished whiskey glass on the desk would have done the job.

He looked into the bedroom. She was curled up on her side, asleep in the center of the bed. He knew a moment's bitterness that she could look so peaceful when his gut was knotted with tension. Then she turned restlessly in her sleep, murmuring the half words, half nonsense he'd heard the other night. No, she had no more peace than he did.

Mitch returned to the computer room, closing the door behind him. After a swallow of the lukewarm diluted whiskey that Kira had left, he opened the KeySpy program and called up the log. He clicked on yesterday's date, since midnight had arrived almost an hour earlier.

Mitch scrolled down the screen and checked the first entry. She'd logged on at the Whitman-Pierce site, but her keystrokes other than her password had been minimal...until five minutes later. Feeling lower than a thief, Mitch read the message she'd typed.

Don,
Do you think the attached is authentic? I'm worried. Call me when you can.
Kira

She wasn't alone in her worry.

"*What* was authentic, dammit?" Mitch asked.

He downed more of the tepid drink and then went to the Web site's back-door address Kira had used. He began reading through the mail she'd left on the server. It didn't take long to accept that after she'd forwarded whatever this alarming something was, she'd wiped it from the server. He couldn't find it in her sent-mail folder either.

If he'd ever had any real computer training, Mitch was sure he'd have been able to somehow retrieve the message from the guts of his computer. But really he was nothing more than a devious amateur.

Accepting that he'd hit a dead end, Mitch returned to the keystroke log.

What he saw next nearly rocked his faith in her honesty. Kira had been searching the phrase *bearer bonds*.

A couple of years had passed since his Commercial Transactions class, and bearer bonds had been touched on only briefly. Still, Mitch knew one thing for sure—in the United States at least, there was no legal and justifiable reason to be dealing in them. He also couldn't imagine that she'd searched the words out of random curiosity. Not after eleven at night, when he'd earlier made love to her until she'd cried exhaustion.

"What a total goddamn mess," he said, then drained the rest of the whiskey.

He might be an analytical man, but he was also out of avenues. She loved him. She'd said so, even if it was in the act, so to speak. He wouldn't let her take it back and he wouldn't lose her by showing himself for the sneaky bastard he'd proven to be over the last twenty-four hours.

He'd wait until morning. He'd stick with her all day. Whatever it took until she worked up the courage to give him the truth.

Mitch printed the log pages and tucked them into a desk drawer. Once he'd shut down the computer and settled the whiskey glass into the kitchen sink, he got ready for bed.

In his absence Kira had moved diagonally across the mattress, leaving him only a wedge of his usual sleeping space. It amused him in a bleak sort of way that a woman so small could take up so much space in his bed...his mind...and his heart.

"Move it over, Highness," he murmured, trying to get her perpendicular to the headboard.

Mitch folded his body into the territory he'd won. Still restless, she rolled toward him and then came more fully awake.

"I've missed you," she whispered.

Three simple words—not even as intimate as the ones she'd given him earlier—and he ached to be inside her. Mitch made love to her hard, hungry and without the words he wanted to give her in return. First he needed the truth.

THE NEXT MORNING, WHILE KIRA was brushing her teeth, Mitch popped his head into the bathroom and said, "See you soon." Since he was dressed for work and she was off to brew coffee, she wasn't sure what that meant, but she nodded anyway.

Fifteen minutes later she arrived at the Village Grounds. Lisa stuck around after opening the shop long enough to give a few wedding updates. The heart-shaped butter pats were no more. Her dress had been fitted to perfection. And in a true stroke of weirdness, her great-aunt had given them a massive concrete gargoyle as a wedding gift.

Kira asked Lisa if she could stay long enough for Kira to make a couple of calls. She had weirdness of her own to deal with, and nothing so benign as a concrete gargoyle. While Lisa tended the coffee bar, Kira slipped outside and walked across the street to the village green. A woman—and Kira would bet it was Lisa's mother—was on her knees at the edge of the gazebo replacing flower beds of red impatiens with flats of the pale pink variety. Pink was more romantic, no doubt. Kira tactfully pretended not to see her.

She pulled out her phone and dialed the office. Susan answered on the second ring.

"Hey, Susan, it's Kira."

After answering some questions other agents had left with the receptionist, Kira got down to the business that most concerned her.

"Has Roxanne picked up her car yet?" she asked.

"No, it's still in the lot. I thought you said she was gone for the whole week."

"I did, but you know how she likes to change things up. I though she might be back by now."

"Not a sign of her," Susan said. "No calls, no nothing."

Kira frowned. "Do me a favor. Check her office and see if her briefcase is still there."

"Hang on while I put you on hold."

"Okay." While she waited, Kira watched Lisa's mother tuck uprooted red impatiens into the empty plastic packs from the pink.

Susan returned. "It's gone. But, then again, I don't remember seeing it there all week."

Okay, so Roxanne probably knew that she had the wrong PDA. The question was why she cared.

"Kira, is everything okay?" Susan asked. "I've been worried all week…since you asked me for Don's number. It didn't help that Don called and asked me stuff about Roxanne."

Kira worked up the most reassuring voice she could: "Things are a little sticky right now between Roxanne and me, that's all. It should clear up in the next couple of weeks. I promise."

Someone was walking from the back side of the gazebo toward Lisa's mother. It was Mitch.

"I know that you and Roxanne haven't been getting along too well lately," Susan was saying into her ear at the same time Kira was trying to pick up snatches of conversation between Mitch and the flower swapper.

"No, we haven't," Kira said. "And, Susan, if you see anything outside the norm at the office, call Don right away, okay?" Mitch had apparently left Lisa's mom to her gardening, because he was headed her way. "I have to run. I'll talk to you later."

Kira didn't even wait for Susan's goodbye, tucking the cell phone into her purse with the hope of avoiding any Mitch-type questions. The call to Don would have to wait a couple of minutes.

Mitch leaned down and kissed her after he'd arrived.

"This is a pretty conservative town. Isn't there an ordinance against that?" she teased.

He smiled. "Only if we're naked."

She looped her arm through his. "So, do you want to walk me back to work?"

"Absolutely." While they walked, he said, "How would you feel about going out for a nice dinner tonight?"

"Like a date?"

"A date," he agreed. "I'd like to take you to the Nickerson Inn."

The Nickerson was a quaint old place high on a hillside overlooking Lake Michigan. As Kira recalled, it served the most elegant meals in Sandy Bend. She knew that Mitch—the fluff lover—was stretching far to please her in offering this meal.

"I'd love to go," she said, smiling up at him.

When they got to the door, Mitch opened it and ushered her in, then followed. She had assumed he'd be going back to work.

"I'm in the mood for a coffee," he said at her curious look.

He lingered even after he'd been given his coffee, making Lisa laugh and blush with talk about what a beautiful bride she was going to be tomorrow. When he jokingly mentioned that her mom was across the street uprooting the park in favor of a pink theme, she shot out the door. Kira imagined that if Lisa were drawn as a cartoon character, she'd have more steam coming out of her ears than the espresso machine she'd abandoned hissing into a pitcher of milk.

Kira took over behind the counter.

Mitch went to the window and gave a low whistle as both of them watched Lisa lecture her mom.

"Nice job," Kira said. "Get the mother of the bride killed the day before the wedding."

Mitch laughed. "Hey, it's not as though I arrested her. That would have really ticked Lisa off."

Mind on her cell phone, Kira said, "Why don't you go across the street and mediate?"

"No way. I'd rather step into a prison riot than deal with a day-before-the-wedding family spat." To make it clear he wasn't moving, Mitch grabbed a stool from the front counter, carried it back to the coffee bar and tucked it where he wouldn't interfere with the customers—or give her a moment of privacy.

"Is that today's paper?" he asked, pointing to a stack of newsprint Lisa must have left by the bakery case.

Kira tossed the newspaper to him with technically a little more force than what was required. "Read away."

After making a couple of fruit smoothies and ringing up the orders, Kira tried again.

"Don't you have to go walk a beat or do whatever it is you do all day?" she asked.

He looked at her from over the top of the paper. "Nope. I'm done."

She glanced at the clock on the back wall. "You worked for—what—an hour?"

"I got a call from another officer who needed to switch shifts for next Tuesday. I'm sprung. And I was already off until Sunday night, too."

Which was all wonderful, but she still needed to call Don. It was time to get down and dirty.

"As long as you've decided to make yourself a fixture, would you mind watching the store for a few minutes?" she asked.

Mitch set aside the paper, then shook his head. "I don't know how to make lattes."

Kira grabbed her purse and came around the counter. "Fake it."

"Where are you going?" There was an edge of panic to his voice. She would have thought that, as a male, he'd get a kick out of the new toys he could play with.

She came close and spoke in a low, confiding tone. "I'm going to the ladies' room. I think it might be that time of the month. I'm feeling a little crampy," she said, laying one hand low on her belly for added effect.

That shut him up. She figured he was considering himself lucky that she hadn't sent him to the market to buy tampons.

The shop had one small unisex bathroom at the very back. After glancing over her shoulder to make sure that Mitch had parked himself behind the counter, she shut herself in. And just in case he didn't fully buy her story and decided to come eavesdrop, she turned on the sink taps full blast before calling Don.

His secretary quickly connected him.

"Is that water running?" he asked.

"Yup."

"I don't think I want to know where you're calling from."

"You don't," she said. "Did you get my e-mail from last night? Do you think it's really Roxanne?"

"Yes, but the Internet service provider won't just hand over customer information, so it's a tough one to prove very quickly. What do you have that she could need?"

Kira told Don about the PDA mix-up and how last night she'd gone through every file.

"Just because you can't see a file doesn't mean it isn't there. It's simple enough to hide one and password protect it."

When it came to that sort of technical stuff, she'd take him at his word. Still, she had her doubts about Roxanne's level of attention.

"I don't know," Kira said. "We're talking about someone who stuck her business passwords in a shopping list."

"Maybe she's more careful with things that mean more to her." Don paused a second. "I've corroborated the bearer-bond rumor, so if there's a hidden file, it could be worth millions. Literally."

He had a point.

"Did you talk to your attorney yesterday?" Don asked.

At her continuing silence, he said, "This is serious stuff. Do it, Kira."

She looked at her reflection, pale and pinched, in the bathroom mirror. It was as though she'd aged five years in less than five minutes. "I will."

After their call ended, Kira shut off the water and gave herself a moment to work up a calm facade. It was already Friday afternoon. Would it be so horrible to steal a day or two of happiness before everything came tumbling down?

She would call her father on Sunday. He was well connected, far better suited for the job of finding her an attorney than she was. And it wasn't as though too much more could go wrong in less than forty-eight hours.

She'd spend what time she had left with Mitch, then give him an easy out of their relationship. He deserved that much, at least.

After sticking her cell phone back in her purse, Kira left the bathroom. Mitch was at the register.

"False alarm," she said in a cheerful voice as she nudged him aside.

If only she could say the same thing about Don's call.

13

FINE DINING AND TORTURE could be found under the
same entry in Mitch's thesaurus. He and Kira
weren't even dressed to leave for the restaurant and
already he was uptight.

Scowling at his reflection in the dresser mirror,
Mitch reknotted his tie for the third damn time. Tie
finally neither too long nor too short, he picked up
the small red velvet box he'd retrieved from his safe-
deposit box at the bank in the early afternoon.

His mom had died when he was just a little kid.
As time had passed, a lot of his memories of specific
events had faded. He still remembered her laugh
and the way she'd always smelled sweet to him, as
if she'd just been baking cupcakes. And he remembered this....

Mitch opened the box and touched the delicate
necklace that lay on its white silk lining. His mother's
family had been farm people and had had little
money for luxuries, so this was a simple piece. Once,
he'd shown the necklace to Dana, who had a better
eye for jewelry than he did. She'd said that the pinkish gold was called rose gold and that the cut of the
small diamond it held was old.

The necklace was one of the few keepsakes he had
from his mother. She'd always worn it, and his dad

had later told him that it had been handed down from her grandmother. Now Mitch wanted Kira to have it. He wanted her to see that he meant the necklace as a symbol of the trust they should have in each other. He was damn sure that the subterfuge and avoidance she'd thrown his way was rooted in panic and he was positive that once they got past this garbage he wanted her in his life.

He couldn't believe he was moving to the level of metaphor, but words hadn't exactly worked between the two of them. Worse, shadowing her today had only put her more on edge. He knew that she'd called someone from the bathroom of the Village Grounds this morning and he knew that she'd seemed sad and subdued the rest of the day.

Mitch snapped shut the box and stuck it in his blazer pocket. He was asking a lot from a simple piece of jewelry, but he didn't know what else to do. He'd never failed at much. To do it the first time in such a colossal way would be a killer.

Kira had closed herself in the bathroom. After fifteen minutes of cooling his heels in the living room, Mitch wondered whether she'd ever come out.

He came closer to the door. The scent of a warm and spicy perfume lingered in the air, but he couldn't hear a thing.

"Are you still alive in there?" he asked.

"Stop hovering. I'll be out in a few minutes," she said.

Duly chastised, Mitch returned to the living room. True to her word, Kira appeared not long after. He stood, but it was pretty much an involuntary reflex, not a show of manners.

"Wow," he finally managed to say.

While he'd been in the bank, Kira must have been shopping. He knew that she deserved more expansive praise for the way she looked in her short, sleek and low-cut black dress, but his tongue seemed to have grown uncooperative.

She twirled once and then said, "So, you like it?"

He nodded. Even with their troubles, he'd have to say that he was one lucky, lucky man.

As it turned out, Mitch got lucky on a number of counts. First, they were seated on the screened porch off the dining room, a comfortable place where he could look past the green treetops to the blue of Lake Michigan stretching to the horizon. Second, along with the fine food and fancy sauces that a woman like Kira had probably cut her teeth on, the menu also had stuff a guy could eat—cow and everything.

During dinner they talked about the old days and old friends. For a while it didn't feel to Mitch as though whatever she was embroiled in today hung over his head like an anvil, ready to flatten him. He could almost imagine what life would be like once they were past it.

He waited until after the meal had been cleared to give her the necklace.

"I have something for you," he said, pulling the box from his pocket and setting it in front of her.

A pretty tinge of pink climbed her cheeks. "It's really for me?"

He nodded. She seemed so floored that he wondered if all the guys she'd dated had been faced with the same problem he'd had—not knowing what to get a girl who had everything.

Kira slowly opened the box, then touched one finger to the necklace. Her obvious delight was gratifying. "It's beautiful and so delicate."

"It was my mother's." His throat felt thick when he spoke.

"Your mother's?" she echoed. Something he'd peg as dismay flashed across her face. "Mitch, I can't take this."

"Why not?"

She looked down at the tablecloth, then back at him. "It should stay in your family. It wouldn't be right for me to accept it."

"But you're the woman I want to have it."

"I'm—I'm leaving on Sunday," she said in a rush. "Remember how I'd told you that I had a little glitch in my business?"

He nodded.

"I need to fix it now. Life's going to be crazy for a while. I don't know how long it will be until I can come back to Michigan again and I totally understand how busy you are finishing off school and with your work. This is just...bad timing. For both of us."

She closed the box and handed it back to him. Mitch left it on the table, a marker of all that was screwed up between them. If he didn't know about her concerned e-mail and the computer research she'd been doing, he'd have thought that she was dumping him. But he did know and recognized her talk as an attempt to let him extricate himself.

Problem was, he had no intention of doing that. His time in the hospital had taught him that he was tough enough to wait out almost anything.

Curiosity and a sense that they were playing some sort of game of brinksmanship drove him to ask, "And if I want to come to Florida?"

She looked as though she wanted to cry. Hell, he nearly did. Or at least go punch a wall.

"I don't know, Mitch. As I said, there's a lot I have to do. Let's just wait and see."

Mitch knew there was a moral to this evening and he wasn't crazy about being on the ugly end of it. Devious guys didn't deserve to be happy. He took the necklace and returned it to his pocket.

DINNER WAS FINISHED, AND IT felt to Kira as though her brief fantasy of an idyllic Dollhouse Cottage life was, too. Mitch was a generous man, kind enough to try to keep conversation flowing when they both had run out of words.

"Let's take a walk toward the water," he said. "The sun will be setting soon."

Because she wasn't ready to go back to the cottage, Kira agreed. She hadn't planned on telling Mitch so soon that she'd be leaving, but when he'd tried to give her his mother's necklace, she'd had no choice. Accepting it would have been wrong, as would dragging him into the middle of her problems.

They headed to a broad stretch of beach with a boardwalk that lay west of the Nickerson Inn. As she and Mitch walked, she wanted to hold his hand or his arm—anything to try to regain the connection she felt fading. When he led her out onto the pier, at least she had an excuse to do just that.

"Would you mind?" she asked, taking his hand. "High heels and I get along for only so long."

He squeezed her hand once, then wrapped it into the crook of his elbow. They walked past fishermen and other couples strolling. People greeted Mitch. He gave them a restrained greeting in return.

At the end of the pier they stood just apart from a small group waiting for the orange-red globe of the sun to finally touch the water. This time of year it was a long wait. Kira would guess that it was nearing nine and the sun yet had a distance to travel.

She was feeling weary, and it wasn't from the hour. Doing the right thing was very tiring exercise.

"What time Sunday had you planned to leave?" Mitch asked in a low voice.

She didn't want to talk about this. She'd done enough to spoil her last hours in town already. "I don't know…afternoon maybe."

More people gathered on the pier. The sunset was taking on almost a Key West-type festive atmosphere. Kira began to feel out of place, and apparently Mitch did, too.

"Let's head to land," he said.

As they walked past the edge of the picnic area that was adjacent to the state park's beach, Kira hesitated. At a table just ahead sat a man and woman. He was paging through a magazine and she was chatting on her cell phone. Kira was sure she'd never seen the man before, but the woman looked vaguely familiar. As they walked past, Kira scrutinized her. Middle-aged, brown hair, bland expression…

She shrugged off the moment, thinking the woman must look like someone she'd once shown a house to. When they were five or so yards past, Kira paused and looked back. Recognition hit her like a punch. Kira's bad leg gave a little, and she felt her ankle wobble.

Mitch steadied her. "Are you okay?"

"Sorry. Stupid shoes," she murmured, trying to sound unaffected as her mind raced. It had been only days but over fifteen hundred miles since she'd seen that unremarkable woman…in Coconut Grove. Kira was almost certain that she was the same woman she'd seen parked in the blue minivan the night Roxanne had disappeared.

Suddenly dinner wasn't sitting too well. Not with trouble hot on her heels…

MITCH WOKE AT SEVEN ON Saturday. His bed was far too empty for comfort, since Kira had decided she wanted to sleep on the couch. She'd thought it would be better that way. Better for whom, he wasn't exactly sure.

He was about to head out the front door for a lengthy, mind-clearing run when he stopped long enough to watch her struggle to roll to her side, her legs tangled in the sheet she'd put over herself. He didn't like witnessing her discomfort.

Mitch walked to the couch, bent down and kissed her forehead. When her eyes opened, he said, "You're moving." Without giving her time to protest, he scooped her up, carried her to his bedroom and settled her on the bed.

"I'll be back later. Sleep, since I'm betting you didn't all night."

After stretching he began to run his standard loop through the downtown area and out to the beach. Preparations were in full swing for Lisa and Jim's wedding, which was at eleven. Mitch crossed the street to check out the action. A large white tent was being erected on a portion of the green. Tables and chairs were being delivered, and other workers were there, too. Mitch jogged by a white-panel florist's van parked about a block down from the green, no doubt waiting its turn. He smiled at the woman in the driver's seat, and she gave him a quick smile back.

As he continued his run, the florist lingered in his mind. He'd seen her somewhere before, and it wasn't in a flower shop. Mitch knew the best way to make the connection was to stop thinking about it and let his subconscious simmer. Sooner or later it would come to him. It always did.

KIRA WOKE TO FIND MITCH sitting on the edge of the bed. In his hand was a mug of coffee.

Once she'd sat upright, he handed it to her, saying, "You'll have to risk homemade, since the Village Grounds is closed today."

"Thanks. I'm sure it's wonderful." She took a sip, then worked on waking more. "So, what time is it?"

"Ten," he said with a casual nod toward the clock.

"Ten?" Kira pushed the mug back at him. "The wedding's in an hour." She scrambled from beneath the covers. "I don't know what I'm wearing and all I have is a card for them."

"Relax. It's casual, so you don't need to barricade yourself in the bathroom for hours. And the gift I bought can be from both of us. I forgot to buy a card, so we'll use yours."

Kira felt as though she was living on two levels. There was the outward, blissfully normal Sandy Bend Saturday full of social events. Then there was the deeper, upsetting knowledge that nothing was as it seemed.

"Thanks," she said, then accepted the mug again.

"When I ran this morning, I did some thinking, and here's what I'd like. I'd like today to be special…memorable. I accept that you plan to leave tomorrow, but let's not have that carry over into today, okay?"

She nodded. "I'd like that, too."

"We have Jim and Lisa's wedding, then dinner out at Cal's place. After that I plan to bring you back here and make love to you until maybe you change your mind about tomorrow."

"Mitch, I can't—"

He raised his hand, palm outward. "Nope. No negativity."

"Okay."

Mitch stood. "I'll be out on the back deck. Come get me when you're ready."

Kira showered, then fussed with her hair, ending up with it pinned into a knot. She pulled on one of her sleeveless silk tops and a flowing floral skirt perfect for a wedding on a green. Then she joined Mitch and they walked downtown together.

After the disastrous near wedding in Chicago, Kira had decided that if she were ever actually to do the deed, she'd want something more casual. Something like what Lisa had. The white gingerbread of the green's gazebo had been draped with a fat white organza ribbon that shone iridescent in the sun. The folding chairs set up for the guests to watch the ceremony were covered in white fabric with a bow at the back of each. The aisle was marked by baskets of flowers, with white roses, purple Japanese iris and whimsical daisies in the mix. At the back of the gazebo a harpist was playing.

It was perfection, Kira decided. Mitch took her hand and led her down the gentle slope to the seating area. Others Kira knew from town were gathering. She saw Mrs. Hawkins from the market on the arm of a tall, older man, which Kira found surprising, since the market owner had been widowed for years.

"Who's with Mrs. Hawkins?" Kira quietly asked Mitch.

"That's Len Vandervoort, her husband. She remarried last year but kept Hawkins as her last name not to confuse folks at her market."

Kira was pleased for Mrs. Hawkins. The sight of the couple gave her hope, too. Maybe by the time she and Mitch were in their eighties they'd have managed to get this love thing right.

Cal and Dana were seated a few rows from the back. Dana spotted them and waved them over. When the usher came to take Kira's arm, she told him they'd like to sit by the other couple. Dana and Cal stood as they arrived.

In what was one of the shocks of Kira's life, Cal leaned forward and gave her a kiss on the cheek.

"It's good to see you," he said.

Kira managed a polite thank-you to Cal as she sat. So this was what it felt like to belong…. Pity she was learning when it was too late.

"Dinner's at seven," Dana said to them.

"Can I bring anything?" Kira asked, recovering her poise.

"Just yourselves. And don't let Mitch make you late. I'm baking walleye in parchment paper, and the fish will turn to leather if it's in the oven too long."

They chatted until a violinist came forward and stood beside the gazebo. Silence fell as the minister, the groom and his ushers lined up. The violinist began to play. A trio of bridesmaids came down the aisle before the traditional wedding march started.

Everyone rose and turned. Lisa was, as Mitch had predicted, beautiful.

Kira didn't usually cry at weddings, but she began to tear up. She knew it was a reaction from the emotions that had buffeted her the past few days, but understanding the source didn't help. She did her best to stop the tears from escaping and ruining her makeup, but it was a losing battle.

As Lisa joined Jim at the altar, Kira felt a square of fabric being pressed into her hand. Mitch had handed her a handkerchief. He followed up with a quick kiss to her temple. It was going to be so very hard to leave this man.

After the ceremony they joined everyone in a tent at the far end of the green. She tried to be cheerful. She met Lisa's Jim and thanked them both for having her to the wedding. She ate more than she should have and avoided alcohol altogether. She was weepy enough already. Once the band had set up in the gazebo, she danced with both Mitch and Cal. Still, she felt overwhelmed.

While Mitch was dancing with Dana, Kira walked to the edge of the gathering, seeking a little less crowd, a little less noise. Sightseers stood on the sidewalk that bordered the green, a few taking snapshots of the wedding. In all the years she'd visited Sandy Bend Kira had never figured it especially photoworthy. Now her perspective had changed.

As the tourists moved on, Kira glanced across the street at the Village Grounds, where someone had painted *Just Married* in bright red letters on the front window. She smiled at the sight. Then she noticed something that made her smile fade. It was the woman from last night—and maybe last week. This time she was walking past the Village Grounds. Spooked, Kira hurried back to the reception, where she stuck to Mitch's side. After a while she had calmed down enough to let go of his hand.

Afternoon stretched toward evening. Kira saw no sign of the mystery woman again, though that was no surprise, since Kira made sure to keep to the middle of the reception throng. Dana and Cal left around four, clearly intent on reliving some wedding—and honeymoon—memories of their own before dinner.

Over time the reception turned into a town celebration, with more food and more people arriving. Kira expected that it would still be going strong at midnight. It was nearly six-thirty when Mitch suggested that they head back to the house, grab his car and head out to Cal and Dana's.

Fifteen minutes later they were on the road. Cal and Dana lived on the Brewer family farm, several miles into the countryside. Kira was blissfully relieved to have this break from town and from the potential of spotting the mystery woman. She leaned back, closed her eyes and put her fate in Mitch's hands for a few minutes.

Sandy Bend was behind them when Mitch made a sharp right turn onto a dirt road. Kira sat upright and braced her hands on the dashboard.

"Where are you going?"

He glanced her way. "I decided to take the scenic route."

Had he not chosen a road bounded on both sides by asparagus fields and little else, she might have bought in. The harvest was through and the stalks remaining had begun to grow tall, sliver-green and fernlike. The view was pretty enough—for the first half mile or so.

The back roads around Sandy Bend ran fairly straight. Kira soon realized that he was driving in a large square that would take them back to the main, paved road into town. At one point he slowed to let a truck gain on and then pass them.

"You could probably afford to pick it up a few miles an hour," she suggested. She didn't want to be responsible for petrified walleye at dinner.

Mitch barely responded. When they'd returned to the main road, he once again headed east into the countryside. She relaxed until he pulled into the mouth of another road and made a U-turn toward town.

"Where are we going?" she asked.

"Don't talk."

A minute or so later he muttered a blunt expletive. He looked so grim—almost furious—that Kira was actually scared.

"Mitch, what's wrong?"

"I said don't talk."

"But you're heading the wrong way, and Cal's expecting us."

He glared at her in response.

In a matter of minutes they had pulled into the drive at the Dollhouse Cottage. He strode to the door, looking once over his shoulder to tell her to hurry. Once inside he led her to the kitchen, where he looked out the back door before closing it and turning to her.

"Is there any reason someone would want to follow you?"

14

SWEAT BROKE OUT ON KIRA'S palms, but she kept her voice level. "Follow me?"

"Yeah. A dark green Taurus with two occupants."

It was possible, but she far preferred living in denial.

"Are you sure?" she asked.

He turned away from her for a moment, almost as though he couldn't stand the sight of her.

"I want you to come with me," he said when he'd turned back. He wrapped his fingers around her wrist and led her into his office. There he pulled out a sheaf of papers. "I loaded a keystroke-logging program on my computer so I could track you. I don't know what exactly you've been doing, but it has nothing to do with selling houses. I don't like being followed. In fact, it really pisses me off. Now, can you tell me what the hell's going on?"

Horrified, Kira pulled the papers from his hands. "You've been spying on me? How could you?"

"I told you not to use the computer."

"That's no excuse!"

He rubbed between his brows with the fingers of his right hand. "What choice did you leave me?"

"All you had to do was ask me to go."

Mitch walked away to adjust the blind over the

window so that the outdoors was totally obscured. "After a while it wasn't an option."

She tossed the papers into the wastebasket by the desk. "And spying was?"

"No. What I did sucked, okay? But we'll get to my sins later. For now, since I can guarantee that we're going to have visitors of some kind in the near future, I think you'd better tell me what's been going on. And once you're done, I'm getting Cal over here."

Mitch pulled out his desk chair and sat.

Kira was a mess. Anger and fright knotted her stomach. She felt betrayed yet strangely relieved at the same time. Clasping her hands to hide their trembling, she began to speak.

"Roxanne, my partner at work, took off just before I came to Sandy Bend. The circumstances weren't the best. She was with a couple of guys I didn't like the looks of. I got a threatening call, and some more goons were at my house. I wasn't sure what was going on, except it wasn't good."

She paused, looking for some sign of receptiveness in Mitch but finding instead a face devoid of expression.

"Go on," he said.

"I hired an investigator through a friend, and he suggested that leaving town might make some sense. I picked Sandy Bend because no one would expect it." She didn't add that her thoughts of him that afternoon had probably subconsciously urged her north, too.

"And since you've been here? Have you heard from your friend? Learned anything from your investigator?"

"I stumbled on the fact that Roxanne has been

running lots of money through our client escrow account. Things just weren't adding up. I began to worry that she was into something really bad. Roxanne's not exactly an angel."

"I know all about Roxanne."

"How?"

"The usual way," he said flatly. "So, where's Roxanne now?"

Part of Kira didn't want to tell him anything more. But the rest of her knew the time for evasiveness was past. If she didn't give him the truth now—no matter how helpless it made her look—everything they'd shared in the past week would become meaningless.

"I'm not totally sure where Roxanne is," she admitted. "I got an e-mail from her on Thursday night telling me to come home because she needed something from me and her business associates knew where I was anyway. When I received it, I contacted Don right away."

"Don?"

"The P.I."

"You called this guy in Florida instead of looking across your pillow and talking to me?"

"I didn't want to involve you."

"It can't have escaped you that we *are* involved."

Kira knew he was speaking out of hurt, but she was hurting, too. "You know what I mean. And there was no solid evidence that the sender was really Roxanne. It's pretty easy to appear to be whomever you choose in cyberspace."

"It doesn't matter who sent it. Kira, it was a stone-cold threat."

She nodded. "I know, and I thought I could handle it. Then last night at the beach and again today at the wedding I saw a woman who I think was with the guys at my door in Florida."

"Caucasian, short brown hair, about five foot five, maybe forty years old?" he asked.

She nodded.

Mitch swore. "And you didn't share this with me, either?"

She had no doubt now that he was furious and she definitely wasn't going to ask how he knew about the mystery woman.

He stood. "You haven't changed. I can't friggin' believe it. You haven't changed at all. You're still the same selfish and reckless person, aren't you?"

"That's not fair, Mitch."

"But it's true. Let's put the facts together." He began to pace the small, crowded room. "You flee Florida because your missing partner is involved in something that appears to be criminal. You get an e-mail from her saying her associates know where you are. You get followed and you still don't bother to tell me. What were you thinking?"

"This wasn't some sort of plot against you. This wasn't even about you." She was going to be screaming if she didn't calm down, and she'd given up screaming a couple of years ago.

Kira drew a deep breath, then slowly exhaled before continuing. "When I came to town, I didn't know for sure that anything bad was going on. It could have just been Roxanne taking off on a sudden vacation. God knows she's done it before."

"And the men at your door who scared you so much that you took off? Maybe they were bible salesmen, huh?"

"Once I was gone it didn't feel so ominous anymore. They were there, and I was here."

"And when you discovered they were looking for you? Why not then? Why didn't you come to me then? Kira, you've risked your life!"

"I know." She paused to swipe at a tear beneath her right eye. "At least I do now, but I didn't want to drag you into my mess. Here's the last of it—by accident, I ended up with Roxanne's PDA when I left town. Don thinks there's a hidden file that she wants. And he thinks it has something to do with a big amount of bearer bonds that some drug kingpin's missing."

Mitch gave a humorless laugh. "And I'm not being fair in saying that you're still selfish and reckless? Right."

He walked out of the room. Kira stood there, her arms wrapped around her middle as though she could hold in the pain. A few minutes later she heard Mitch in the bedroom talking to Cal on the phone. She went into the bathroom and gathered some tissues. Sooner or later she was bound to snap, and it wasn't going to be pretty.

Ready for the storm to come, she sat in the living room and waited. Cal arrived about fifteen minutes later with an officer he introduced as Cathy.

"Cathy will be staying here tonight," Cal said to Kira. "It's a precaution, really. I've put in some calls to see if the folks who followed you are from any other law-enforcement branch. Usually we get a courtesy visit when they're around, but not always."

Kira nodded, clutching her stack of tissues. "Okay."

Mitch came from the direction of the bedroom, duffel bag in hand.

"Are you going somewhere?" Kira asked.

He wouldn't meet her eyes. "You'll be safe here."

She didn't even care that she had witnesses to her panic. She just wanted him to stay. "Don't leave me tonight. Please."

"I have to. I can't deal with you right now. I'm ticked off and I've said too much already." He scrubbed a hand over his face. "Tomorrow, okay?" he said, then left.

But he'd forgotten...tomorrow, she'd be gone.

Before Cal took off, Kira said, "Tell Dana I'm really sorry about the walleye."

And that, of all things, was what started the tears coming. Overcooked fish.

MITCH HAD WANTED A MEMORABLE day, and damn but he had gotten it. As he drove the last miles to his brother's country place, Mitch tried to calm enough to think rationally. It was a losing battle.

He pulled up to the lodge, which was really an old barn that Cal had converted into a bachelor's weekend retreat. It sat empty more often than not, since Dana understandably wasn't crazy about the place Cal used to take all his women. Now Cal rented it to hunters during hunting season and loaned it to buddies the rest of the year. Since it was summer and Cal's buddies had been there, at least Mitch was guaranteed a full beer fridge—one of the many marvels of the place.

He unlocked the front door and headed across the slate floors and thick wool rugs straight to the small, glass-fronted cooler under the bar counter. Without much regard for what he was choosing, he pulled a bottle of imported German brew and opened it. Then

he stalked to the fireplace and scowled into its empty
depths.

He'd really blown it, not connecting the woman
in the florist's van with the odd tourist he'd seen on
the beach. It should have clicked and it hadn't. He
hated being taken by surprise, hated missing things.
It wouldn't have changed the outcome of the day, but
at least he'd feel better.

He was furious with Kira and furious with himself.
Oh, he'd figured maybe she was in a little financial hot
water. If it were just a money thing—even one of ques-
tionable legality—he could have forgiven her for
keeping him on the outside. But to be under siege
from threats and still not trust him enough to ask for
help?

"Unforgivable," Mitch said. And he damn well
meant it, too. A guy had his pride, and his had been
supremely violated.

The thing that let him know he was a total sucker?
He still loved her, dammit.

He just couldn't bear looking at her.

As soon as Kira had conquered the last of her residual sniffles, she got the number for her father in London. She wasn't thrilled with making the call, but
there was no one better to find her a top criminal attorney. Clearly, Mitch was out of the question as a resource.

Kira dialed her dad and gave him the lowdown
on how she'd managed to mess up her life in less
time than it used to take her to choose a nail-polish
color. She was calm and factual about it, inviting
none of his I'm-in-charge-now behavior.

Really, he was very obliging considering she'd

been forced to wake him in the middle of the night. He'd even offered to fly home immediately. She'd told him not to change his schedule. Now that she had his help on the attorney front, she could handle the situation.

By midnight she'd finished making her plans for the next day. She was going to leave her car at her parents' lake house and have one of Cal's officers drive her to the Grand Rapids airport, where she would fly to Miami. Waiting there would be the attorney her father had retained. They would then deliver Roxanne's PDA to the Miami police, and Kira would give a statement.

She slept restlessly on Mitch's bed until about five in the morning, when she gave up. Cal arrived at seven, saying he'd take her to the airport himself. When she asked about Mitch, all he'd say was, "You're going to have to give him some time."

Kira's suitcase was loaded into Cal's trunk when Mitch pulled into the drive. Her heart leaped, but then dived when she caught the closed expression on his face.

"I'll take her," he said to Cal.

Cal scrutinized his brother. "You sure?"

"Yeah."

Her suitcase was transferred to Mitch's trunk, and Kira began what she was sure was going to be the longest hour-and-a-half drive of her life. They'd been on the road for nearly forty minutes and were heading east on I-96 before she found the courage to speak.

"I don't want to leave things like this between us," she said. "I can't stand feeling as though you hate me."

Mitch was silent for a moment, then said, "Kira, I don't hate you. I just—"

She knew what words were coming next. "Don't say it."

She couldn't bear hearing that he didn't love her.

"Maybe you could let me explain why I behaved the way I did?" she asked.

"Okay." Kira noted the way his knuckles shone white as he gripped the steering wheel. She was fighting a battle she probably couldn't win, but she had to try.

"I know a lot of people think I've had it easy, but there's a price that comes with being a Whitman. When I was growing up, nothing was unconditional—especially not love. You know my accident when I was sixteen?"

He nodded.

"My dad was furious. I felt like I was being convicted for behavior unbecoming a Whitman. After that I tried so hard to earn his love. I involved him in every decision. I'd follow his every rule until I thought I'd go crazy. Then I'd end up committing some act of rebellion."

She glanced at Mitch, who at least looked as though he was listening. "Of course after each grand rebellion I'd step back in with Dad's plans, which is how I almost ended up marrying Winston. When I realized that I was now going to make two people miserable for life instead of just one, I found the nerve to cut my ties. It was drastic, but it was the only way I'd be strong enough to do it."

"I'm glad you figured it out, but I'm not sure what that has to do with this past week."

"Here's the thing…. When I decided that I needed to stand on my own, I guess I did it with the same passion that I used to devote to being my dad's follower. I hadn't really thought about this until last night, after you left, but now I think I get it.

"By pushing you out of my life, all I did was prove that I'd swung too far in the other direction. I didn't want you to think that I was still the same weak person. Add to that my fear that if you were involved with me, I'd somehow wreck your chances for your dream job. And there we have it, another classic Kira disaster. All of which boils down to I'm really, really sorry."

He nodded. "Thank you. And I'm sorry for spying on you. That was wrong. Dead wrong."

"Flawed person that I am, I've already decided there's nothing I can do but forgive you." Kira watched him as she spoke and thought she might have even caught a brief smile. She pulled together the rest of her courage and continued.

"So, I guess what I need to know now is whether there's any way you can love me, horrible flaws and all. Because I love you—headbanger music, marshmallow fluff and all."

"Kira…" He shook his head. "Damn, this is hard. I do love you, but I can't live with you. I've never sunk to spying on anyone in my life, and it scares the hell out of me that I did it. I don't know who I am with you."

He loved her, *but…*

More conditional love.

"I see," Kira said, then turned her attention out the window. The countryside was nothing but a teary blur. She didn't speak again, except to tell Mitch which airline she was flying out on. Mitch offered to come into the terminal with her, but she told him it wouldn't be necessary. He pulled up to the curb, switched off the car and got her belongings from the trunk.

She meant to thank him coolly, then walk away. Love got the better of her, though. "I don't suppose I could have one last hug? I really need it."

He wrapped her in his arms. Her heart turned over when she felt him kiss the top of her head.

"It's been interesting, Highness. With you, it's always interesting."

Ten days later…

KIRA HAD HAD ENOUGH OF "interesting" to last her a dozen lifetimes. When she'd been met at the airport in Miami, her new attorney had informed her that she'd be speaking to the FBI, not the local police. With the international flow of bearer bonds and the activity of the drug cartel involved, the case was under the federal government's jurisdiction.

It seemed that Cal's instincts had been correct. The woman who'd been following Kira wasn't one of Roxanne's associates but a federal employee. And Kira had been followed for months before she'd even noticed. That at least gave her some comfort about the FBI's skill level.

The thugs who she'd seen at her door weeks earlier were just that, at least. And as of this morning all of them were under arrest. It was also the first morning she'd actually had time to go back to work.

She'd spoken to her staff, telling them she'd understand if anyone chose to leave because she was certain that listings were going to die off until the publicity cooled, but it was her intention to continue the business. She knew a few of the more aggressive agents would jump ship quickly, but a few would also stay. Susan had made it clear that she'd be at the front desk as long as Kira would have her. As soon as Kira could afford it, she planned to repay Susan's loyalty by helping with her college expenses.

Kira closed her office door and phoned Mitch, thinking he deserved an update after the hell she'd put him through. She wasn't nervous about calling, since she didn't really expect to catch him. He was seldom home, according to Cal, who'd called yesterday to check on her. Still, after she dialed, Kira took a stupid sort of comfort in knowing that up in Sandy Bend the phone was ringing in the Dollhouse Cottage.

"Hello?" a male answered after the fifth ring.

Kira was tempted to hang up but instead collected herself enough to say, "Mitch?"

There was a brief pause before he said, "Kira, is that you?" His voice sounded almost rusty.

"Yes. I—I thought maybe you'd like to know what's going on down here."

She got another pause, then he said a quiet "Sure."

Kira gripped the phone tighter and closed her eyes. She hadn't thought it would be this hard to hear his voice again. This heartbreaking.

"They arrested Roxanne today. From what my attorney has been able to piece together, I guess Roxanne had been operating a money-laundering business, buying and delivering bearer bonds. On top of that, she was in huge debt. She decided to keep a few of the bearer bonds that she was supposed to deliver, figuring she'd just take the money and flee the country. She wasn't fast enough. When the owner's associates picked her up that day, she told them I had the bonds."

"Nice," Mitch said.

"I get the feeling she wasn't too fond of me," Kira joked, though once she had, she wished she could pull the words back. She wasn't sure Mitch was too fond of her, either. "Anyway, she gave up on that after a few hours and admitted that the bonds were in a safe at a storage facility, except she was so freaked out, she couldn't remember the combination to the safe. It was in the PDA—"

"Which you'd accidentally taken," he filled in.

"So, anyway, Roxanne's in jail, the owner of the bonds and his enforcers have been arrested, and now I get to untangle my life."

"I'm glad you're safe," he said.

That, she supposed, was a start.

"How are you?" she asked.

"Tired. School's a bitch and I haven't been sleeping well."

Her throat grew tight. "Me, either."

"I miss you," he said, "and I don't like missing you."

"Maybe if you came down for a visit…?"

Her tentative offer was met by silence. "I don't think I can do that," Mitch finally said.

"Then, you take care of yourself," Kira replied because there was nothing else left to be said.

"You, too. 'Bye."

And with that, it was over.

Kira looked out her window at the action on the street. People strolled and laughed. Cars drove past, filled with even more souls busy living life. She couldn't be the only one with a broken heart, yet she was letting it conquer her.

She turned from the window. It was time to forget the Dollhouse Cottage and the first man she'd ever loved. It was time to get on with life.

15

Four months later...

GRAY WASN'T ROXANNE'S BEST color. As Kira's ex-partner was led from the courtroom following her sentencing, her suit and skin had taken on the same hue. Kira wasn't surprised. Roxanne had accepted a plea agreement—seven years in exchange for her full cooperation in the cases pending against her associates. According to Kira's attorney, the sentence was far less than what Roxanne could have served. She'd be relatively young when released. But Kira knew that for Roxanne it might as well be a lifetime. She'd be ready for BOTOX and her first tummy job by the time she hit the street and she wouldn't have the money to pay for it.

Roxanne glanced back over her shoulder at the gallery, and her gaze locked with Kira's. It wasn't a friendly or even a regretful look. Again Kira wasn't surprised. Roxanne had decided early on that her legal troubles were Kira's fault. If Kira hadn't mixed up the PDAs, she wouldn't have been caught. The fact that Roxanne had been under surveillance for months prior to the mix-up couldn't shake her from this conviction. Kira didn't care. Roxanne was no longer her problem. And those problems that she did have, she'd never stubbornly insist on bearing alone again. She'd learned *her* lesson, just too late.

Kira walked from the chill of the air conditioned federal building and into the strong Miami sun. She still loved this area and knew that she would continue to build a satisfying and busy life here. She just regretted that it was a life alone.

HOT, SWEATY AND TOTALLY NOT acclimated to the Florida sun, Mitch tugged at the collar of his polo shirt. If he'd had a plan, right now he could be saying that he'd met with an unexpected complication. But he didn't have a plan, other than knowing that he'd had enough.

Enough of finding his bed too big and his life too empty.

Enough of doubting himself.

Enough of wondering nearly every damn minute of the day what Kira was doing.

Now he knew that at least one of the things she was doing was waving at the guard outside her damn gated community.

"This gonna take much longer?" the cabbie asked as Mitch considered yet another approach to wheedle his way past the guard.

"Doesn't matter. The meter's running, isn't it?" Mitch replied.

The cabbie muttered something, then pulled out his cell phone and began to talk to someone in a Spanish so fast that even Mitch, who was fluent, couldn't catch it.

The guard—a middle-aged man with a uniform so starched that it hurt to look at it—wasn't receptive to logic, the sight of Mitch's Sandy Bend Police shield or begging. The best Mitch could figure to do was make the guard feel involved in the situation so he might show some level of empathy.

Mitch gave the guard his best I'm-a-trusted-member-of-the-community smile. "Mind if I step out so we can talk?"

The guard backed into his shack, reminding Mitch of a hermit crab. "Stay in the car, sir."

Mitch took his hand off the door handle. "Look, I appreciate that you're doing your job and that my name's not on the list." He gestured at the guard's clipboard. "But there must be some process for the times when a homeowner forgets to leave word."

"I can call Miss Whitman," the guard offered.

"I already told you, I'm trying to surprise her."

"Sorry, then. You'll have to move along."

"I didn't come here all the way from Michigan just to 'move along.' Is there another contact listed?"

"Her office," the guard said grudgingly.

"Perfect! Now, if you'd just let me borrow your phone?" He opened the car door.

The guard closed the lower half door to his little white shack. "Stay *in* the car, sir!"

"Then you call Susan—she's the receptionist. And—"

"I don't think so, sir."

Mitch was losing patience. Susan knew he was coming. The only rational step he'd taken was calling Kira's office yesterday to confirm that she was in town.

"Fifty bucks to make a call," Mitch said to the cabbie, who was still talking away.

"Seventy-five," the cabbie shot back.

"Done."

After that, it was magic. The guard took the phone, confirmed it was Susan and agreed to let Mitch in. Slowly the gate rolled back. Mitch relaxed. He was almost home.

KIRA HAD NEVER SEEN SUSAN behave so oddly. She'd barely gotten in the door from Roxanne's sentencing and her receptionist/assistant was trying to push her back out. Kira might have to rethink that assistant role if this was the help she'd be getting.

Susan lingered in Kira's office doorway, unwilling to leave. "It's been a really stressful day for you. I think you should go home and relax."

"I've got work to get through," Kira said.

"So take it home and do it by the pool. You've got this wonderful new house and you've barely taken the time to unpack."

"No big deal. I've covered the essentials."

Susan stalked toward Kira's desk, then braced her hands on it. Her threatening stance would have worked a little better if she weren't grinning. "You're not getting this, are you? Let me repeat, you *need* to go home."

"And you *need* to get your blood pressure checked or something. You're not usually this crazed." Kira began tucking papers into her briefcase. "I don't know what's up with you, but I'll go home just to get some peace."

Susan laughed. "I knew you'd see it my way."

As Kira drove home, she considered how far she'd come in rebuilding her life. It had been a miserable few months proving that the company hadn't profited from Roxanne's extracurricular activities, and the stakes had been high. Kira would have had to forfeit the business as Roxanne had her precious Porsche, her home and her freedom.

Kira had been smart enough to know that she couldn't survive those rocky months on her own. She'd gone to her father and worked out the financing arrangements to have Whitman Enterprises invest. It was an arm's-length transaction—no strings, no manipulation, just one businessperson negotiating with another. She was now Whitman Enterprises' southern branch, and so long as her numbers stayed good, life would be golden.

It felt wonderful being back in the family fold—better than she'd thought possible. She'd invited Steve and Hallie down for a visit during Steve's winter break. They had accepted, and Kira was already excited.

Kira pulled her car into the driveway of the house she'd bought as soon as her finances had been in the clear. Rose Cottage was a 1920s guesthouse to a larger property that had been razed years before, making way for a small, gated community.

Her home was little more than eleven hundred square feet, but for one very heartfelt reason, she'd fallen in love with it at first sight. Rose Cottage was Mitch's Dollhouse Cottage done Florida-style. The house's stucco glowed a warm pinkish-white in the afternoon sun. The sight of her one extravagance— a small stained-glass inset above the front door— made her smile grow.

Kira stepped out of the car and was assailed by music. Her first thought was that she was in deep doo-doo, since the noise was decibels and decibels above what the community rules permitted. Her second thought was that she didn't care.

The music blasting from Rose Cottage wasn't hip-hop or techno or even country. It was pure, unadulterated headbanger rock, still popular with only one person she knew: Mitch.

She grabbed her briefcase and headed to the front door. A note had been taped there. Welcome home, it read. Step inside.

Attached to the mirror in the front entryway was another note reading Look down. On the small console table beneath the mirror was a gift. Open me said its tag.

Kira's hands shook as she peeled back the flowery wrapping paper that had been stuck together with about two yards too much tape. Finally inside she found a red velvet box.

She opened it and had to stop herself from getting all weepy. Over the necklace was yet another note. This has been waiting for you.

Kira set aside the note and gently lifted the necklace from its white silk bed. It took a few tries to get it on and the clasp closed, but she eventually managed. When she had it in place, she took a moment to settle her hand over the gold-set diamond and make a silent promise to Mitch's mother that she would take the very best of care both of the necklace and of Mitch.

Speaking of whom…

"Mitch?" she called, but then realized that the music was more muted in the house than it had been outside. She hurried to the patio door, then stopped before opening it, overwhelmed with love and relief and even a good case of nerves.

Dressed in a black bathing suit, he was stretched out in a lounge chair by the pool, sunglasses on, books and papers all around him.

"Don't screw this up," she muttered to herself, then went outside to join him. First stop was to the portable stereo he'd plugged in by the back door. He looked up when she turned down the volume. Mitch pulled off his sunglasses.

As she neared, what she saw in his eyes gave her the courage to be calm. She saw doubt, worry and apology. But most of all she saw love.

"Hey," he said, setting aside the notebook he'd been paging through. "You're home early. Susan said you usually came home around six."

"Let's just say I got hurried along."

When she drew close enough, he pulled her on top of him. He smelled of sunblock and salty skin, and because she couldn't resist, she kissed him. Once their mouths touched, the control they'd both been holding on to so tightly let go. One kiss became a dozen—deep, searing and unending—yet it still wasn't enough. Mitch whispered hot words of desperation, of how much he missed her and burned for her. And then he said the words she wanted most: "I love you."

Kira held her breath, waiting for that *but*.... When it didn't come, she rejoiced. "I love you, too. I have since...well, since I figured out *how* to love."

After giving her another kiss, Mitch resettled her so they were facing each other, tucked tightly together in the lounge chair. He brushed a stray lock of hair from her forehead.

"Once I got past acting like a wounded animal, I spent a lot of time thinking over the past few months," he said. "The way I see it, the only thing that messed us up last time was a whole lot of pride. You wanted to prove you could stand alone and I was busy trying to prove I could control the woman who'd spent her teenage years stomping on my heart."

"But—"

He kissed her silent. "I know—we've both changed. You showed me that when I drove you to the airport back in June. You tried to let me in, but I was still too hurt and full of myself to understand what you were doing. I've checked my ego at the door, Kira, and I'd like to stay if you'll have me. I plan to take the Florida bar exam in February, then find myself a job—eventually as a federal prosecutor but until then whatever I can get. I'm going to be underfoot a lot until then. Do you think I'll fit in your life here?"

She smiled, glancing back at her tiny Rose Cottage. "I'll tell you exactly how we're going to fit. Hot..." She kissed him once. "Tight..." This time he kissed her. "And perfect," she finished.

And because Kira Whitman was an independent woman of her word, that's exactly how it worked out.

1

Spring 2005

Chance Mitchell had never been obsessed by a woman in his life. He sent a glance down the table to where Detective Natalie Gibbs was sipping a glass of white wine. He continued to study her as she tucked a stray curl behind her ear. The two women seated next to her could be described as equally attractive, but ever since he'd joined his friends for a celebration at the Blue Pepper, his gaze had kept returning to Natalie.

At nine o'clock the popular Georgetown bistro was crowded. Customers were lined up three deep at the bar, and a salsa band was playing on the patio. In some corner of his mind, Chance was aware of that, just as he was vaguely aware of the ongoing conversation at his table, but his focus remained on the fascinating detective.

Her hair fell to her shoulders, and in the dim light of the bar, the red gold curls looked as if they might burst into flames at any moment. He wanted to touch those curls. He wanted to touch her—slowly and thoroughly.

Chance took a long swallow of his beer, but it did little to cool the heat that burned inside of him. Oh, he was obsessing all right, and he wanted to know why.

What he felt for Natalie had begun the first moment he'd seen her. They'd both been working undercover for different agencies, and she'd been disguised as a man when she'd walked into his art gallery. From the instant their eyes had met, there'd been a connection. He'd felt a curious shock of recognition that had registered like a punch in his gut. And in spite of the fact that he'd been completely fooled by her disguise, he'd been instantly attracted to her. To *him*.

So far, he hadn't acted on the attraction. During the three days that he and Natalie had joined forces and worked as partners, the cool, aloof redhead had kept him at arm's length. And he'd let her. That's what he couldn't quite figure out. He was a man who knew how to get what he wanted, but Natalie Gibbs had him hesitating in a way he couldn't recall doing since he'd been a teenager.

Perhaps it was time he put a stop to that. She didn't look quite so cool tonight. Maybe it was the clothes. When they'd worked as partners, she'd always worn a jacket and slacks—the standard uniform of a woman who worked in a man's world. But tonight, the shirt she wore left her arms and throat bare, and the lacy, sheer fabric revealed curves as well as skin.

His eyes shifted to the V-neck that ended just where he imagined the valley between her breasts began. He let his gaze lower to her waist. He could imagine unbuttoning them one at a time—very slowly, drawing out the pleasure for them both.

Even as the images filled his mind, the tightening in his gut turned raw and primitively sexual. Why in hell was he hesitating? Desire was something he was familiar with. He could handle it. Or he could walk away. Couldn't he?

He took another swallow of his beer.

"You all right?"

Chance tore his gaze away from Natalie to face the two men seated beside him. Tracker McBride had asked the question. But it was Lucas Wainwright who was studying him thoughtfully. Seven years ago, Tracker and Lucas had worked with him in a Special Forces unit, and in the last two weeks, they'd had the opportunity to work together again to crack a smuggling ring operating in D.C. Tonight, they were supposed to be celebrating the successful closure of the case, and this was the second time he'd lost track of the conversation. Thanks to Detective Natalie Gibbs.

"I think he has his eye on the fair detective," Lucas said.

Tracker's look turned speculative. "Really?"

Knowing that the best defense was a good offense, Chance said to Tracker, "Have you and Sophie set a date yet?"

Tracker's gaze went to the tall blonde sitting to Natalie's right. "No comment."

Lucas grinned. "I hear from Mac that Sophie is talking about a fall wedding."

Chance bit back a laugh at the expression on Tracker's face and shifted his gaze to the third woman at the other end of the table, Dr. MacKenzie Lloyd Wainwright. Mac and Lucas had been married for a year, and they were expecting a child. He'd never envisioned either of his friends marrying and settling down.

"Now that Lucas and I are pretty much spoken for, it's your turn," Tracker said.

Chance held both hands out, palms up. "Not a chance in hell." Then he laughed as his friends winced at the pun. He just wasn't the marrying kind.

It wasn't that he didn't like women. He did. And you could italicize the plural. Not that he had ever involved himself with more than one woman at a time. Going down that particular path had always seemed to him to be a way too complicated if not downright suicidal. He'd always made sure that his relationships were simple, uncomplicated, and a lot of fun while they lasted. *Permanent* wasn't a word that existed in his vocabulary. Hell, nothing was permanent—not in his life.

"I don't know," Tracker said. "Sophie says that there's a real spark between you and the detective."

The sudden ringing of a phone had all three men reaching for their cells. Whoever was getting the call, Chance figured he was saved by the bell. Lucas opened his and a second later said, "I'm going to have to take this in a quieter spot." Rising, he signaled Tracker to come with him. The two friends worked together now. Lucas ran his family's company, Wainwright Enterprises, and Tracker headed up security for him.

Chance sipped his beer and found his gaze returning to Natalie at the other end of the table. When she glanced up and met his eyes, there was a moment, one long moment, when everything else faded. A heated conversation at a nearby table, laughter from the bar, even the low sound of a saxophone became just a buzz in his ears. The faces of the other two women at the table blurred, and all he could see was Natalie.

Twin sensations assaulted him—the hard punch

to his gut and a strange flutter just beneath his heart. No—this wasn't the reaction he had to just any woman. Why did this particular woman have this kind of effect on him? A part of him wanted to find out; another part of him wanted to run.

The realization had a spurt of panic moving through him. No woman had ever made him want to run before.

"Hey." Tracker's amused tone only penetrated when he felt the nudge to his shoulder. Turning, Chance discovered that Lucas had moved to help Mac from her chair. "Our party's breaking up," Tracker said. "Mac's tired, and Sophie and I can walk back to her place. Do you need a lift back to your hotel?"

"No," he said as he rose from his chair. It had been years since he'd allowed himself to run away from anything. That part of his life was over. He was flying to London in the morning. And there was one thing he was going to do before he left. Chance moved with Tracker down to the other end of the table.

"Sorry to be such a party pooper," Mac said, stifling a huge yawn.

"I'm the one who yawned first," Sophie said. "The last few days have been hectic." Then she smiled at Natalie. "But you should stay. Chance is an excellent dancer, and the music is good."

"No, I—" Natalie began as she rose from her chair.

"Sophie's right on one point," Chance said. "The music is very good."

"Please. Don't let me break up your evening," Mac said, taking Natalie's hand and squeezing it. "Stay and have at least one dance. If I weren't asleep on my feet, I'd drag Lucas out. There's nothing more romantic than dancing under the stars."

"What's one dance?" Sophie said softly as she kissed Natalie's cheek.

Chance waited until the two couples had taken their leave. "We don't have to dance if you're afraid of that Latin beat."

Natalie's eyes narrowed as she met his. "I can dance to that if you can."

It was just the reaction Chance had hoped for. The one thing he'd learned from working with the beautiful detective was that she was never afraid to take a risk. That was his key, he realized as he took her hand and led her toward the patio. If he framed his proposition in the right way, they'd be taking a different kind of risk together before the night was over.

If you enjoyed what you just read,
then we've got an offer you can't resist!

Take 2 bestselling
love stories FREE!

Plus get a FREE surprise gift!

Clip this page and mail it to Harlequin Reader Service®

IN U.S.A.	**IN CANADA**
3010 Walden Ave.	P.O. Box 609
P.O. Box 1867	Fort Erie, Ontario
Buffalo, N.Y. 14240-1867	L2A 5X3

YES! Please send me 2 free Blaze™ novels and my free surprise gift. After receiving them, if I don't wish to receive anymore, I can return the shipping statement marked cancel. If I don't cancel, I will receive 4 brand-new novels each month, before they're available in stores! In the U.S.A., bill me at the bargain price of $3.99 plus 25¢ shipping and handling per book and applicable sales tax, if any*. In Canada, bill me at the bargain price of $4.47 plus 25¢ shipping and handling per book and applicable taxes**. That's the complete price and a savings of at least 10% off the cover prices—what a great deal! I understand that accepting the 2 free books and gift places me under no obligation ever to buy any books. I can always return a shipment and cancel at any time. Even if I never buy another book from Harlequin, the 2 free books and gift are mine to keep forever.

150 HDN DZ9K
350 HDN DZ9L

Name	(PLEASE PRINT)	
Address	Apt.#	
City	State/Prov.	Zip/Postal Code

Not valid to current Harlequin Blaze™ subscribers.

Want to try two free books from another series?
Call 1-800-873-8635 or visit www.morefreebooks.com.

* Terms and prices subject to change without notice. Sales tax applicable in N.Y.
** Canadian residents will be charged applicable provincial taxes and GST.
   All orders subject to approval. Offer limited to one per household.
® and ™ are registered trademarks owned and used by the trademark owner and or its licensee.

BLZ04R   ©2004 Harlequin Enterprises Limited.

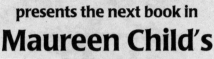

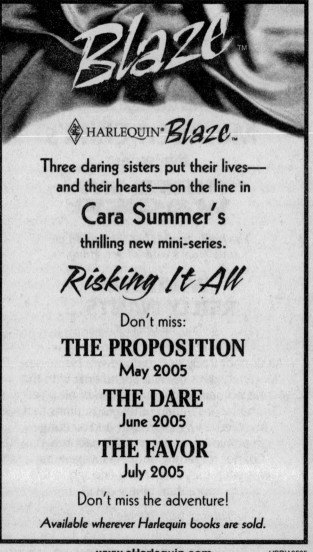